Stars, Life and Intelligence:

Being a Darwinian and a Believer

Terry Kelly SJ

ATF PRESS
Adelaide

National Library of Australia Cataloguing-in-Publication entry

Author: Kelly, Terence J.

Title: Stars, life and intelligence : being a Darwinian and a believer / Terry Kelly.

ISBN: 9781921511691 (pbk.)

Subjects: Bible and evolution.
Evolution (Biology)--Religious aspects--Christianity.
Religion and science.

Dewey Number: 231.7652

Cover design by Astrid Sengkey

ATF Press
An imprint of the Australasian Theological Forum Ltd
P O Box 504
Hindmarsh
SA 5007
ABN 90 116 359 963
www.atfpress.com

Table of Contents

Introduction

Chapter 1 Universe of Evolution

Chapter 2 From Mere Matter to the Living Cell

Chapter 3 The Progress of Life: From Simple Cells to First Appearance of Modern Body Forms

Chapter 4 Emergence from the Sea: Adaptations, Extinctions and the Final Arrival of Mammals

Chapter 5 Homonisation: the Speedy Process to Homo Sapiens

Chapter 6 Laws of Nature Plus Change Guide Evolution

Chapter 7 Darwin's Evolution: a Theory for Today

Chapter 8 The God of Evolution: Dawinism and the Contemporary Believer

Chapter 9 The Christian God and Evolution

Chapter 10 Purpose in a Fractured World: The Kingdom of God

Epilogue

Introduction

Chapter Overview

- Is the question purposeful creation or evolution?
- The wonder of evolution
    * Only a theory?
    * More than chance?
- Science: a powerful but limited discipline
- Chance or God? A false dilemma?
- Plan of the book
    * The story of evolution
    * Philosophical and theistic reflection on evolution

1. Purposeful creation or evolution?

There is a simplistic mantra around today linking evolution and religion. It is reducible to a logical dilemma.

> Either a purposeful creation or natural selection
>
> Natural selection, 'Yes'
>
> Therefore purposeful creation 'No'.

A convincing case can be made for the operation of natural selection in the process of evolution. Seemingly this adds strength to the above logical dilemma. If one equates creation to a literal account of the first chapter of the book of Genesis, one would have to agree with the conclusion of the dilemma. However, the Genesis account was put into its final form about two millennia before the advent of science as a serious discipline. It is an affirmation of the supreme mastery of God over the material universe in the context of the geography and cosmology of 2500 years ago. One needs to look beyond the primitive science and work out if the religious assertion can be intelligible when considered alongside the scientific picture of today. One needs first of all to abstract the religious assertion from the accompanying primitive science and ask whether the religious assertion can sit well with today's science.

2. The wonder of evolution

2.1 'Only a theory'?
The story of evolution by natural selection is ultimately a theory, but much more than 'only a theory'. Fossil evidence dating back over three billion years shows in retrospect an evolving scenario from primitive cells to many sea based organisms, ever more complex with time, then to land based organisms which subsequent to evolutionary changes were made more able to explore and colonise the land. Eventually there was a very rapid transition to full intelligence. The fossil evidence is well confirmed by DNA studies. Comparing DNA sequences of different animals can show investigators when species diverged. As the whole process is guided by the laws of nature as well as by chance, one can say the process is evidence of purpose. Then one can ask the question: is God involved in this? One view stops at science and says the combination of the laws of nature and chance is the only

necessary explanation. God is superfluous. As Laplace said to Napoleon, 'I have no need of that hypothesis'.[1]

2.2 Chance not a sufficient explanation
Others look at the laws of nature and enquire firstly why they are mathematical and wonder about an overriding intelligence to fashion such laws. Secondly why are the laws fitted to cause such a remarkable series of transitions? The possibility of chance mutations can be associated with a property of DNA whereby elements can swap positions and do so with a certain amount of regularity. The laws then select the advantageous changes. Only favourable chances are selected. One can say, with this variety of chance there is a power and designer at work. Chance-laden DNA and Nature's Laws are the work of the one God.

3. Science powerful but limited

Science is a powerful discourse; it has unravelled for us the workings of nature, and technology has enabled us to apply the findings in many ways to further advance knowledge, to perform complex tasks, to further communication, and to make life easier and more exciting. But there are boundaries and limits to science. Firstly, the final models of how nature is working are never the final word; they are always awaiting 'falsification', never blessed with certain 'verification'. Secondly, the deeper one goes towards hoped-for truth the more one is confronted with counter-intuitive models such as quantum theory, 'spooky action' at a distance, dark energy of the vacuum, the Big Bang. Thirdly, science cannot advance beyond the questions accessible by scientific experiment. Questions about purpose and God, right and wrong, good and evil, are not accessible to science. Scientific conclusions, however, can then be subjected to reasonable analysis, philosophical reflection, aided perhaps by religious beliefs.

4. Chance or God? A false dilemma?

Is the above dilemma a false dilemma? Can purposeful creation and natural selection both be true?

Such are the features of evolution, one can argue strongly the case for a purpose. One can at least say belief in God sits well with evolutionary theory. To come to this conclusion we need to extend and improve our image of the God of Abraham, Moses and Jesus. God is intelligent, subtle, powerful – a respecter of the freedom with which the Divine will has endowed creation itself and *homo sapiens*.

'Either a purposeful creation or natural selection' is, therefore, a *false dilemma*. A case can be made out for 'purposeful creation via natural selection'.

5. Plan of the book

5.1. Part 1: The story of evolution
As many students do not study biology, and hence lack acquaintance with evolution, the first five chapters of the book are involved with expounding the agreed features of the evolutionary process. In the first chapter, there is a brief account of the general evolution of the Cosmos, and a more detailed account of the formation of the Earth which sets the scene for coming journey of life. Chapters 2, 3 and 4 take the reader from the first cell, to the Cambrian Explosion in the depths of the sea, to the emergence of vertebrates from the sea to the land, and their consequent development in the new environment. Chapter 5 is the story of the rapid progress from the first bipedal ape to *homo sapiens*.

5.2 Part 2: Evolution and theism
The next five chapters are involved with evolution as a process, and philosophical and religious reflection on the process. Chapter 6 analyses the laws of nature and chance. Chapter 7 describes Darwin's experiences and his theory of evolution by natural selection. The slow acceptance of natural selection is mentioned and the question of evolution in the theory of evolution itself is raised. Chapter 8 examines carefully how evolution by natural selection is consonant with God as a Designer. It

1. 'Je n'avais pas besoin de cette hypothèse-là.' Well known response to Napoleon. Rouse Ball, (1908). Accessed 2/5/2009: *Pierre-Simon Laplace*. Wikipedia.

further considers the laws of nature, and then outlines views of selective theistic biologists and other academics. Chapter 9 looks at the Christian God in relation to evolution. It discusses how to interpret the various creation accounts in the light of scriptural research and modern science. Following this, it treats Deism, Yahweh the God of the Jews, Intelligent Design, and begins a discussion of Jesus.

The final chapter is an explanation of Jesus' mission, what he meant by the kingdom of God in relation to miracles, incidents, parables, leading in the end appropriately to the final kingdom as spoken about by Jesus and in the Book of Revelation. The beginnings of the kingdom on Earth and its fulfilment in the 'new heaven and the new earth' are the ultimate goals of evolution. Natural selection finishes with the arrival of *homo sapiens* who then is constrained freely to undertake to build the kingdom and await its final revelation.

6. Acknowledgments

Thanks:

- to my sister Katherine Kelly, who spent many hours on the formatting and layout.
- to Paul Marks, the Head of Science Department at St Ignatius' College Adelaide, who advised me about the biology.
- to Gerry Wake from Sydney for offering resources and encouragement.
- to my fellow Jesuits for their material support and encouragement.
- to Astrid Sengkey of ATF Press for expert work on pictures and diagrams.
- and finally to Hilary Regan at ATF Press for asking me to engage upon this work.

Chapter 1
A Universe of Evolution

Chapter overview

- The Universe began at the Big Bang has evolved through many stages
    - ⋆ The beginning
    - ⋆ An expanding chaos of particles
    - ⋆ Star formation
    - ⋆ The formation of elements
- The formation of earth
    - ⋆ Oceans
    - ⋆ Tectonic plates
- Ice Epochs
- Extension: Origin and necessity of the Moon

1. A history of change

Throughout human existence, it was thought that everything on earth, especially the stars in the sky had always been the same with the exception of the seasons, night and day; and the occasional catastrophe. Even as recently as the 1930s the scientific consensus was the stars had always remained static. The proposal of Georges Lemaitre (priest and scientist) that there had been a beginning was rejected, even by the great Albert Einstein. The scientific consensus of the later second and early third millennia is that there was a beginning. Ever since then there has been change in the cosmos, and within this change, there have been stages of development.

1.1 The beginning

It all began some 13.7 billion years ago with what is referred to as the 'Big Bang' where a unique birth occurred cosmically. Space, time, energy came into existence. Space expanded taking with it all the particles and photons that appeared. An article entitled *'From Big Bang to Big Bounce'*,[1] proposes the present universe emerged from the ruins of a previous universe which had contracted to a 'big crunch'. Do we have 'an eternal series of expansions and contractions with no beginning and no end'? asks the writer.[2] According to an article in another scientific publication[3] , there are too many unsolved difficulties with the physics of the bounce. Michael Turner, in this article is quoted as saying 'this is an old idea and the bounce problem still remains. Very exotic physics is needed'. Cosmologist Andrew Linde is also quoted in the same article as saying that the bounce is '. . . fundamentally flawed. The bounce idea is plagued by numerous unsolved problems. We don't know how to go through the singularity at the bounce.' Roger Penrose, mathematician and cosmological theorist, delves more deeply into this theory and is dismissive of any possibility of a bounce.

> but to my mind, it is even more geometrically implausible that highly irregular singularities that result from collapse can magically convert themselves into (or glue themselves to) the extraordinarily smooth and uniform Big Bang that each new universe would need if it is to acquire a respectable Second Law (of thermodynamics) of the kind that we are familiar with.[4]

1. Anil Ananthaswamy, 'From Big Bang to Big Bounce', in *New Scientist*, 200/ 2686 (2008): 32–3.
2. *Ibid*, 32
3. Peter Rodgers, 'Cyclic Universe Runs into Criticism', in *Physics World*, 15/Jun (2002): 8–15.
4. Roger Penrose, *The Road to Reality* (London: Johnathan Cape, 2004), 762. The Second Law (of Thermodynamics) need not concern us here apart from the fact it is deemed necessary for the formation of structures

Penrose calculates the chance of a new Big Bang having the required smoothness so that a life potential universe could emerge from it is 1 in $10^{10 \text{ to power 123 zeros}}$. This is not 10^{123}, which is unimaginable; but it is an ultra-huge number, far greater than all the elementary particles in the universe. The 'big crunch' would not result in the smoothness associated with Big Bang requirements. On the contrary, it would be highly chaotic.

1.2 After the bang[5]

The immediate physics is highly speculative. So transferring to what may not seem immediate, (but is not even a millionth of a second later) there has formed a very hot mixture of quarks, electrons, other particles, and units of radiation called photons. After one second, protons and neutrons have formed from the quarks. For the next two minutes some nuclear fusion took place, converting many of the protons and neutrons into helium4 so that twenty-five per cent of visible matter is now helium. From three minutes to 380,000 years all this matter expanded chaotically. The temperature then

- Cosmic evolution
  - Energy → protons/neutrons/electrons → nuclei → atoms →
  - Gas clouds → denser spots →
  - Stars [1st generation] →
  - Supernovae → gas clouds seeded with elements → stars [2nd generation] →
  - Planets
- The Laws of Nature bring about these processes

fell enough for electrons to combine with the protons to form hydrogen atoms; and with the helium nuclei to form helium atoms. The mixture of atoms would seem to have been uniform in density, but it was not. Behind the scenes mysterious dark matter had been aggregating into regions of higher density, due to quantum events in the actual Bang. The newly formed atoms were attracted to the denser regions; the aggregations of matter formed clusters and filaments of galaxies, leaving spaces (voids); and stars began to form within the galaxies.

2. Stars

2.1 The formation of a star

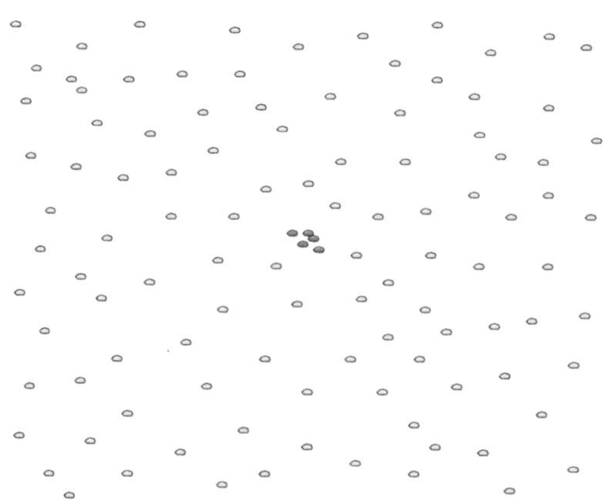

A slightly denser region of a hydrogen/helium cloud would develop by chance. This would preferentially attract other atoms.

The slightly denser spot then would preferentially attract more matter at a greater rate. So a giant gas cloud contracted. It contracted due to the force of gravity. This is an attractive force, which pulls on everything. The matter within the cloud, at the centre, pulled on the matter further out, causing it to be drawn in.

5. For detailed account see Terry Kelly, *Reason and Religion in an Age of Science* (Adelaide: ATF, 2007), 81–85.

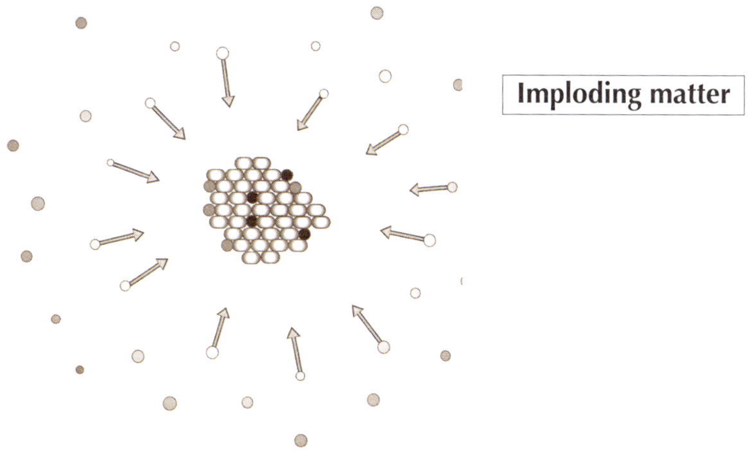

As this denser region grew more and more dense, matter was attracted to it faster and faster. The centre became much denser, therefore exerting more pull. Matter was being attracted to the centre at faster speed, which in turn caused the centre to further increase its density, leading to an even faster build–up in the centre. This caused the pressure to increase, which was accompanied by an increase of temperature. The huge sphere of dense gas began to glow, but this was only the start. After some time the temperature became so high that nuclear fusion took place—a gigantic nuclear explosion—trillions of hydrogen bombs continually exploding.

The hydrogens combined to form helium producing more heat, this heat enabling the fusion to continue indefinitely. The mass of the product is less than the mass of the hydrogens. The loss of mass (m) became energy, heat energy and light. $E = mc^2$. The sphere of gas lit up brilliantly, becoming the Sun. The heat generated enabled many more fusions.

The original outpouring of matter from the 'Big Bang' was seventy-five per cent atomic hydrogen and twenty-five per cent helium4. The first suns to form by the process described above were composed of hydrogen and helium, the hydrogen then fusing to form more helium and so the star shone brightly.

2.2 The formation of the other elements of the periodic table

Where did the Sun get all the other ninety-two elements? The Sun is a star, but one which was not formed at the earliest stages of star formation. It had to wait until the earlier giant stars had formed. These stars manufactured all the ninety elements within themselves, and delivered these to space and hence to other gas clouds. The giant early star spent millions of years synthesising the elements. It finally imploded spectacularly; rebounded from this implosion, and spilt all the elements into space.

2.3 The formation of the Sun

These elements journeyed in space and collected in various remaining gas clouds. It was one of the element–laced gas clouds that contracted to form the Sun and planets. The Sun began as a huge gas cloud laced with all the other elements. It contracted gravitationally like the earlier stars and increased in pressure and temperature. It finally ignited as a continuous nuclear fusion event.

2.4 Formation of rings of matter

This hot sphere of gas contracting to form our Sun was initially rotating. As it contracted it left off circles of matter at various intervals, which were rotating with the Sun, as demanded by the principle of conservation of angular momentum.

Each orbit is initially one gigantic circular dust and rock storm. The larger rocks in the circles exercised more gravity, just because they were larger, and attracted more of the rocks to themselves.

> In the very early history of the solar system, the earth was a molten planetoid, half the size it is today, but growing rapidly by gobbling up rubble that had condensed from the dust cloud swirling around the young Sun.[6]

6. Ian Plimer, *A Short History of Planet Earth* (Sydney: ABC books, 2001), 13.

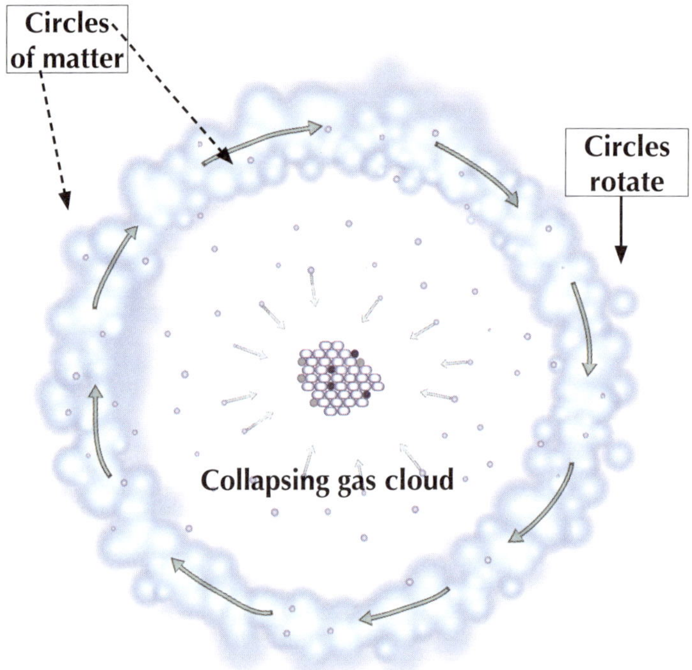

The rocks in these circles of matter exerted gravitational forces on each other, causing them to come closer and grow larger. What was to become earth was a large rock, among the millions of rocks of all sizes from kilometres in diameter to dust, whose gravity attracted the nearby omnipresent dust and rock in the orbit.

2.5 Planet forms

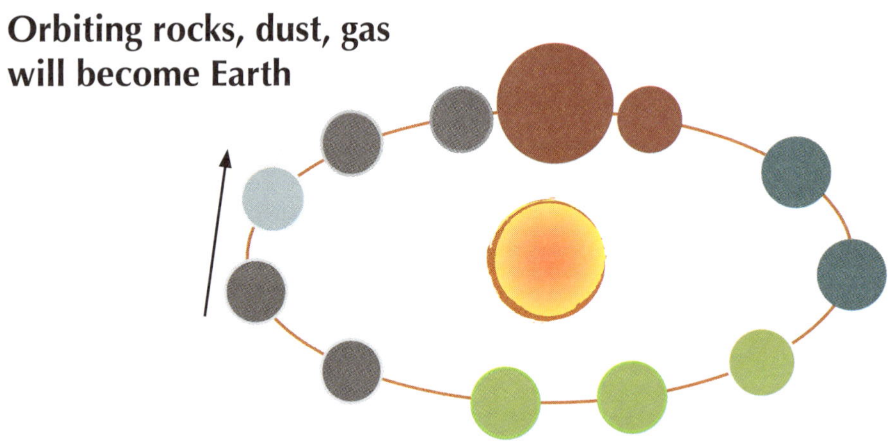

Ultimately one large sphere of matter was left in each orbit – a modern day planet. In one orbit the matter did not coalesce; this is the asteroid belt. The relative closeness of the huge planet Jupiter, and thus its large gravitational influence prevented these rocks from coming together.

2.6 One last large collision

In its early life, the earth was struck by a Mars-sized object—a molten mass about the then size of the earth. This caused dislodgement of part of the earth, which resulted in the moon. The moon still recedes from the earth at some centimetres per year. The rest of the bombarding object became entrenched in the centre of the earth. This mass contained great stores of iron. Thus earth now has an iron core, which can conduct currents. As a result of this collision, earth grew to two-thirds of its present size. Over the next fifty million years it completed the collection of most of the remaining rubble, and grew to its present size.[7]

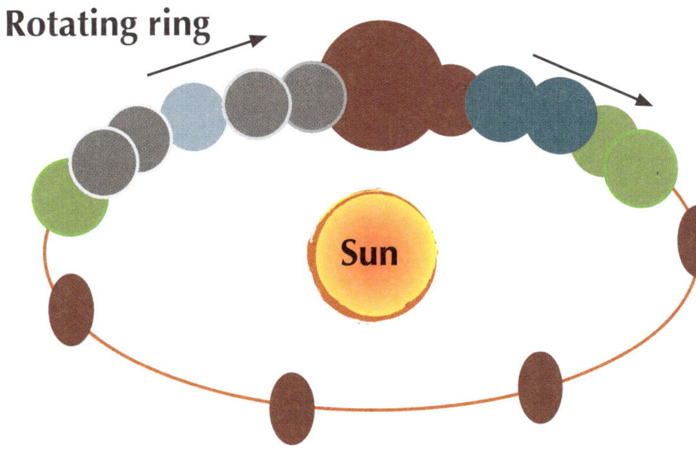

3. Tectonic plates

As the earth cooled, parts of the surface solidified. It did not form a continuous solid outer spherical shell, but formed separate regions of solid, which are known as tectonic plates.

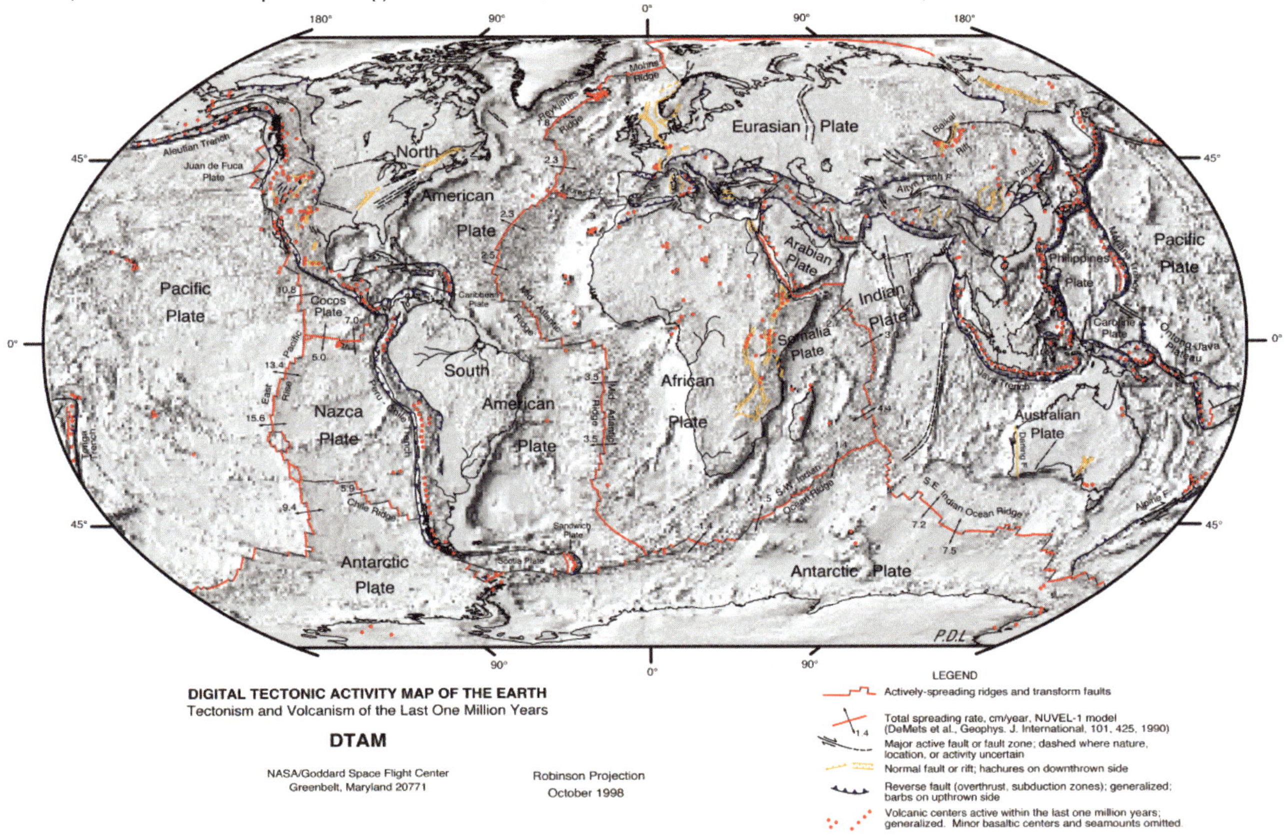

G221.001

There are seven main plates and various small ones. On average, they are eighty kilometres thick, and move relative to one another about a few inches a year. If two land plates collide head-on, they form a mountain range. For example, Himalayas are still growing. When land and sea plates collide, the sea plate is drawn under the land plate, and the rock is transferred down into the molten region and is melted. The Pacific Ocean floor is currently being forced under the plates involving Japan and South America, and being fed into the mantle. If two sea plates move away from each other, the opposite happens; molten rock emerges from the gap and adds itself to the sea floor. Thus there is a recycling of rock. If two plates move in opposite directions sliding past each other, in the manner of

7. *Ibid*, 17.

two trains going in opposite directions, they form fault lines. Therefore the formation of mountains, events on the sea floor, and earthquakes can be explained with reference to the tectonic plates.

The rise of mountains—a slow process—can alter climate in one part of the world, causing either large increases in rainfall in some areas, or droughts in other areas[8]. This can affect the evolution of animals by changing the environment. Drought conditions especially need development of new features to survive. The changes occur very slowly, giving species time to adapt at an equally slow rate by natural selection over many generations. When they move into different latitudes, the continents they carry experience changed climate; over billions of years, the climate may change from cold to tropical, exerting a significant influence on the survival or enhancement of species—both plants and animals.

Though they do not form a continuous unbroken spherical shell, the plates cover almost the whole surface, remaining separate. They float on the next layer of molten rock.

After the crust formed, molten rock spewed up through volcanoes and the spaces between the tectonic plates, continually adding rock to the surface. The oldest rocks still at the surface are 3750 million years old, and contain no fossils. But, they have a ratio of isotopes of carbon suggestive of organic origin; however this could have other explanations. A huge asteroid bombardment 3900 million years ago would have wiped out all life at this time if it had formed.

4. Later development of planet earth

4.1 Bombardment

From 4500 million years ago (mya) to 3800 mya the earth was continually bombarded by comets, dust, and asteroids. The many effects on the earth have been obliterated because of water, but how it was impacted can be deduced by looking at the moon's surface, which has had no wind or rain to change it, and would have been subjected to similar showers of debris in the so-called 'Late Heavy Bombardment'.

4.2 Oceans

As the earth cooled, it was bombarded by millions of comets, which were loaded with water, so that the surface was initially surrounded by dense water vapour. This finally became liquid water as the temperature cooled.

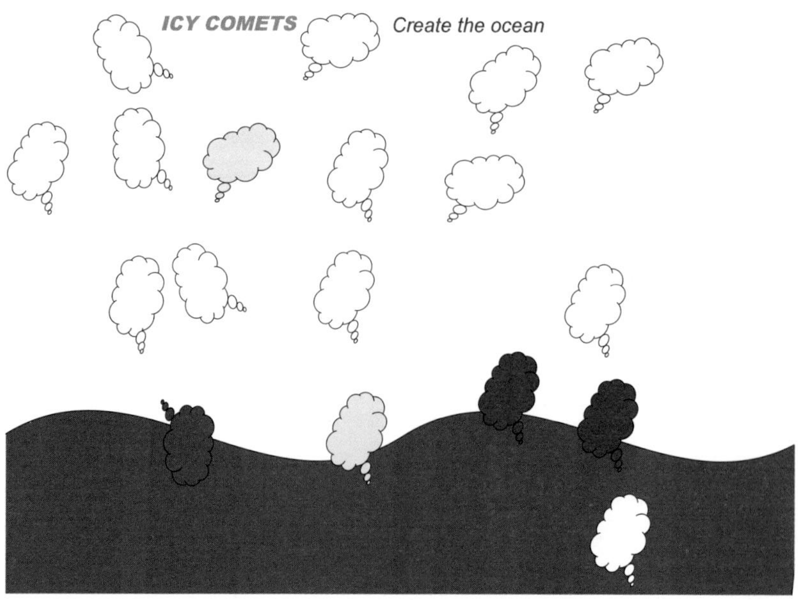

8. See page 39 chapter 5.

The period from 4150 to 3800 million years ago was an opportunity for the formation of life. Prior to this, there were regular impacts of planetoids, which vaporised the whole ocean. The ocean then remained as steam for a number of months, during which the atmosphere had a temperature of over 1000C.

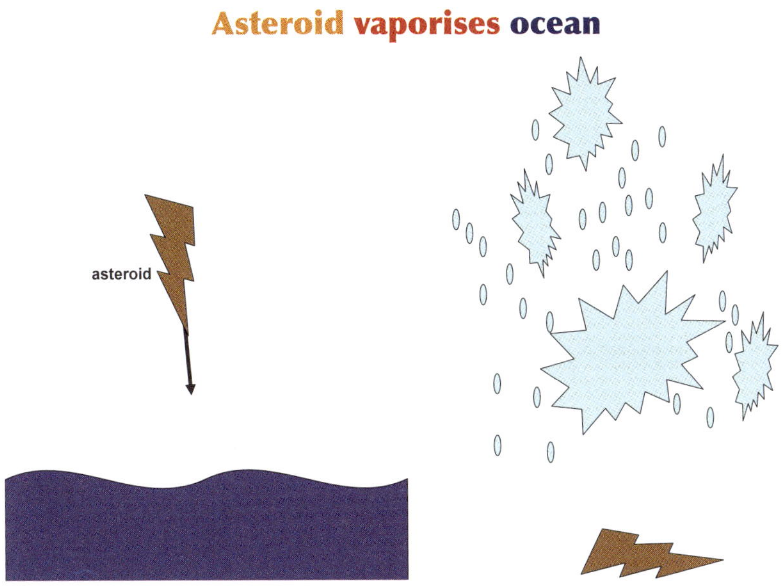

4.3 Atmosphere

The matter coalescing to form the earth, not only contained more massive atoms which formed solids, but also lighter atoms which naturally formed gases. The present atmosphere is not a typical cosmic atmosphere, which was lost early on. It rather has originated from within the early earth, and expelled through volcanoes. The early atmosphere was thought to have contained nitrogen, methane, ammonia, carbon dioxide, sulphur dioxide, hydrogen sulphide, but no oxygen. Earth was not only bombarded by water–bearing missives, but was continually subjected to showers of rocks and boulders as it attracted the remains of the rocks in its orbit to itself. Thus it was not a safe environment.

4.4 Formation of the hot interior

The collisions involving planetesimals, asteroids, smaller rocks, plus the radioactive elements from the original matter—cast off from the shrinking Sun and from the moon-making collision—caused the planet to heat and melt. The heavy metals, mostly iron, flowed to the centre, making the centre three and half times the density of the crust. The radioactive metals within the molten centre have kept it hot and molten to this day. Moon craters show how much the earth was being bombarded four billion years ago. The earth's cratered surface is lost because of volcanic output, and rocks emerging from under the surface at spaces between the plates.

4.5 Vulcanism

Many volcanoes joined the molten interior to the newly formed surface. These constantly spewed forth lava onto the surface.

Due to the tectonic plates, the surface was not a continuous crust like the outer layer of a tennis ball. It was a set of contiguous, mobile but disconnected islands of matter, touching each other, so that the surface is continuous.

5. Ice epochs[9]

5.1 Ice ages and interglacials

The last few million years are known as an Ice Epoch, consisting of a series of lengthy Ice Ages—glaciations—which are interspersed with much shorter warmer periods—interglacials. We now live in an interglacial period of an Ice Epoch where residual ice from the glaciation remains at the poles. In the Ice Age component of the Ice Epoch, a thick ice sheet would cover Europe from the North Pole to the British Isles, part of France and even further south in a more extreme glaciation. This would potentially destroy the plant life and much of the animal life, or cause the migration of animals to the south. Similar Ice Epochs have occurred from 1200 to 1000 million years ago, from 750 to 600 million years ago, and from 320 to 250 million years ago. Thus during each of these periods, there have been long periods of glaciation interspersed with short interglacials. In the long periods between the epochs, no ice existed on the earth's surface and temperatures were much warmer. Ice is not normally a feature of the earth's surface.

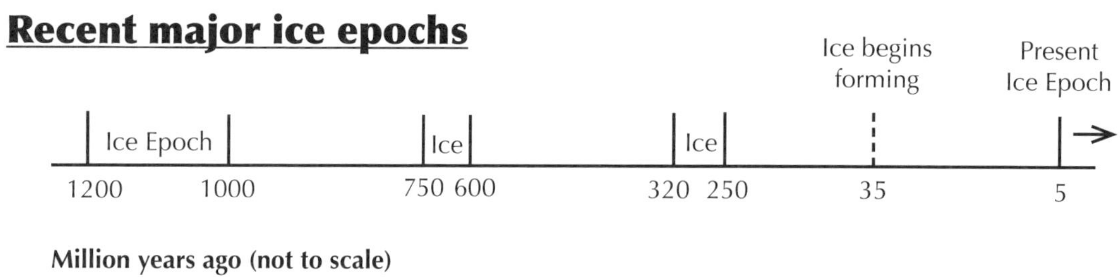

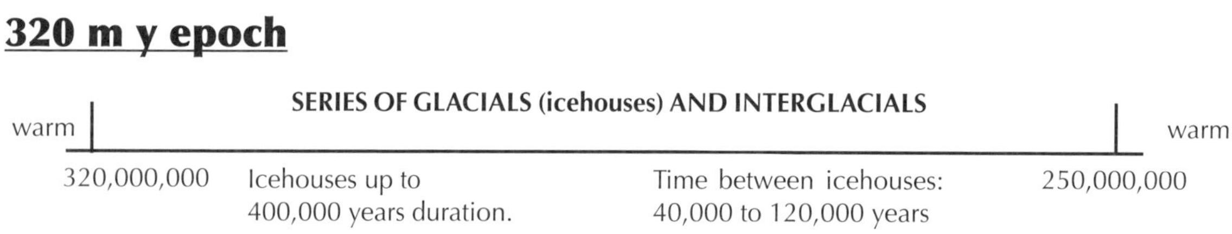

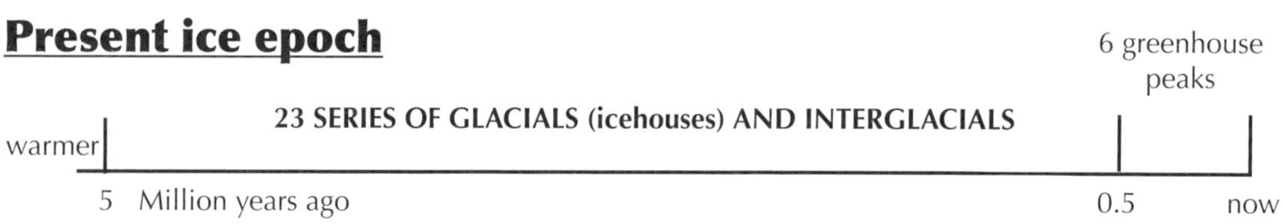

5.2 Milankovich Cycles[10]

Milutin Milankovitch, a Serbian, worked out three variables associated with the earth's spinning and circling. His extensive research showed a link between these cycles and the glaciation/interglacial events during the current Ice Epoch. His research covered thirty years during which his ideas were at times dismissed.

The three cycles involve variations in axis-tilt, in orbital eccentricity, and in angle of spin wobble.

9. John and Mary Gribben, *Ice Age* (London: Allen Lane, 2001).
10. http://www.homepage.montana.edu/~geol445/hyperglac/time1/milankov.htm>

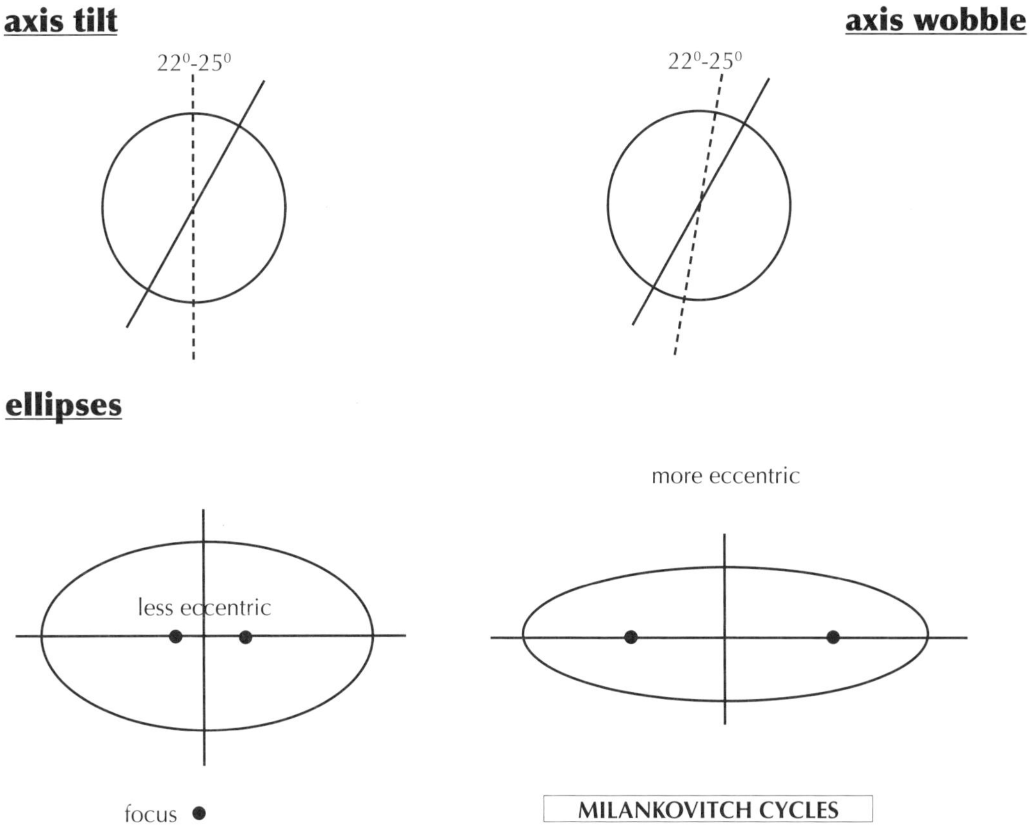

5.2.1. Axis tilt

The earth does not spin at 90^0 to the plane of its orbit, but its axis of rotation makes an angle with the plane of orbit. At present this angle is 66.6^0, or the angle between the perpendicular to the plane and the axis of rotation is 23.4^0. This angle is maintained during the whole year's journey around the Sun, and will be maintained to all intents and purposes for years to come. However there is a long term built–in cycle to this angle of tilt. Over the course of 41,000 years, it has varied between 22^0 and 25^0. At its maximum, the effect on the hemisphere enduring winter is greater, and sufficient to lower the amount of heat reaching the ground in higher latitudes so as to favour glaciation. Over thousands of successive years. this has been enough to bring about an ice epoch. Lower obliquity causes Polar Regions to receive less seasonally–contrasting solar radiation, which produces conditions more favorable to glaciation. Changes in tilt influence the relative strength of the seasons, but the effects of the tilt cycle are particularly pronounced in the high latitudes where the great ice ages begin.

When the tilt is less, less heat arrives at the Poles in summer, causing the build–up of ice.

Tilt increases

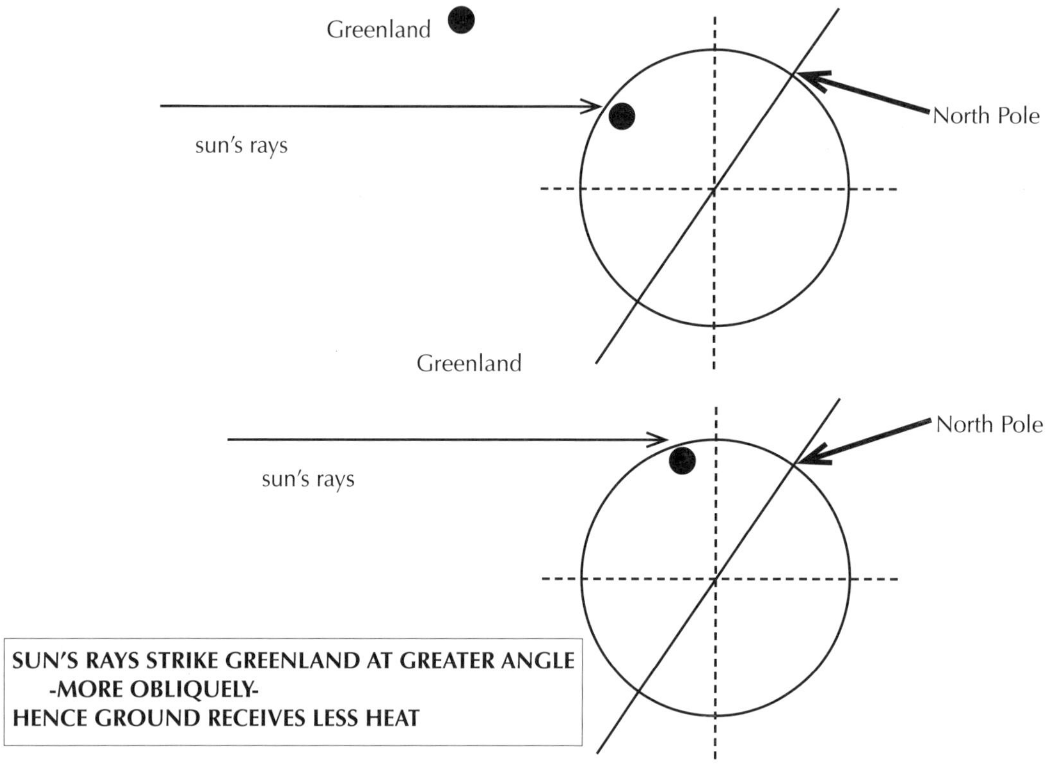

5.2.2 Wobble

The second cycle is the wobble. A top as it spins wobbles; so does the earth. The line joining the geographic North and South Poles changes direction; and the direction of the earth's spin axis relative to the stars varies. This direction can change, whilst maintaining the same tilt. The spin axis points differently towards stellar constellations. It describes a circle of 26,000 years periodicity.[11] An increased angle again affects the amount of solar energy reaching the ground at higher latitudes for the hemisphere enduring winter. This has a period of 23,000 years, and is due to the gravitational pull of the Sun and Moon on the earth.

5.2.3 Eccentricity

The earth's orbit is not a circle; it is an ellipse. This is a geometric figure, which can be well described, simply, by algebra. An ellipse resembles a circle pulled out of shape, such as a football oval where goal–to–goal is longer than wing–to–wing. The Sun is not at the centre, because there is no geometric centre as for the circle; it is at a focus. There are two focuses (foci): if they are far apart, the ellipse is said to have high eccentricity, and it tends to be a longer, thinner figure. However, if the foci are close, the ellipse approaches to the shape of a circle. If they coincide, you have a circle.

When the orbit is more eccentric—more elliptical—the earth is further from the Sun at the furthest point. Thus the hemisphere experiencing winter at that time will receive less heat from the Sun than if it were in circular orbit, or in a less eccentric orbit.

5.2.4 The three Cycles together can cause glaciation

Together, the three can cause glaciation: if the three negative influences occurred simultaneously—and they would remain coincident for centuries—the build–up of ice is on the cards. Conversely if during an ice age, the three influences all favoured more heat, the ice would melt. Ice may still be at the poles during an interglacial and when astronomical influences were again more negative, a new glaciation will begin. At present, only the wobble favours glaciation, with tilt and orbital eccentricity not favourable to glaciation.

11. J and M Gribbin, *Ice Age*, 23.

The escape from Ice Age conditions, beginning 18,000 years ago, required the combined influence of all three astronomical cycles to drag the earth into a peak of warmth about 6000 years ago. Orbital eccentricity changes combined with a shift in the wobble of the earth, (boosted) the heat of the Northern Hemisphere summers, just at a time when the tilt of our planet reached a maximum, putting the summer Sun particularly high in the sky.[12]

6. Extension: origin and necessity of the moon

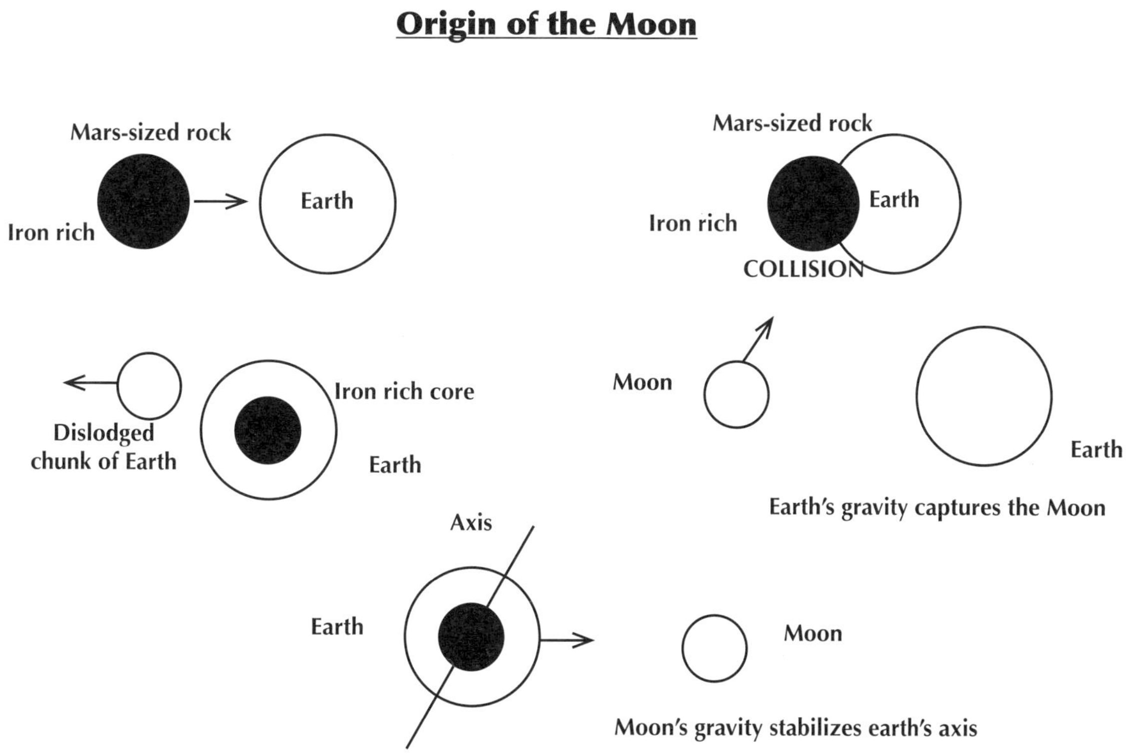

6.1 Origin

The favoured model today is the 'giant impact' model. As matter accreted to the early earth, other large rocks were still rotating in the earth's orbit. One of these, the size of Mars collided with earth. The heat of the gigantic collision melted the earth's surface so that a large part of the impacting object disappeared into the molten mantle. The earth's centre has an abnormally large percentage of iron, and this is accounted for by ascribing to the impactor a large percentage of iron in its make-up. The collision dislodged a large amount of matter from the earth which was ejected into space. The moon has the same percentage of oxygen in its makeup as the earth, not as a gas, but combined with other elements. Other meteorites have quite different percentages of oxygen. This is good evidence that what is now the moon was once part of earth. The moon is still moving away from earth at a few centimetres per year. It is much larger than satellites of Mars, larger than Pluto, and with the earth really forms a double planet system.

6.2 Necessity

The existence of the moon seems to have been a necessity for the history of the evolution of life. The gravitational effect of the moon on earth enables the axis of tilt to remain within its 22^0 to 25^0 boundaries. If this gravitational effect were absent, the earth's axis of tilt would swing much more wildly, changing climatic conditions too often and too violently for natural selection to work.

12. J and M Gribben, *Ice Age*, 89.

6.3 Iron core

The other pro-life spin-off for this collision theory is the presence of iron in the core. Iron is a conductor, and electric currents continually pass through the iron. These currents have the effect of producing the earth's well-known magnetic field. Magnetic fields produce forces on moving charged particles. Many dangerous high-speed cosmic charged particles thus have forces exerted on them as they near the earth. The force deflects them from the earth, so that organic life is spared lethal radiation.

Chapter 2
From Mere Matter to the Living Cell

Chapter overview

- A discussion of 'what is life'?
    - * Reductionist: Life is physics and chemistry
    - * Vitalist: Life is caused by a 'vital principle' in addition to physics and chemistry.
    - * An emergent phenomenon: the whole is greater than the sum of the parts
- The nature of DNA
- Complexity of the cell
    - * Its parts
    - * Its chemicals
- Transition from non-life to life
    - * Historical problem
    - * Today's problem

1. Deep time

Geological time is measured in eras. The scales of time are unimaginable to us. It seems as though life began before 2500 million years ago, before the first era in the scheme below. Bacterial remains have been dated as far back as 3800 million years ago, 3.8 billion years ago.

GEOLOGICAL ERAS

- Million years ago 2500 - 545 Proterozoic
- 545 – 495 Cambrian
- 495 – 438 Ordovician
- 438 – 417 Silurian
- 417 – 362 Devonian
- 362 – 290 Carboniferous
- 290 – 248 Permian
- 248 – 206 Triassic
- 206 – 142 Jurassic
- 142 – 65 Cretaceous
- 65 – 0 Tertiary

2. What is life? question and answer exploration

It seems that biologists are quite reluctant to define life.[1]

Ultimately life is a cell.

Question: What is life?
Answer: Life occurs when a whole lot of functions are integrated—they all work together for the

1. Frank E Buldenholzer, 'What is Life? Current Scientific and Philosophical Perspectives', in *The Cosmos in Becoming*, edited by Teresa Wong Yai Chow *et al* (Adelaide: ATF Press, 2008), 201.

good of the whole. The living thing sustains itself, defends itself, reproduces itself.
Question: Can you explain how a whole lot of processes act together in harmony ?
Answer: There are three theories about this:

1) *Reductionist:* Life can be totally explained by the properties of the particles that make up the living thing—and the laws of chemistry, electricity, mechanics.

2) *Vitalist:* A 'vital force' organises the chemical reactions, the mechanical laws, the electrical impulses to act together. Aristotle taught that every living thing has a vital force, a soul. A plant had a vegetable soul which enabled it to grow, integrate nourishment into itself, reproduce itself; an animal had an animal soul which, in addition to the capabilities a plant soul has, enabled it to experience sensations of sight, hearing, touch, smell, be aware of other animals, experience emotions, have memory; a human has a soul which in addition to all this enables the human to reason, and gives the human freedom.

3) *Emergence:* As matter becomes more complex it develops new properties which are not reducible to the properties of the constituents. New laws emerge suitable to the new realities. The laws of biology are not reducible to the laws of physics and chemistry. Biology depends on physics and chemistry, but something new has emerged with the increase in complexity.

Question: Can you say a little more on *Emergence*?
Answer: Ernst Mayr[2] sharply differentiates biology from physics and chemistry.
Classification of life phenomena reveal new properties arise at every level of increasing complexity.

The ladder of complexity/awareness

Mind, intelligent conciousness, thought, free will.

↑

Sensation: seeing, feeling, hearing, memory, taste, smell

↑

Groups of cells coordinated together

Macromolecules

↑

Molecules

↑

Atoms

↑

Protons, neutrons, electrons, neutrinos

↑ ↑ ↑ ↑ ↑ ↑ ↑ ↑ ↑

Quarks, gluons, electrons, neutrinos

Each group potentialities depend on the previous groups' laws. But for each group, new properties, laws emerge, which are not reducible to laws of lower groups.

Large molecules associated with life are much more complex than anything in inanimate nature. Cells are more complex than these molecules. The behaviour of cells cannot be reduced to the laws of physics and chemistry. The processes of reproduction, metabolism, growth, show so many interactions between parts that a complete knowledge of all the parts gives only a partial explanation.

Properties of atoms, rocks, the dynamics of stars, and the operation of gravity remain fixed. But the properties of living populations change with time. In the living world every individual is unique; not so in the inanimate world where one molecular structure fits endless individuals.

2. Ernst Mayr, *What Makes Biology Unique* (Cambridge: Cambridge University Press, 2007), 36–37.

Principles of entropy are not applicable in living systems. Non-living systems left to themselves degenerate, become more disordered; not so living systems. Principles of entropy apply to the living thing plus its environment. As the living organism thrives, its surroundings become more disordered.

Question: Can you simply explain complexity?
Answer: All matter is constructed from smaller units. Let us start from the smallest units and work our way upwards. The smallest units of matter are quarks which form protons and neutrons which form nuclei, which together with electrons form atoms.

Up-quarks + down-quarks → Protons + neutrons
protons + neutrons → nuclei.
nuclei + electrons → atoms
Atoms + Atoms → molecules
Molecules + Molecules → more complex molecules (chain)
(more complex molecules)^n → polymers
Polymers + polymers→ more complex polymers
more complex polymers + + + → DNA
DNA is a long string of millions of units in a particular order. This is complexity.

Beginning from the bottom of the diagram below, the increasing complexity of matter is shown, ending with the molocule DNA. The properties of each level cannot be regarded as the sum of the properties of the constituents.

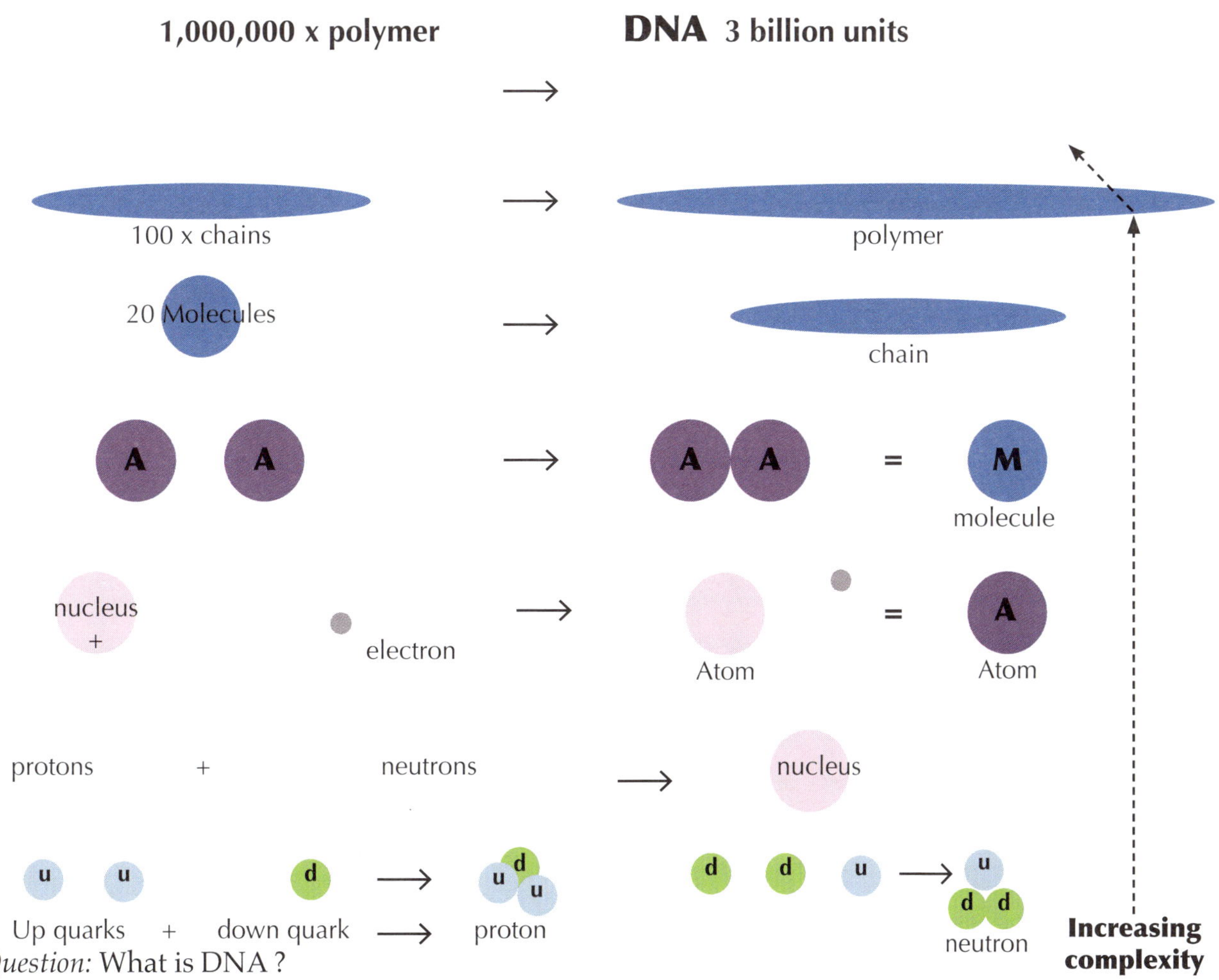

Question: What is DNA ?
Answer: Deoxyribose Nucleic Acid
Question: Can you be less scientific?

Answer: DNA can be thought of as strings of letters. Each letter designates a chemical. Each three of the letters—each 'codon'—forms a word.

3 billion bases in a line

◄..................... **TCGTGACGGCCATCACGCCCCGAATTGAACCGT** ....►

◄..................... **TCGTGACGGCCATCACGCCCCGAATTGAACCGT** ....►

◄..................... **TCG TGA CGG CCA TCA CGC CCC GAA TTG AAC CGT** ....►

Each 3 [triplet] [codon] represents a word

Question: could you explain 'letters'?
Answer: A chemical compound is likened to a letter. Each letter stands for a chemical compound known as a base.
There are four bases involved. These four bases function as a four letter alphabet:
A, T, G, and **C.**

Question: You said DNA can be thought of as a string. Could you explain string?
Answer: One string of human DNA would be 150 km long if each letter was magnified to this size: ATTGGAACCCACGCTTAGACATTATGG......All these 'letters' are joined, joined by chemical bonds.

Question: Is there more than one string?
Answer: There are forty-six strings in the nucleus of every cell of every human being. They are wound together in pairs. So there are twenty-three pairs. If all the information were typed, it would fill 1,000,000 pages. The whole human genome, all the information on all the strings, has now been revealed. Only about one third of the letters appear so far to have meaning.

Question: How can chemicals be called information?
Answer: Each triplet (codon) of letters is a word: ATT GGA ACC CAC GCT TAG ACA TTA. Each of these is a three letter word.

Question: What does this mean?
Answer: Each codon means a specific life-chemical – an 'amino acid'. Each codes for a particular acid, that is, attracts a particular amino acid to itself.

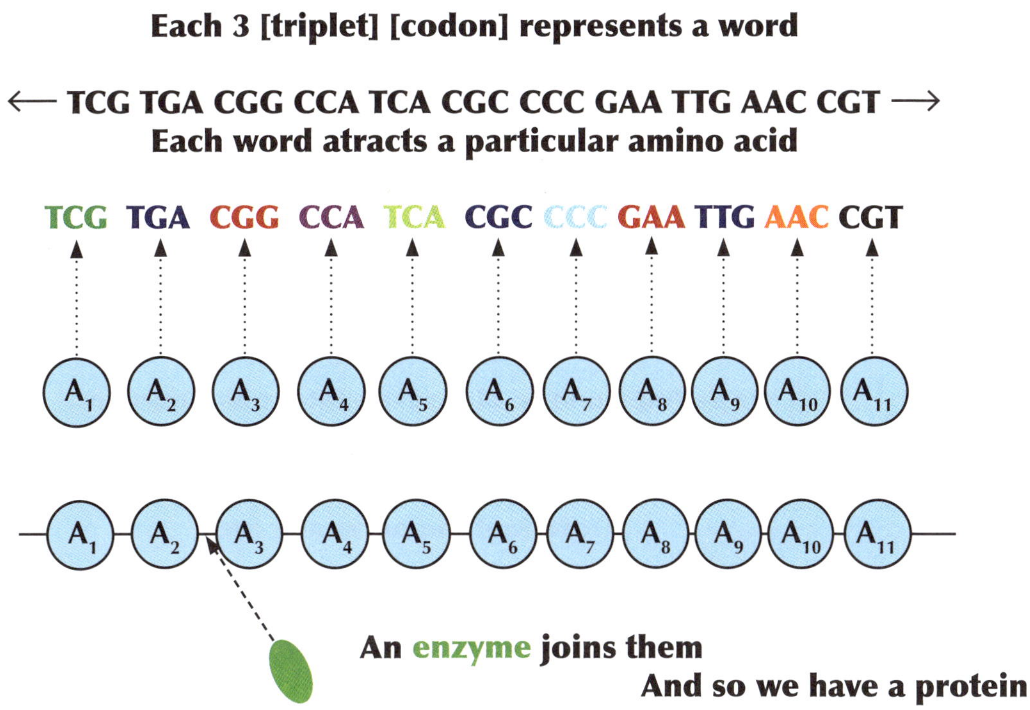

Question: What does that mean?
Answer: Each 'word' attracts its own acid to it, and the acid attaches itself to its word:

TCG	TCA	CGG	CCA	AAC	CGT
acid$_1$	acid$_2$	acid$_3$	acid$_4$	acid$_{10}$	acid$_{11}$

That is, if the triplet is exposed in the cell, it will attract that acid to itself. For example, TGC may be programmed to attract NH_2-$(CH_2)_{10}$-COOH.

A set of triplets (codons) in succession will attract a set of different amino acids in the correct order to form, for example, an anti-body. At the beginning and end of this set of triplets are triplets, which mean start and stop. So, a particular compound with the right number of acids and no more—and in the correct order—is formed to perform a specific function. The acids are joined by the action of molecules with that designated task at an assembly point.

Question: Then?
Answer: A worker chemical— an enzyme—links them; and we have an anti-body, or a digestive juice, or dopamine or adrenalin; and they are released from the assembly area and find their way out of the cell.

New protein off to deal with a virus

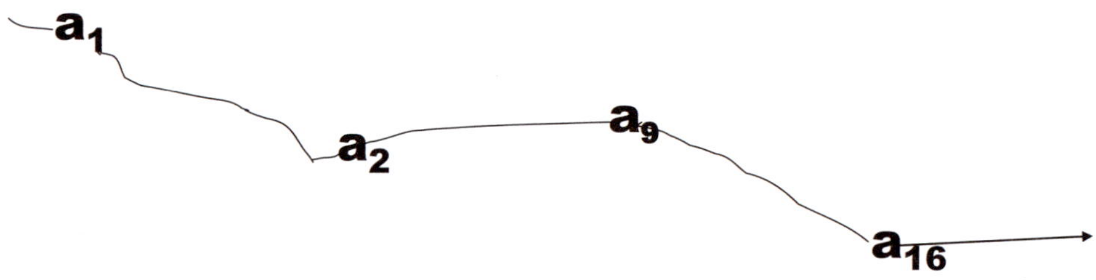

Or perhaps one to digest the latest hamburger

Or to fuel the adrenalin rush

Question: How often does this happen? How many proteins are formed?
Answer: Many life compounds are formed from various amino acids present in the cytoplasm of the cell. There are 100,000,000 known antibodies for various viruses and bacteria. The cytoplasm is the fluid surrounding the nucleus; it is the nucleus that contains the DNA.

Question: Could you summarize all that?
Answer: DNA is not life, but it contains the instructions to build and operate a living being. It needs a cell to function.

3. The cell

3.1 The elements within a cell

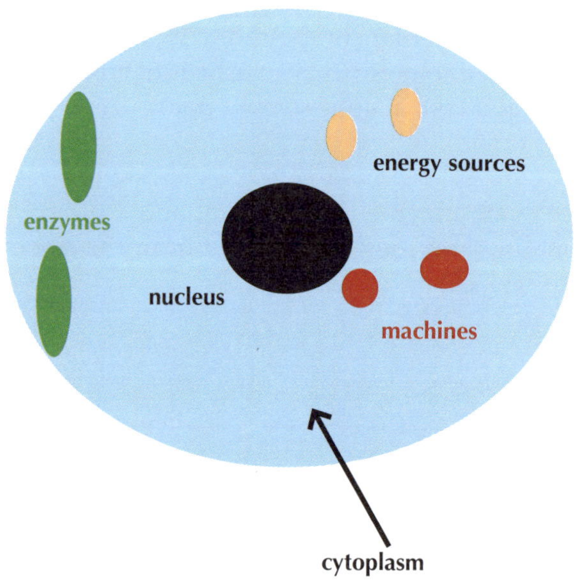

The cell is the fundamental unit of living matter. All living things are composed of one cell or of many cells. A cell has a diameter of about 0.001 cm; one hundredth of a millimetre. It can be seen under an ordinary microscope. Robert Hooke was the first to develop the microscope and the first to see the cell. Cells make up all the organs.

3.2 The cell at work

The cell is like a factory. A factory needs a control centre, a power source, workers, a product, transport within the factory, and a means of getting the product out and raw materials in. The cell has all these:

- *Control centre:* this is the *nucleus* where decisions are made about what work the cell will do.
- *Factory proper,* the cytoplasm: the fluid filling the cell. Here the work is done. Here are found the machines, the facilities for transport, power sources, the materials for constructing molecules needed in life processes.
- *Power source: Mitochondria:* these create mobile packets of energy which are used in the many chemical reactions that occur in the cell every minute.
- *Fuel:* the fuel is ATP—adenosine triphosphate. It is made by the mitochondria.
- *Nutrients:* these come in from the outside. They are enclosed in little bags, vacuoles.
- *Chemical agents, machines:* The newly arrived nutrients are then encountered by lysosomes (little bags) which contain enzymes and acids. The lysosomes pour the enzymes and acids into the food vacuoles containing the nutrients. The acids and enzymes break down the nutrients to usable portions, which are then spilled into the cytoplasm, and used to form various proteins.
- *Workers, Ribosomes:* These help assemble the amino-acids which have been attracted to the appropriate regions of the unzipped DNA.[3]
- *Export facility:* the proteins for export are attracted to the Golgi Apparatus. They are in sacs and move from here to the surface of the cell from where they are released.
- *Factory wall:* the cell membrane is impervious to most molecules.
- *Gateway:* antennae proteins control chanelling devices for getting the molecules in or out of the cell.

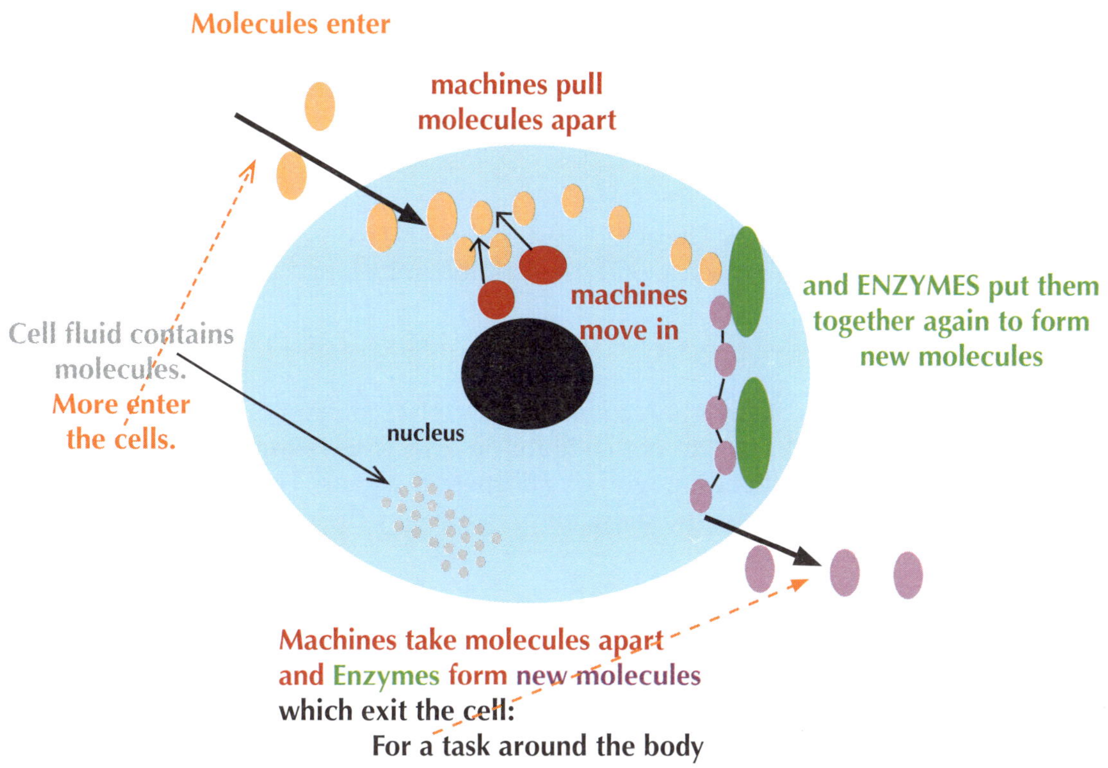

3.3 Chemicals and processes associated with the cell

3.3.1 Proteins.

A protein is a molecule designed (by years of natural selection) to do a specific task. Each protein can do one task. It may be an anti-body, a digestive enzyme, a neurotransmitter, an emotion associate such as adrenalin. A crucial feature of a protein is its shape, which fits it to react with another molecule. If the other molecule is an invader, it sticks to it and nullifies it. If the other molecule is a complex

3. Actually a copy of DNA called RNA.

molecule, it sticks to it and breaks it into simpler constituents. If molecules need to be joined, it finds them and joins them.

A particular chemical conversion may involve a series of steps. The appropriate enzymes for each step line up in the required order to facilitate the steps.

An enzyme has a region within its structure with a pattern which somehow complements a part of a molecule on which it acts. The shapes match, the enzyme sticks, and the reaction is then facilitated.

3.3.2 Amino acids

These are molecules from which proteins are built. There are about twenty amino acids which can be used to build proteins. For chemistry students they have the general formula NH_2-$(CH_2)_n$-COOH. A protein is built from any number, between fifty to 2000 amino acids. The acids are arranged in an order which gives the protein a particular shape, which fits it for its task. There are millions of possible shapes—100,000,000 possible anti-bodies for example. Once formed, the protein bends into a three dimensional structure. If the order of amino acids is changed, the shape of the protein changes, changing its function. This happens in gene mutations.

3.3.3 Nucleic acids

1) DNA

This is the molecule previously described. A long string of phosphate units and sugars provides the structure on which the four bases are attached. The order of the bases (G, T, A, and C), is crucial. A bacterium has one double helix with three million bases. The human has twenty-three double helices each with three billion bases.

2) RNA

When the DNA is due to unzip at a particular location to provide the blueprint for the engineering of a protein, the engineering does not happen within the precinct of the nucleus. Nothing except messages can enter this region. Instead, the DNA sends a copy of itself, unzipped in the required region, into the cytoplasm. The copy, RNA then does this work. There are two connected varieties of RNA which work in concert.

3.3.4 Gene

The gene is a set of adjacent codons. The active part of the DNA consists of the four bases A, T, G, C arranged in order, a continuous sequence of the 4, 3 billion units long.

....**TAG**TTTTCCTGGCCTACTGTTGCTGATGAAGGACGAGGGTACTTGAAAGACCAG**TAA**....

Each three of these bases is one word. A codon (base triplet) corresponds with an amino acid.

But codons TAA, TAG, and TGA do not code for an acid. They simply mean stop. A sequence beginning with one of these and ending with one of these is a gene. The triplets (codons) between these stops attract their amino acids, and the acids are joined by the ribosomes.

3.4 Synthesis of a protein (worker chemical).

- A message comes to the DNA that a protein is to be made. The message may come from inside or outside the cell.
- Within the nucleus an accurate copy is made of the required region of the relevant DNA strand. This is RNA.
- The RNA which has a copy of the order of the codons (triplets) involved moves from the nucleus to the cytoplasm.
- Particular acids are attracted to each triplet of the RNA, as explained before.
- Ribosomes interact with the RNA and attach the lined-up acids to each other.
- When the ribsomes reach the stop triplet, the protein chain is released into the cytoplasm, and then out of the cell into the body.[4]

4. Two copies of RNA are actually involved. Transfer RNA collects the acids in correct order, and takes them to the

3.5 Mutation

If one letter in a codon is changed, this codon attracts a different amino acid, so that the resulting protein produced is different. When this happens spontaneously by chance, you have a mutation. In a small percentage of cases this changed codon, meaning a changed gene, confers on its recipient an advantage which over the course of many generations may produce individuals more fitted to the prevailing conditions of climate or predation, and hence more successful individuals in a given species. Over many generations involving millions of years, the accumulation of such changes may result in new species. Another method of mutation is if codons change places.

4. A working model of a cell

Build your own e coli

Each atom a coloured bead

COST at 5c/bead: $4 billion

1 cm diameter

WEIGHT
of finished model: 10,000 tonnes

TIME
Hire 1000 staff–click one bead every 5 seconds, working 8 hours a day, 5 days per week, needs *35 years*

PLACE: Hire a cathedral

The *e coli* is a bacterium, comprised of one cell only. Within dimensions of a thousandth of a millimetre long and two thousandths of a millimetre wide, it has an enormous number of units.

Try to build a model[5] of the one cell which is the bacterium *e coli*. Let each atom be a bead of diameter 1 cm. The beads representing carbon, hydrogen, oxygen, nitrogen, phosphorous and sulphur have different colours. If you employ 1000 staff each working five days per week putting one bead into place every five seconds, this would take 35 years. The weight of the product would be 10,000 tons, and it would need a large cathedral to house it. Weak magnetic forces would have to be factored into the design. 2000 enzymes need to be able to find the molecules on which they are to work to provide the running of the cell. Then energy has to be supplied so that enzymes can move to find the molecules on which they have to work. Each ribosome would be a machine with 270,000 beads, and there would be 30,000 of these machines. The cost would be $4 billion.

5. What explains a living thing? Further questions and answers

Question: What is a living thing?
Answer: A living thing = something that *feeds* itself, *reproduces*, *defends* itself, whose parts work in *harmony*, all because its cells contain DNA.

---

ribosomes, where messenger RNA is waiting to receive them, allowing the ribosomes then to connect them.

5. A G Cairns-Smith, *Seven Clues to The Origin of Life* (Cambridge: Cambridge University Press, 1993), 16–21.

- The *Reductionist* would say the properties of the living thing are explained by the properties of the DNA which can be explained by properties of the bases, which are explained by properties of molecules, which are explained by properties of atoms, which are explained by properties of protons and neutrons, which are explained by properties of quarks.
- The *Vitalist* would say a 'vital force' is present in the living thing to organize the matter.
- The *Physicalist*[6] [The scientist proposing emergence] would say as matter complexifies, new properties arise ['emerge'] which are not reducible to the properties of the parts.

Question: Can you explain emergence again?
Answer: Think of it this way: the human is more complex than the animal, which is more complex than other living things, which are more complex than cells, which are more complex than atoms. As the structures become more complex, the behaviour becomes more sophisticated. More abilities which were not there before appear.

Question: Would you be more specific?
Answer: A single cell feeds, reproduces, and its activities are coordinated.

A multi-celled unit's cells work together: the unit swims, eats others.

Animal: In addition to having single cells with coordinated activities, and many cells which work together, the animal also sees, hears, tastes, touches, remembers, learns.

Human: In addition to what the animal has, the human also knows, knows that it knows, experiences a self, knows it will die, is unsatisfied, can be free from forces of natural selection and so, can freely change life.

All these powers emerge in the organisms as complexity increases.

Question: Is this the product of chemistry?
Answer: Two things could be said:

1) The greater complexity enables the spiritualness seemingly already potentially inherent in matter to express itself.
2) The new properties revealed by matter as it becomes more complex are not predictable from a knowledge of the parts.

Question: Could you explain the second one?
Answer: When you build a house, you can envisage the finished product before you put the parts together. When you put the parts of a living molecule together, you cannot predict the property of life, memory, thought from the properties of the parts. You get something more.

Question: Why do molecules evolve in the direction of higher forms of life?
Answer: The ones on the path to life and more life seem to be the stable ones. There seems to be an inner urge to follow this path, and end up with consciousness.

> There is still something mysterious about evolution, with its apparent groping towards some future purpose. Things at least seem to organize themselves somewhat better than they ought to, just on the basis of blind chance evolution and natural selection. It may well be that such appearances are quite deceptive. There seems to be something about the way that the laws of physics work which allows natural selection to be a

6. Buldenholzer, 'What is Life? Current Scientific and Philosophical Perspectives', *op cit*, 206–220.

much more effective process than it would be with just arbitrary laws. The resulting apparently intelligent groping is an interesting issue.[7]

Question: Is this 'natural selection'?
Answer: Partly; but 'survival of the fittest' which is the result of natural selection, does not include the ability to write music, compose poetry, solve problems involving $\sqrt{-1}$, e^x, or the phenomenon of giving your life for another.

6. Non-life → Life

6.1 Historical issue
Three centuries ago, before the advent of suitable instruments, most people believed new life arose spontaneously from dead matter. Evidence for this, for example, was the maggots that arose from bad meat.

6.1.1 Francesco Redi
In the mid seventeenth century, prevailing wisdom was that maggots formed naturally from rotting meat. But in 1668 Francesco Redi took eight jars. In four of them he placed either fish or meat, and covered them with muslin or fine gauze. In the second four, he placed the same fish or meat, but did not cover them with muslin. Maggots eventually appeared in the uncovered jars, but not in the covered ones. He continued his experiments: he put dead flies with meat into covered jars, and living flies with meat into covered jars. Maggots arose in the second case. The life had not come from the non-living flies or meat, but from the living flies.

6.1.2 Lassaro Spallanzi
But views, which had been the common wisdom for many generations, die hard. Most scientists for many years still remained unconvinced: life spontaneously emerged from non-life. About eighty years later, debate was still the order of the day. John Needham, a biologist and priest, thought he had proved spontaneous generation by boiling chicken broth, covering it, and observing micro-organisms to abound some time later.
However, Italian priest, Lazzaro Spallanzani, repeated this with an added control.
He placed chicken broth into a flask, sealed it, created a partial vacuum after sealing, and then boiled the broth. No micro-organisms resulted, but spontaneous generation adherents said all this showed was that spontaneous generation needed air.

Spanzalli

Pasteur

7. Roger Penrose, *The Emperor's New Mind* (Oxford: Oxford University Press, 1989), 416.

6.1.3 Louis Pasteur

Over a century later, the French Academy of Sciences initiated a contest to solve the question. Louis Pasteur entered the contest. He heated meat broth in a flask with a long neck, allowed air to enter, then bent the long neck it into an S-shape. No micro-organisms were detected until he brought the broth into contact with the bent part of the neck where they had been trapped. Thus spontaneous generation died.

6.2 The problem today of the origin of life from non-life

6.2.1. It happened, but how?

However, on a broader scale, the problem remains today. Life developed from non-life, but how? As stars gave rise to the atoms of higher elements, as atoms of elements gave rise to molecules comprised of atoms, (and these two transitions are understood), so it is widely believed non-living molecules gave rise to life, but this transition is not understood. At some stage in the evolution of planet earth, life arose from non-life. Somehow non-living matter had to evolve into living matter; not on the seemingly miraculous scale of fully formed creatures emerging from the rot, but over hundreds of millions of years, life in a rudimentary initial form had to come from non-living matter. Some biologists[8] declare we are nowhere near a solution to the problem, others[9] believe one may develop scenarios in which this could have happened, but declare it is impossible to declare any theorised process is what actually occurred. So it remains an enigma, though biologists anticipate a solution will eventually be found.

6.2.2. General stages of the process

For life to form, simple chemicals would have to interact to form more complex chemicals which then had to complexify further, and form polymers. These would need to be enclosed with some sort of membrane around them. Inside the isolated space within the membrane there would need to be a source of energy and a mechanism for information transfer. How this happened is the object of much speculation. There are chemicals in outer space, the first chemicals on the path to life. Did living cells land on the earth from elsewhere or did it happen on earth? Whatever about this question, the transition from non-life to life would eventually have to be addressed, whether it occurred elsewhere or here on earth.

6.2.3. Building blocks

It is presumed life arose spontaneously from pre-biotic molecules no earlier than 4 billion years ago. The simple chemicals are found in space and are easily synthesized on early earth. Two of these are hydrogen cyanide, HCN, and formaldehyde, HCHO.

Much more complex molecules than these from which chemicals intrinsically involved in a living cell are formed are not generally found on earth, and it seems to need controlled and protected environments to synthesize these—not likely in the chemical wild. The commonest of these more complex molecules found on earth are not those of life. But even if they were, how would the more-complex-still molecules arise from these? This is an unsolved question. The molecules which could make up amino acids can be synthesised in the laboratory, but not seemingly under conditions resembling those of early earth.

6.3 The Miller-Urey experiment

In 1953 Stanley Miller enclosed in a flask what was then thought to be the early earth's atmosphere—hydrogen, methane, ammonia, water vapour. He boiled the mixture for days, and put electric discharges through the bubbling mixture to simulate lightning. After some time he analysed the darkened mixture, and found hydrogen cyanide and some amino acids present. This was a sensational finding at the time, but now it is thought the early atmosphere was different to Miller's mix; it is believed to have been composed of carbon monoxide, carbon dioxide, water vapour and nitrogen. Such an atmosphere in a Miller-type experiment does produce formaldehyde from which sugars

8. Simon Conway Morris, *Life's Solution* (Cambridge: Cambridge University Press, 2003), 44–63.
9. Cairns-Smith, *Seven Clues to the Origin of Life*, 114–116.

could result but it does not produce hydrogen cyanide and amino acids needed for synthesizing the bases in DNA; a biochemical pathway for hydrogen cyanide and amino acids has yet to be found.

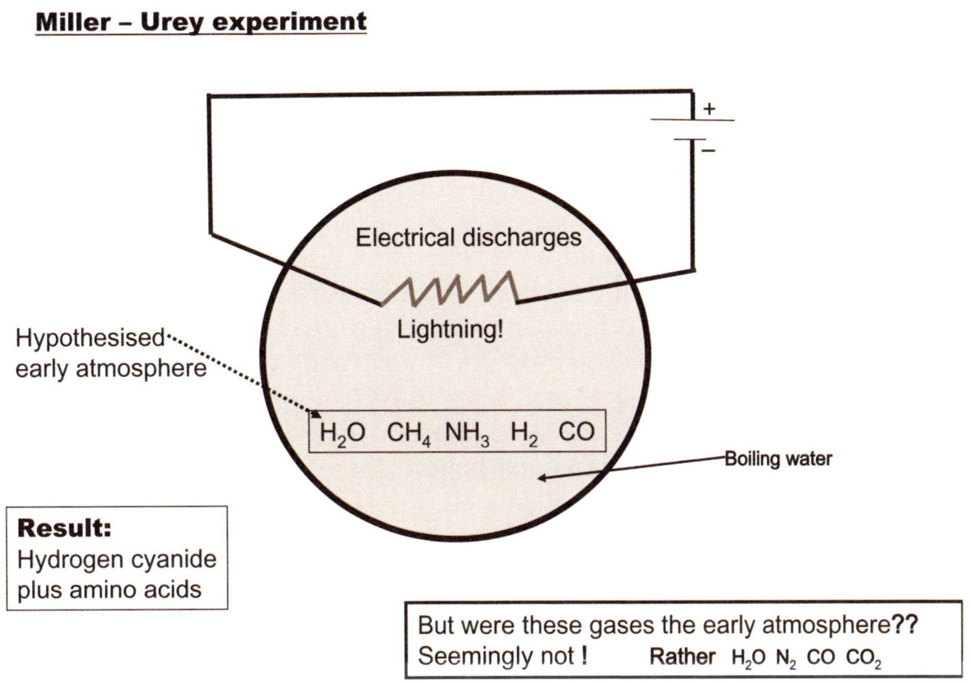

A key life ingredient, ribose,[10] can be formed from the polymerisation of formaldehyde (HCHO), but the yield is low, and good quantities of undesirable tar-like side effects are formed. Careful manipulation of the reaction conditions are needed to produce a satisfactory yield and fewer contaminants. Ribose itself, once formed easily degrades; so could such conditions have allowed its production in non-laboratory conditions? All the laboratory generations of products are far removed from the early earth life in the raw.

6.4 The conditions on early earth

6.4.1 Catastrophic times

What was the early earth of four billion years ago like? The very early atmosphere was composed of hot gases and the earth's gravity was too weak to hold these because the earth at this stage was too small. As the earth cooled and eventually formed a crust, gases escaped from beneath the crust, most of which was water vapour. Water arrived in an endless bombardment of icy comets.[11] Tremendous storms flooded the earth for millions of years, and at times the oceans boiled away due to crashes of huge asteroids, some tens of kilometres in diameter, as the earth was adding to its mass. This caused an increase of gravity and a subsequent increase of ability to hold an atmosphere. If life did arise during these catastrophic times, it proabably would not have survived.

6.4.2 Necessary steps from building blocks to the cell

Once amino acids and other building blocks of life molecules had formed—and the how of this is still unanswered—they had to come together to form all the molecules of life. The eventual result, the cell, would need a membrane, enzymes, ATP to provide energy, nucleic acids with coding bases. How could a four word language be transformed into twenty words coding for amino acids?

10. Morris, *Life's Solution*, 52

11. See chapter 1.

At some point, molecules of the sort we now find in organisms, were made originally without organisms. They were made as a result of processes operating on early earth. They were then organised into the first beings able to evolve through natural selection.

Speculations do not yet touch the conceptual difficulties. Cells are fully working machines of incredible complexity. There is a gap of light years between the simple building blocks and the final result.

6.5 Summary: Difficulties

1) Evolution does not know in advance which pieces would be relevant to a finished product.
2) Functioning cell systems are highly interlocked: all the pieces need each other. None could survive and operate without the others.
3) There are features which could have been otherwise: amino acid alphabet, left-handedness. The fitting together of amino acids and codons demands they have the same handedness. It is hard to see how all the original constituents were left-handed.
4) The enormous distance between the constituents and the finished product.

The stating of these difficulties is not an endorsement of 'Intelligent Design'. Scientists of theistic (non-creationist) and agnostic persuasions believe there is a solution. Many seeming mysteries have been solved. This difficult one will someday also yield a solution. Simon Conway Morris—a discounter of all present theories—is convinced such a process did take place and one day we may understand what happened.

> . . . one should be optimistic. Somehow, we must assume that the problems of combining those molecules that prefer hot springs as against glaciers, not to mention the myriad of often unwanted chemical by-products all ready to gum up a reaction, will be surmounted.[12]

12. Morris, *Life's Solutions*, 67.

Chapter 3

The Progress of Life: From Simple Cells to First Appearance of Modern Body Forms

Chapter overview

- The first cells: Prokaryotes
    - Photosynthesis
    - Stromatolites
- Eukaryotes
    - Protists: one-celled organisms
    - Multi-celled organisms
- Further development: Ediacaran creatures
- Cambrian Explosion
    - Varieties of new life
    - Causes

1. Introduction: When did life first appear?

When did life begin? What is the earliest evidence of life? 3900 million years ago was a time of 'late heavy bombardment'—comets, rocks, asteroids constantly bombarded the earth, causing heat, even to the point of evaporating oceans. If life formed at this time, it would conceivably have been wiped out. The oldest evidence is 3800 million years ago—3.8 billion years. Isotopes of elements are atoms of the element with slightly different atomic weights. Two of the isotopes of carbon are Carbon 12 (^{12}C), and Carbon 13 (^{13}C). The ratio of the proportion of these in organic carbon is different to the ratio of these in inorganic carbon. Evidence suggesting the organic ratio has been found in rocks in Greenland 3800 million years old[1].

Between 3500 million years ago and about 2000 million years ago, life abounded on earth. The cell had developed, DNA and RNA were actively present; cells could manufacture food, but they did not possess a nucleus. The single string of DNA was compacted; it lived in the cytoplasm, but had no membrane around it. These bacteria—prokaryotes—can obtain energy from light, organic compounds, inorganic compounds.

2. The first cells: Prokaryotes

Prokaryotes are bacteria, single-celled organisms, without a nucleus. A single strand of DNA is rolled up and floats in the cytoplasm or clings to the cell wall. They *were* the life form; and they were very numerous between 3.5 and 2.0 billion years ago. They are still numerous today.

Very thin slices of rock, examined under the electron microscope, revealed clear evidence of prokaryotes 3.5 billion years old, and dominating the biosphere until 2.0 billion years ago. They evolved to nucleus-bearing bacteria, but prokaryotes are still present in large numbers and in a great variety of forms. They can live in the gut of animals, and produce methane gas. They can also live around deep-sea hot thermal vents, in sulphur-rich springs, in salty seas, in rock, oil, concrete, or bathed in sunlight.

2.1 Some varieties of present day prokaryotes

There are a number of types of prokaryotes:

1. R Southwood, *The Story of Life* (New York: Oxford University Press, 2004), 14.

- *Methanogens* combine atmospheric carbon dioxide with hydrogen from plant life to form methane, which is released from swamps or from the guts of cattle.
- *Eubacteria* exist by the trillions: in human guts, in the soil, in water. The ones in the soil live around the roots of plants, enabling the conversion of nitrogen to assimilable chemical forms. They react atmospheric nitrogen with hydrogen in organic matter in the quest for energy. Their waste-products are life-necessary elements and compounds: ammonia, amino acids, as well as methane.
- *Sulpholobus* bacteria live in hot springs and convert sulphur compounds in conjuction with the hydrogen from organic compounds or water to sulphur, hydrogen, hydrogen sulphide.
- *Cyanobacteria* convert sunlight, carbon dioxide and water into glucose ($C_6H_{12}O_6$) and liberate oxygen as a waste. They need the green chemical catalyst chlorophyll to bring about this synthesis.

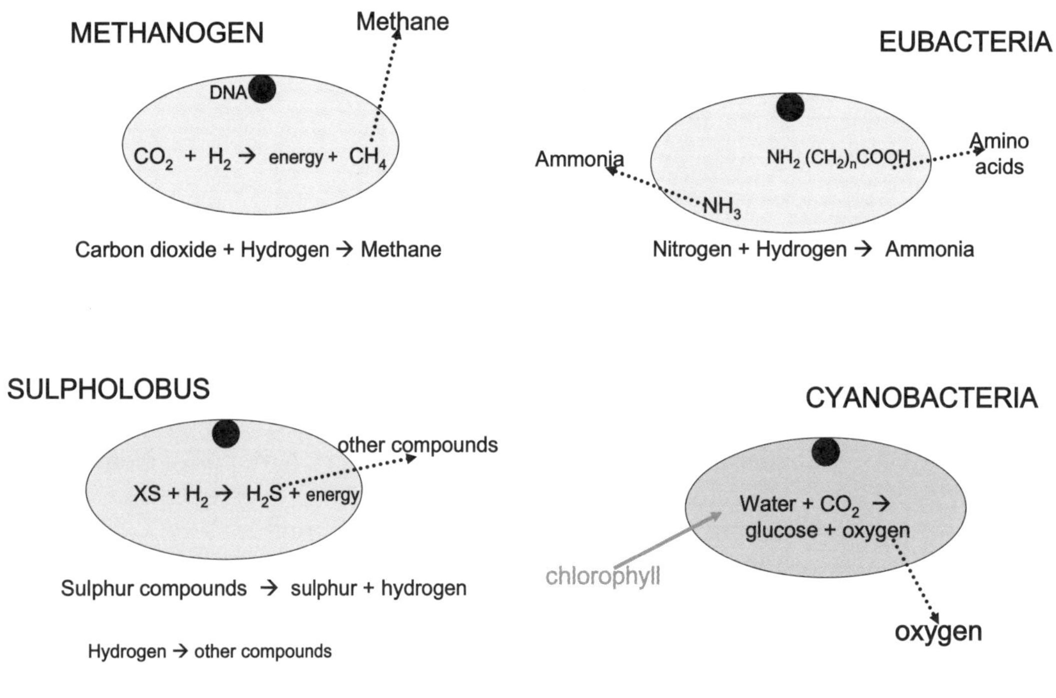

PROKARYOTES – variety and creativity

<u>Question 1</u>. **Life came from non-life, and adapts itself readily itself to any a multiplicity of environments. Do an internet research and find out how bacterial life has spread to almost any environment today.**

2.2 Prokaryotes harvest sunlight and deliver oxygen to the air

Cyanobacteria: The earth originally contained no oxygen in its atmosphere and it is to these glucose-producing organisms we owe the arrival of oxygen in the earth's atmosphere. These organisms live around the roots of plants, enabling the conversion of nitrogen to assimilable chemical forms. They react atmospheric nitrogen with hydrogen in organic matter in the quest for energy. Waste-products are life-necessary elements and compounds: ammonia, amino acids, as well as methane.

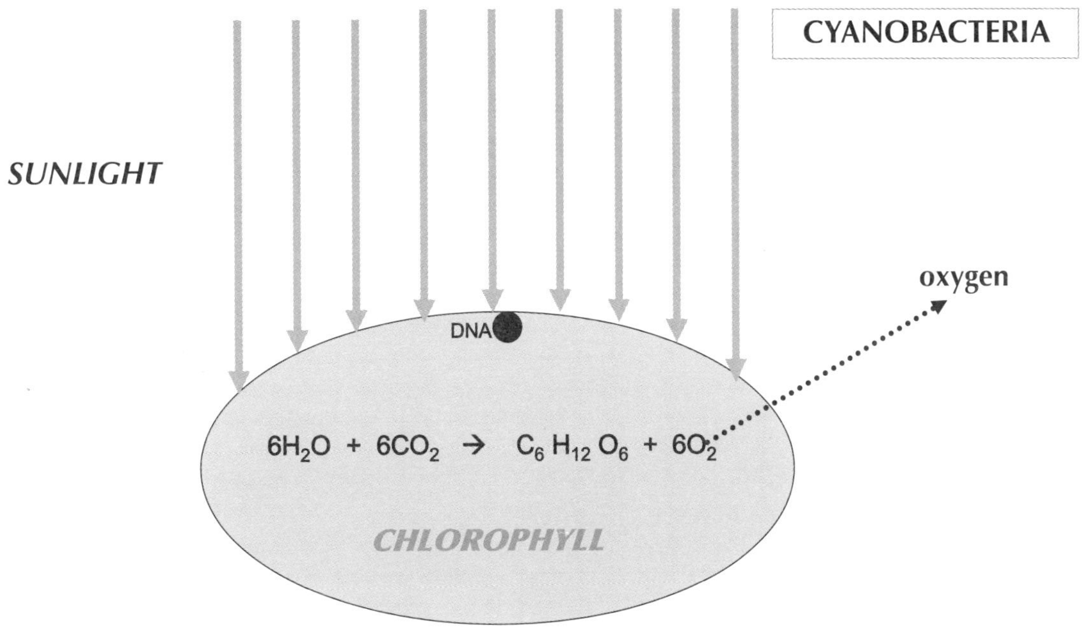

Water vapour + carbon dioxide → glucose + oxygen

Presence of **chlorophyll** necessary for the reaction

3. Stromatolites

These are straight cylindrical structures of limestone or other minerals. Their existence has been known for many decades. They were thought to be merely rock formations. However, the discovery of colonies of stromatolites in protected salty water in Shark Bay Western Australia threw new light on these. They were found to be living colonies. A stromatolite consists of layer upon layer separated by mats. The top layer houses cyanobacteria; the next layer purple bacteria; the next layers other bacteria.

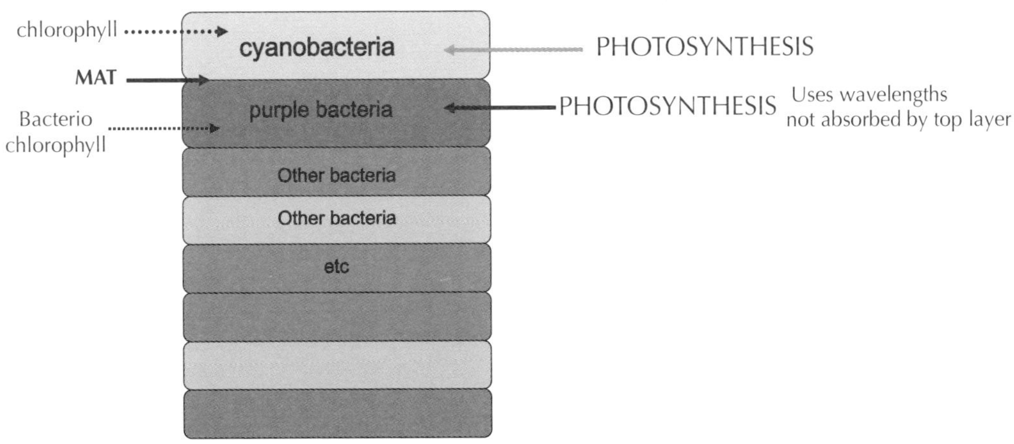

3.1 A working stromatolite

Cyanobacteria harvest sunlight to make glucose in the top layer. Waste products come down to the next layer, which contains purple bacteria. These use the wavelengths of sunlight not accessed by the cyanobacteria in the top layer and, using a different chlorophyll, manufacture glucose, without liberating oxygen. Their wastes fall down to the next layer where other bacteria perform tasks. These include feeding on dead bacteria from above. The layers are very thin.

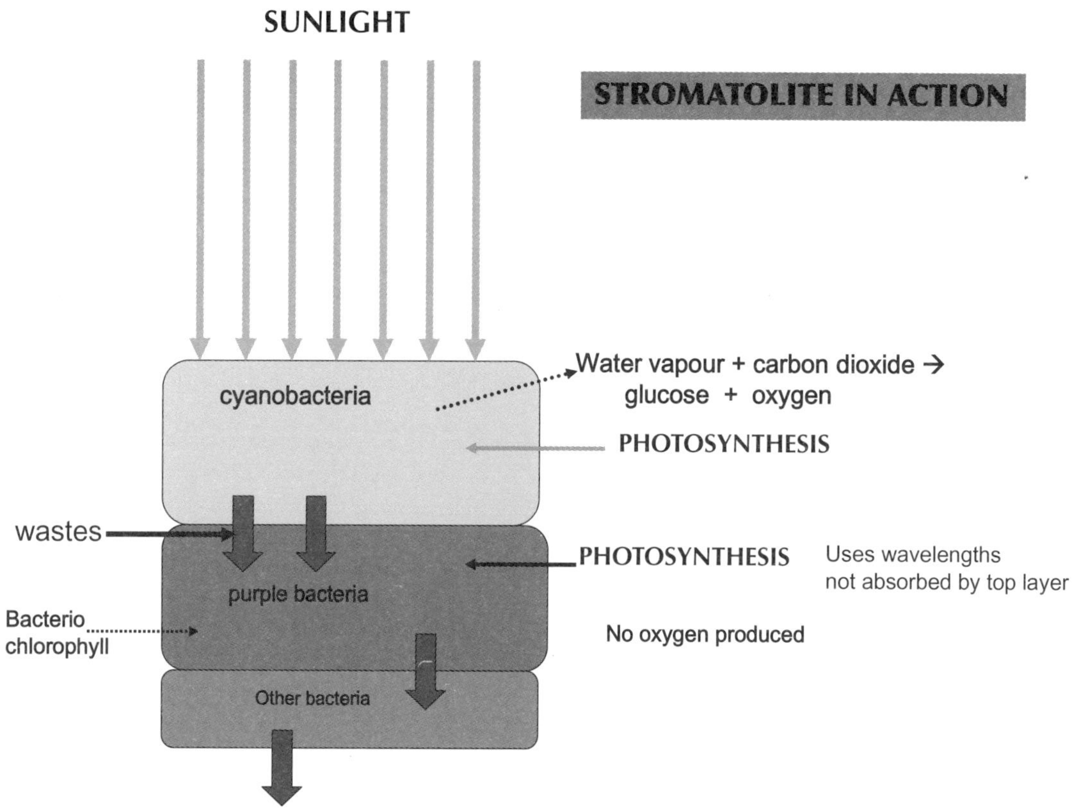

A Stromalite in action

The bacteria in the top layer produce a slime which traps particles of minerals, and gradually screens out the light. When the screening process is advanced enough to block out most of the light, bacteria slide up through the slime and begin making another layer over the top layer. The mineral-laced slime becomes a mat, forming a boundary to the new layer.

3.2 Stromatolite survival today

For about 1.8 billion years, prokaryotes inhabited the sea, poked above the seas in shallow waters as stromatolites, inhabited deep sea vents and rocks under water.

Most stromatolites disappeared after the evolution of other forms of sea-dwelling life. A few stromatolites, such as those in Shark Bay, are in water too salty for other forms of life to attack, and survive to this day. Prokaryotes contribute enormously to the biomass of the earth: forty million in a gram of soil, a million in a millilitre of water.

Shark Bay, West Australia

Question 2. Imagine you are an extra-terrestrial visitor; you land at Shark Bay and see the above sturctures. Would you conclude that life has begun?

4. Eukaryotes[2] 2500 — 600 million years ago

Eukaryotes evolved and developed into many single-celled forms over approximately two billion years. These merged into colonies from which multi-celled organisms developed, all having the more developed eukaryotic cells. Prokaryotic organsims abounded, and still do so today.

4.1 Developments heralding Eukaryotes

4.1.1 The Development of a nucleus

The arrival of eukaryotes is a very significant step in the history of life. The controlling DNA is now not only a separate collection attached to the inner wall of the cell, but this also becomes surrounded by a membrane. It no longer is restricted to one double strand of DNA, but has a number of strands. In cell division the nucleus divides and with it the cell.

4.1.2 Other advances

Other structures not found in prokaryotes are found in the eukaryotic cytoplasm. These are:

- *Mitochondria:* A membrane contains energy-producing material (adenosine triphosphate – ATP) and here energy is produced. The mitichondria obtain substances with energy potential from nutrients in the cytoplasm, and manufacture ATP from these, provided that the cell does not obtain energy from sunlight. Cells may have any number of these; some can have thousands.
- *Plastids:* These are present in almost all plant cells:
    - chloroplasmids: contain chlorophyll and from sunlight, water vapour and CO_2 fashion sugar molecules, which are sources of energy.
    - chromoplasts: contain colour producing chemicals for flowers, vegetables, fruits.
    - Amyloplasts: where starch compounds are stored.
- *Cytoskeletons:* these are filaments which support the cell structure, and help in the movement of materials within the cell.

2. Southwood, *The Story of Life,* 25–35.

- *Microtubules:* have a crucial role in cell division. Roger Penrose has developed an alternative theory for consciousness using microtubules.
- *Actin filaments:* also help in cell structure, and are vital in muscle cells.

4.2 How did developments occur?

An oxygen-dependent prokaryotic cell absorbed bacteria into the cytoplasm which, over millions of years, became mitochondria. The cell also absorbed a bacterium with a flagellum, giving the cell ability to move. Some cells absorbed cyanobacteria—bacteria containing chlorophyll—which became the plastids. The processes obviously benefitted both the host, and the captured organism which gained in protection and access to a reliable food source in the new environment. These processes are referred to as *endosymbiosis*. The developments took hundreds of millions of years.

All cells in higher living organisms are eukaryotic.

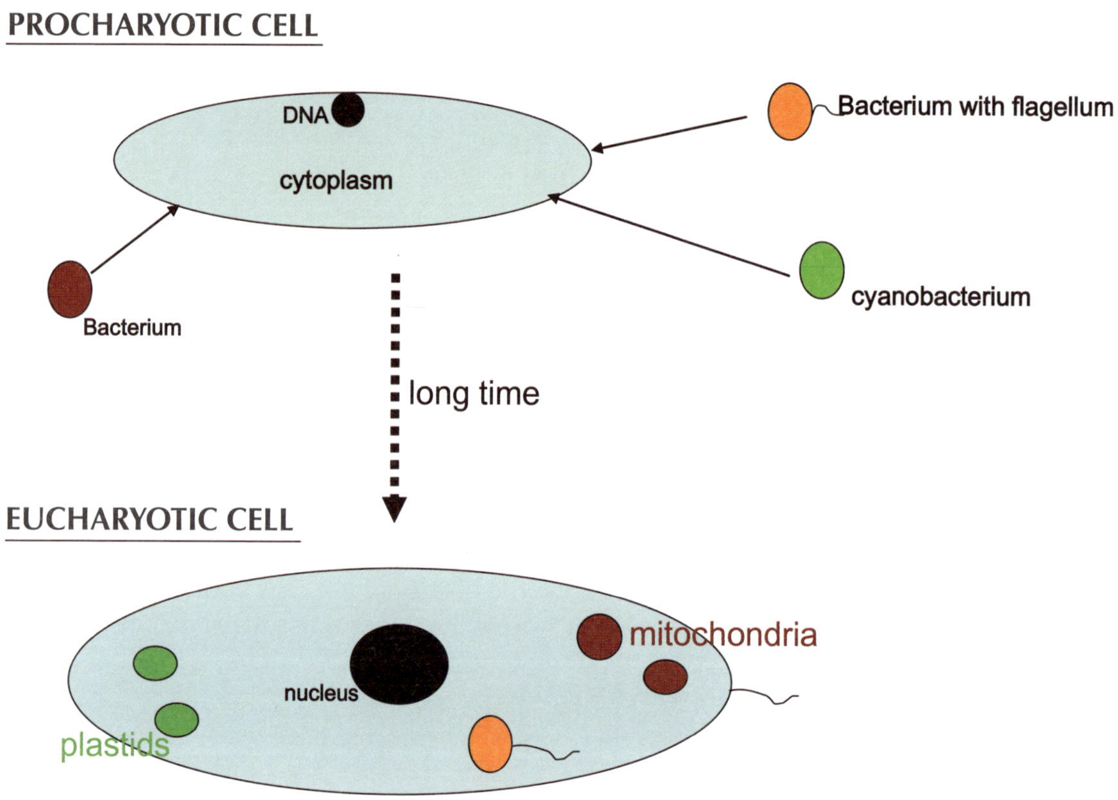

5. More diversified eukaryotes: the protists.

5.1 Single celled organisms

Single eukaryotic cells evolved into a variety of organisms known as *protists*. There are now three main groups:

- Protozoans—those without chlorophyll;
- Algae—those with chlorophyll;
- Fungus-like single-celled organisms.

No other kingdom[3] includes so many cell types: many types of algae, varieties of protozoans, varieties of slime moulds. Included among protists are the vital base of the food chain, plankton. All of these are single-celled independent organisms.

3. One of the three great divisions of natural objects.

The oldest protist fossils occur in rocks over 2000 million years ago. Diverse fossils are found after 1700 million years ago. Today they are very diverse.

5.2 Colonies of single cells

Protists later began living in colonies, but maintaining their independence.

The *volvulina* is a collection of flagellated eukaryotic cells contained in a membrane. These all exist independently.

Volvulina

Colony of independent flagellated eukaryotes

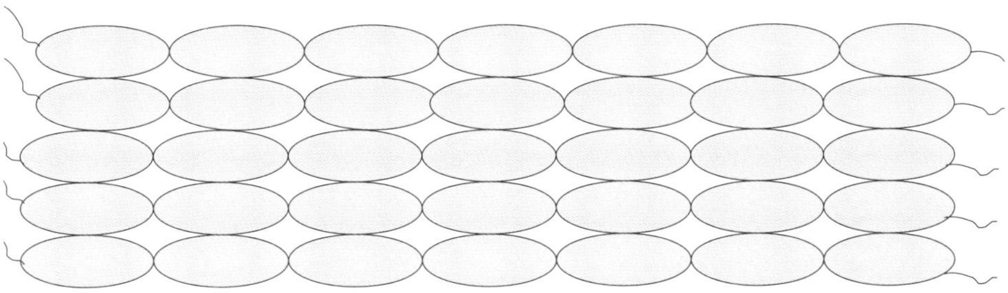

5.3 Sponge – colony of interdependent cells

Many-celled organisms evolved from such single-celled colonies in which various cells had developed different complementary functions. An example of this primitive type of organism is the sponge. Sponges have a cell structure. Here the cells have adapted to perform different functions such as feeding, reproducing, defending. However, they have no nervous system. A sponge does not necessarily die if it is passed through a sieve, and will reform if the cells remain in water. Although there are over 5000 species of sponges, they are an evolutionary dead-end.

Sponge

Colony of cells

various cells had developed different complementary functions

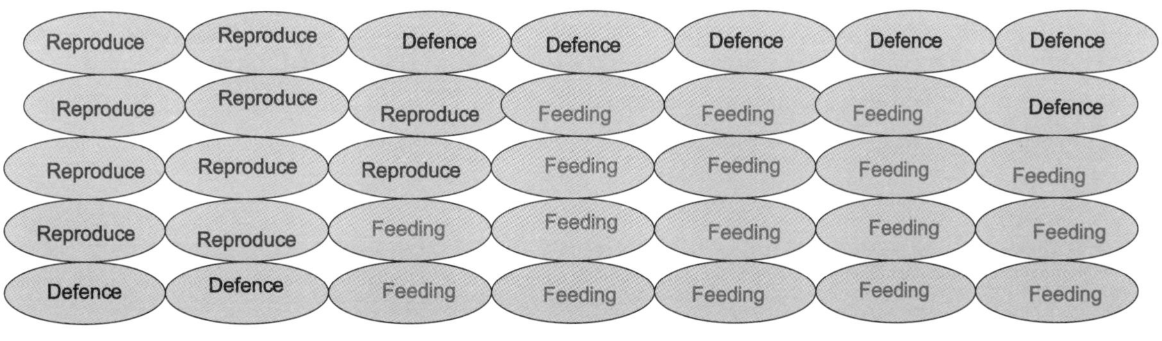

5.4 Multi-celled organisms. Organisms evolve from colonies

There are few fossils to tell us anything about the development to multi-celled organisms. Thus we can only speculate on how this occurred.

From colonies, organisms evolved in different stages. Initially, cells formed in three layers. In the middle layer a cavity formed, later to be filled with organs, heart and blood circulation system.This all apparently happened between 1100 million years ago (mya) and 600 mya. Multi-celled organisms whether plants, animals or fungi lived under the sea. There were no plants or animals on the land, but bacteria thrived on the land as well as in the sea. Much later, multi-celled organisms diversified into worms, insects, crustacians, fish, reptiles, birds and mammals.

Volvulina **Evolutionary development**

Cells develop in 3 layers

Cavity develops inside middle layers

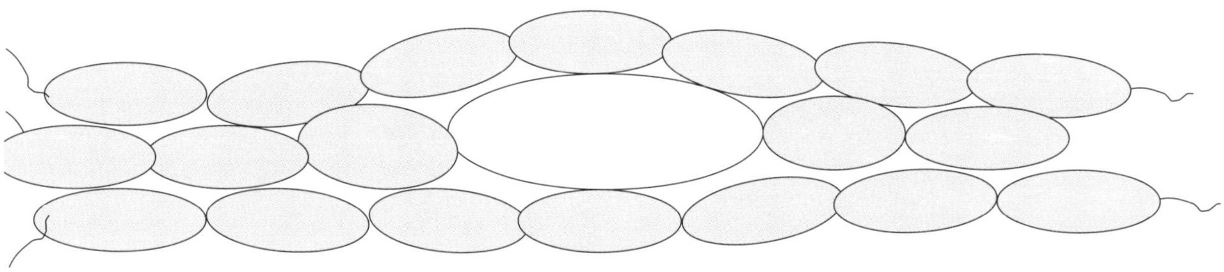

Later inside the cavity organs form

<u>Question 3</u>. **Explain how the progress of life is a step by step process in which matter is revealing an inner fertility.**

5.5 Hydrothermal vents

Much development may have occurred around hydrothermal vents; these are connections between the volcanic under-earth, and the surface through which heat and minerals are conveyed from below. Water within a region of the crust was heated by the molten rock below the crust with the molten rock being much closer to the earth's surface than normal. The superheated water flowed through to the sea bed, carrying a rich assortment of minerals, which later formed a chimney-like structure around the opening.

Life could well have been sustained and could have developed in regions such as these. Such habitats would have been needed during the ice epochs, which occurred 1200 — 1000 mya and 750 – 600 mya. The stage of the glaciation finishing in 575 mya was followed by a surge in life.

Today, bacteria, which convert minerals to energy, form a thick layer at the opening at the sea floor. They also attract other small organisms which feed on them. Snails, shrimps, crabs, fish, and cephalopods feed on these organisms or on each other. Thus there is an independent food chain around such a vent.

HYDROTHERMAL VENT

Life chain surrounds the vent – unique series

Bacteria → plankton → molluscs → crabs

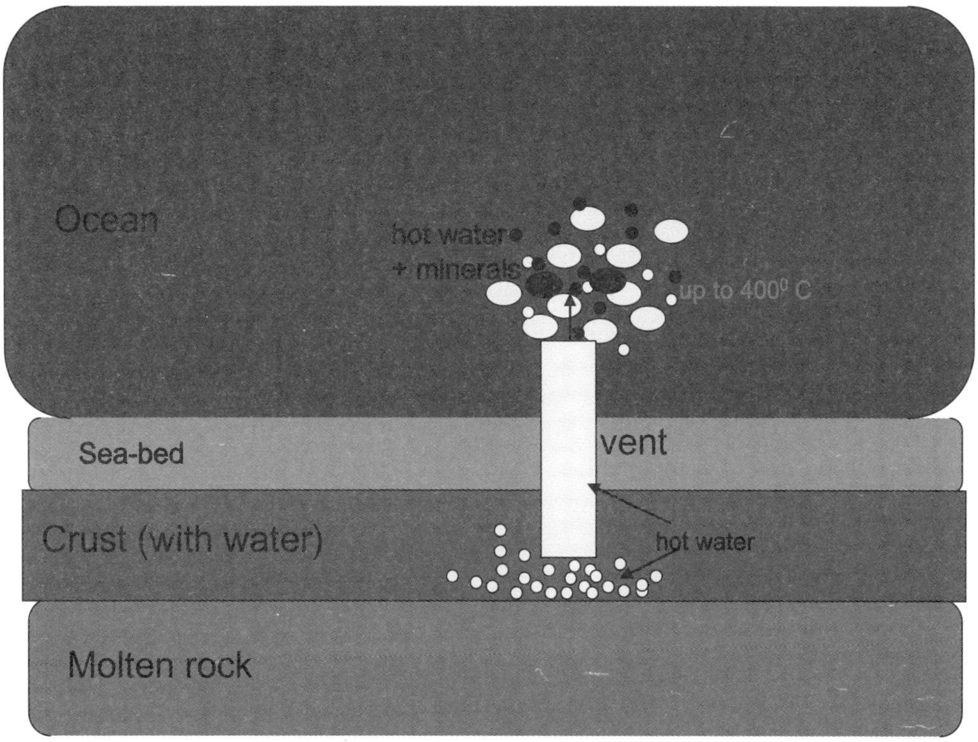

During icehouse events, micro-organisms survived around sites such as geothermal vents. These vents were only first discovered in 1977, and were surrounded by whole food chains—from bacteria to worms, and from molluscs and barnacles to crabs.

Here the temperature of the water in the high pressure environment around the vent may have been as high as 400^{0}C. Today, large colonies of bacteria live in the vicinity, providing the start of a food chain for many unique organisms.

6. A wide variety of organisms develops over 150 million years

6.1 Ediacaran creatures

Fossils of multi-celled organisms dated from about 550 million years ago have been found in various parts of the earth, showing that similar organisms were living at the same time in widely separate vicinities. The collections of organisms are referred to as 'Ediacaran'[4] creatures. These creatures included jelly-fish, worms, leaf-like living organisms attached to rocks, and floating plate-like creatures.

4. Named after the Ediacaran Hills in South Australia, Australia, a source of these fossils.

Popular illustration of Ediacaran organisms

6.2 The Cambrian explosion

The Cambrian explosion was the arrival of a wide variety of new types of organisms quite different from anything that preceded them. Their arrival was over a short geological time, hence 'explosion'. By the end of this era, eleven of the major groups of today's animals had evolved, including chordates—the ancestors of vertebrates. This event heralded the sudden appearance in the fossil record of a significantly increased range of multicellular organisms. In fact, all of today's body forms originated in this era. Moreover, other body plans not extant today have also been found. Minerals ingested by animals assisted in building skeletons, claws, shells, armour, and biting mouthparts. Thus some animals were equipped to attack and others to defend.

A major organism was the trilobite—thousands of species. These were anything from a few millimetres to about fifty centimetres long. They were not swimmers, but lived on the seabed. They possessed an exo-skeleton, and legs with joints.

There were snails, molluscs, cephalopods (ancestors of the octopus), the up to two metre long sea scorpion, and reef builders.

A major extinction at the end of the period obliterated many groups of organisms, but the vertebrate ancestor, the armour-plated fish, survived.

6.2.1 Burgess Shale

530 million years ago a huge mudslide buried thousands of animals—at least 80,000. These animals were not what we see today, but were the species of the Cambrian era [545 — 495 mya]. Not only were there many organisms, but a wide variety. In fact the variety of anatomical designs of the torsos of ocean dwelling organisms was then much greater than those of today's ocean dwellers. Evolution is not the continued progress along a line from single to multi-cells to backbones to brains as we might believe, but there arises a wide diversity of many types of organisms at each epoch. The Burgess Shale was discovered in Canada in 1909. Another site found in China in 1999 yielded evidence of primitive vertebrates among other typical Cambrian animals.

Various Cambrian organisms found in the Burgess Shale:

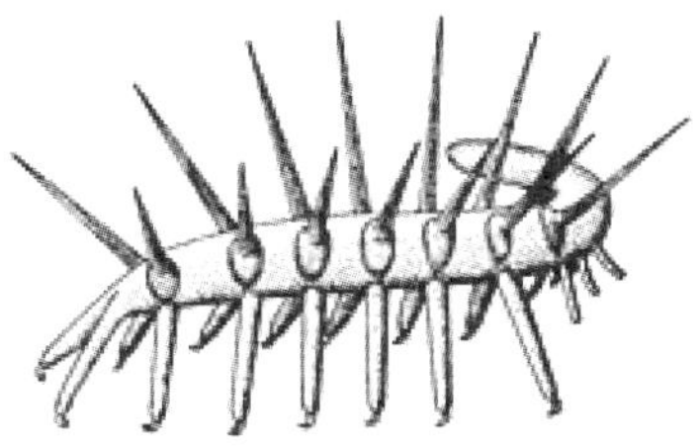

Hallucigenia

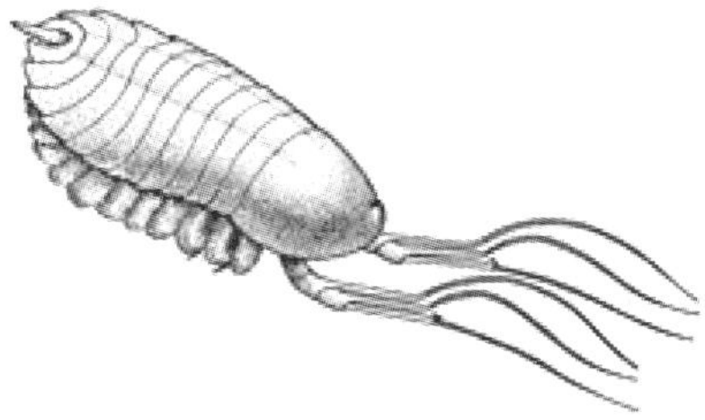

Leonchoilia

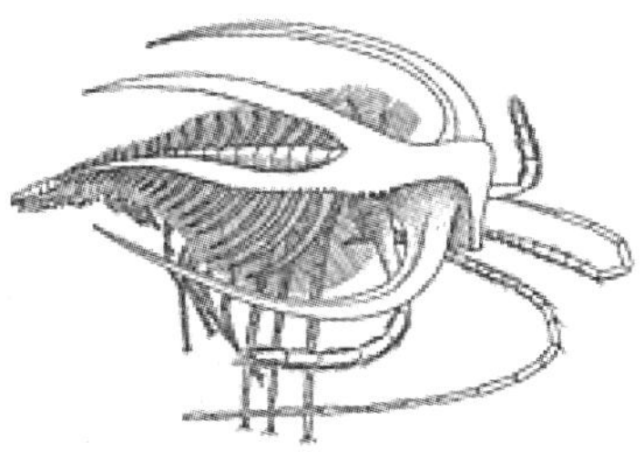

Marella

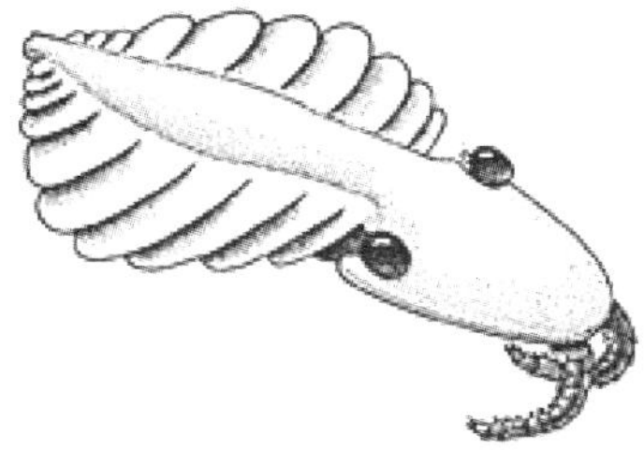

Anomalocharis

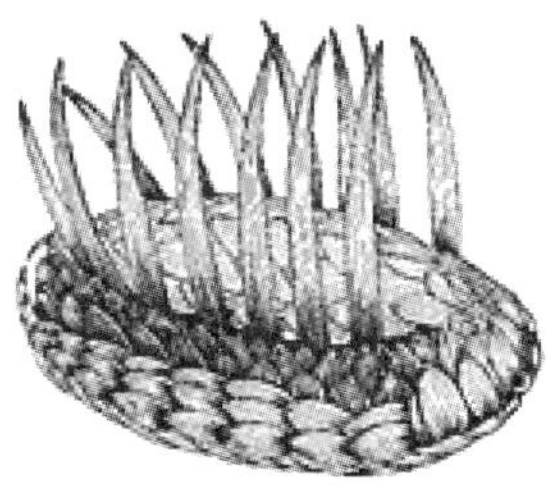

Wiwaxia

Opabinia

<u>Question 4</u>. Life was not only content with occupying every possible niche, but now explodes into multiple new more developed forms. Is there an inbuilt goal in the evolutionary process?

6.3 How did all this happen?

The number of very different species present in the fossil record for the forty million year period suggests that development to basic new forms had been occurring for some time before. During this time there were big environmental changes, which put pressure on the newly developed forms to develop by natural selection.

6.3.1 Possible selective influences

- *Warming of the earth.*

  The 150 million year ice epoch finished about 600 million years ago. The ice epoch was a series of alternating glaciations and 'greenhouse' periods. After this the earth warmed, ice disappeared even from the poles, the ocean deepened by over 200 metres. During glaciation, as water is gathered up into ice, the remaining sea level drops by up to as much as 400 metres. During greenhouse periods, the sea level could be as much as 400 metres above the present level.[5] Such events certainly influence evolution.

- *Increase of oxygen*

  In this short explosion era, the percentage of oxygen in the air increased significantly from under ten to fifteen per cent. This favoured the survival and development of organisms as the percentage of oxygen in the water would increase.

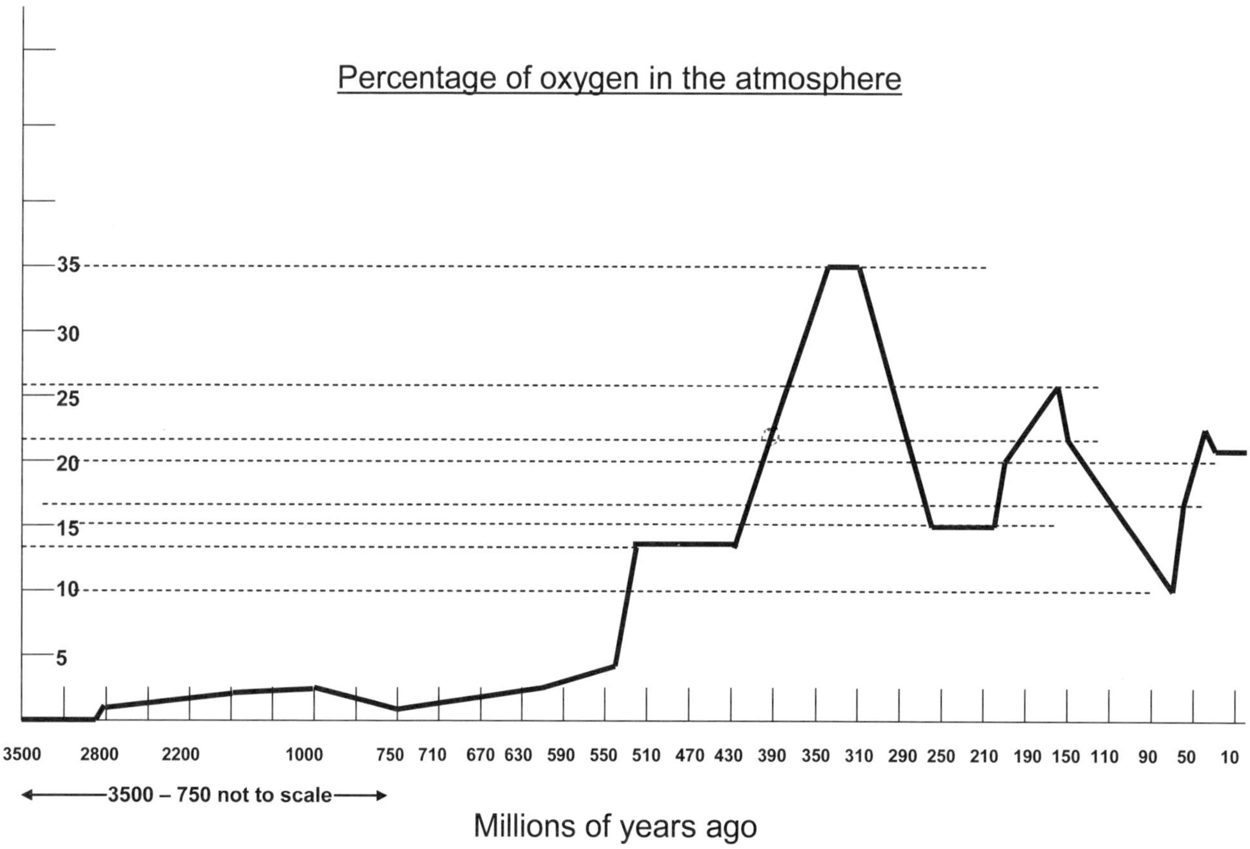

The Cambrian explosion was therefore the exploitation of newly present conditions by animals that had evolved to take advantage of the conditions. This was not a fundamental genetic change[6].

Continental drift. The earth's crust is not a connected solid spherical ring fixed on the top of the next layer. This consists of seven major tectonic plates[7], which are islands of earth crust, floating on the mantle which is liquid. They move some centimetres per year, which may seem slow and insignificant; but not insignificant when geological time is factored in. Moving at one cm / year, in 100 million years, a tectonic plate would have moved 100 x 1,000,000 = 10^8 cm; that is $10^8 \times 10^{-5}$ km, which is one thousand kilometres. Continents can sit over the poles for millions of years, making for a drastic

5. Plimer, *A Short History of Planet Earth* (Sydney: ABC Books, 2001), 38.
6. David J. Bottjer, *Vernanimalcula*, Scientific American August 2005, 43-44
7. Chapter 1.

change in conditions. Tectonic plates may collide and form mountain ranges, which can change rainfall patterns, and hence vegetation. This may result in more lush areas or deserts.

Most of the earth's land was previously concentrated in one supercontinent, Gondwana. Continental drift led to the pulling apart of the various plates leading to many varied conditions which exerted selection pressures on the recently evolved organisms. By the start of the Cambrian, the large supercontinent Gondwana, comprising all land on earth, was breaking up into smaller land masses. This increased the area of continental shelf, produced shallow seas, and expanded diversity of environmental niches in which animals could specialize and speciate.[8] The movement of Tectonic Plates may catapault species into new climatic zones—for example warmer instead of cooler.

Major global rifting occurs in a very short amount of geological time. Great valleys open within the continental shield, rivers pour in and new oceans form. Plate collisions fold earth, and huge mountain chains rise. Volumes of magma spew from the deep. Continents are raised portions of tectonic plates.[9]

6.3.2 Results: basis for a new way forward

The next developments were:

- emergence from the sea,
- becoming more independent of the water by developing the egg,
- developing inner temperature control, thus enabling greater ability to inhabit varying environments,
- and finally developing intelligence thus enabling life to transcend evolution by natural selection.

8. 'Cambrian explosion' at http://www.fossilmuseum.net/Paleobiology/CambrianExplosion.htm accessed 18th April 2009
9. Southwood, 106.

Further Reading

Carl Zimmer, *Evolution: The Triumph of an Idea* (New York: Harper Collins, 2001).

Allan Tobin and Jennie Dushek, *Asking About Life* (Philadelphia: Harcourt College Publishers, 2001).

Chapter 4

Emergence from the Sea: Adaptations, Extinctions and the Final Arrival of Mammals

Chapter overview

- Adapting for land dwelling
- Transitional forms – 'fishibians'
- Five major extinction events
- Evolution to amphibians and reptiles
- Dinosaur dominance for 150 million years
- Dinosaur extinction in the twinkling of a geological eye
- Biospace for mammals

1. The necessity of oxygen

In order to survive on land, organisms firstly needed oxygen in the atmosphere. 3.8 billion years ago there was very little oxygen. The atmosphere contained many gases: nitrogen, carbon dioxide, water vapour, methane, hydrogen, inert gases, and small amounts of others. There is evidence from 2.7 billion years ago, that oxygen was being produced; but its concentration in the atmosphere was low at 0.5%. At that stage, cyanobacteria were involved in the process of photosynthesis—the conversion of sunlight, water vapour and carbon dioxide into glucose, leaving oxygen as a waste product. Oxygen tended to be removed as it combined with minerals; this is the origin of the large deposits of iron oxides in Western Australia. The big numbers of prokaryotic and eukaryotic organisms did not require oxygen for survival, but by 2.4 billion years ago, the oxygen concentration in the atmosphere had increased substantially. The anaerobic (non-oxygen dependent) bacteria were largely wiped out by the more advanced aerobic bacteria, which depended on the newly accumulating gas— oxygen. By 575 million years ago, the oxygen concentration had increased to three per cent and by 545 mya it was five per cent, increasing to thirteen per cent by 520. Between 350 and 120 million years ago the proportion of oxygen increased from thirteen to twenty-one per cent.

Question 1. The presence of the new gas oxygen enabled life to diversify beyond the sea. Was the arrival of oxygen as a 'waste product' of photosynthesis merely another fortuitous accident?

2. Adaptations needed for land inhabitation

No organism could dwell on the land until sufficient oxygen was in the air for respiration and to produce enough ozone, O_3, to screen out the sun's ultra-violet radiation.

To dwell on land, organisms needed major adaptations:

- They needed lungs to breathe oxygen direct. Marine animals extract dissolved oxygen using the gills, which would be ineffective in the air. Associated with lungs is the dual circulatory system;
- Now that these organisms were out of the water, they would need to find other supplies of water to drink.
- Outside the rich supply base of food—the water environment—new sources of food were needed on the previously barren earth. Bacteria were present on the earth, but much more was necessary, such as the evolution of plants.
- Water supplies an upthrust equal to the weight of water displaced (Archimedes' Principle), so that sea-dwelling animals can do without much bodily strength. On land the full force of gravity would be felt, so much improved support structures had to evolve—skeletons. For

example, elephants' skeletons have to support about six tonnes. A whale could weigh more than 100 tonnes because of the water's upthrust.[1]

- Ocean temperatures do not vary much in a particular area. However, land temperatures vary significantly every day; and more so in most latitudes due to the seasons. Land-dwellers required adaptation to deal with these much greater external temperature variations.[2]
- Amphibians returned to the water for reproduction. Other more evolved animals needed adaptations to reproduce—the egg or the uterus.

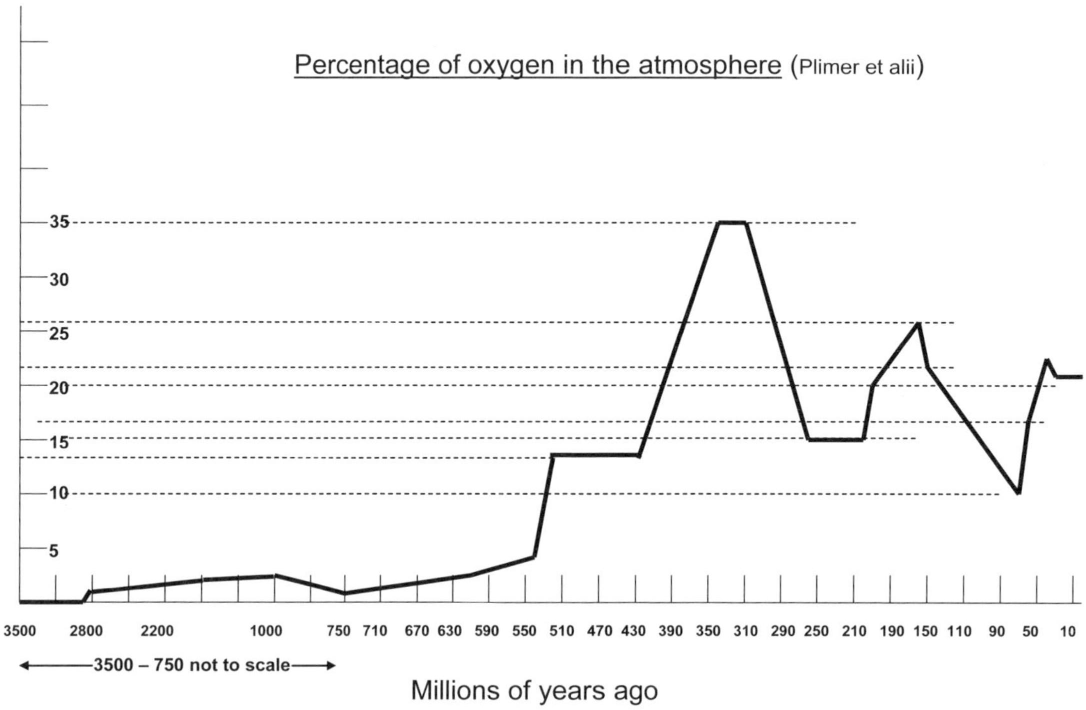

3. The move from Water

3.1 Changes for land-dwelling began in the sea

Question 2. What possessed animals to take their first steps onto dry land half a billion years ago? The body plans of all today's animals appeared in the Cambrian Explosion. But were they not comfortable in the sea?

Why take the risk of this major development? How could such major adaptations take place?

> The colonists needed to evolve a way of breathing air, their senses must have changed to work in their new surroundings, they needed to modify their feeding behaviour, reduce the amount of water lost in excretion, and adapt their sex lives? Why go to all this trouble?[3]

It was not blind purpose that was driving them out of the water, but changes driven by survival of the fittest actually made them ready for this step. Most of the changes needed for land life occurred in the water. 450 million years ago (mya) lungs had been evolving to enable fish to survive in water which did not have the required amount of dissolved oxygen.

3.2 Rotting plant debris a factor

Muscles which performed the task of moving the fins, developed so they could bring about walking on the sea bottom and into the shallows to find rotting vegetation—a source of food. Around the 400

1. R Southwood, *The Story of Life* (New York: Oxford University Press, 2004), 76–77.
2. *Ibid*, 78.
3. Myles McLeod, *New Scientist* (8/6/2002): 39–41.

mya mark, plants had evolved to a greater variety and complexity, rotting vegetation found its way into shallow seas, extending back onto the shore. Some aquatic species found the vegetation a good food source. They were attracted to the shallows, and their fore-fins evolved to help them scavenge among the dead plant matter.

4. Transitional forms

There are fossils of lobe-finned fish, which have the body form of a tetrapod (a four legged animal); their fins were attached to fleshy outgrowths, and there were primitive lungs as well as gills. The front and tail fins of such fish as these developed into legs. Muscles which performed the task of moving the fins, developed so they could bring about walking on the sea bottom, then into the shallows and finally onto land.

Even in fish, fins can be used to propel the organism across land. For example, the lungfish in central Australia can move across land from one pool to another, when the pool is drying out.

Fish fore-fins were stronger than their rear fins, so these developed into legs first. Though predominantly sea dwellers, transitional forms could clamber out of the water, and spend time out of the water. A later fossil showed that rear limbs had developed more strongly, which would have favoured land living. Finds that are dated a little after 340 million years ago show that the fishy creatures that had spent some time on land were now fully land dwellers.

> Perhaps the most complete set of transitional fossils is the so-called 'fishibian' sequence showing the steps by which fish crawled out of the water onto the land during the Devonian period.[4]

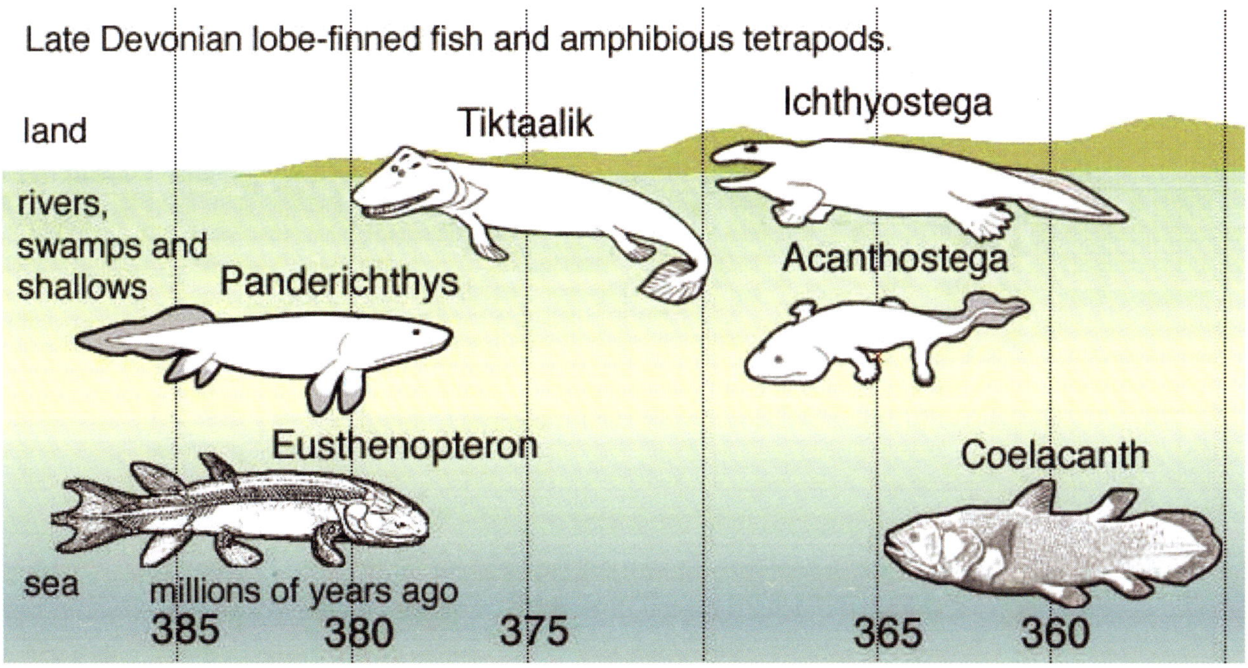

Descendants of lobe-finned fish—like *Eusthenopteron*—exhibited a sequence of adaptations: Panderichthys was suited to muddy shallows. Tiktaalik had limb-like fins that could take it onto land. Early tetrapods such as Acanthostega and Ichthyostega inhabited weed-filled swamps.

Acanthostega is well described on a website:

> One of the best pieces of evidence is a fossil called *Acanthostega*, discovered in Greenland. What's so remarkable about it is that it's a transition fossil. It defies categories. The creature isn't a fish exactly, nor an amphibian, but somewhere in between. It has both lungs and internal gills. It has a tail like a fish, but limbs something like later land crea-

4. Donald Prothero, 'What Missing Link?' *New Scientist* (1/3/2008): 37.

> tures. Before the discovery of fossils like Acanthostega, scientists hypothesised that the evolution of limbs was a result of the transition from water to land. However, *Acanthostega's* limbs weren't capable of supporting the creature's weight. Although it had hands and feet, it appears that its limbs evolved for use in water in swamps, and only later in evolution were adapted for walking on land.[5]

Kenneth Miller gives an account of an important *Acanthostega* fossil find which put paid to the assertion there are no missing links:

> Paleontologists have recognized for years that the earliest tetrapods retained scores of fish-like characters, but this specimen of *Acanthostega* was so well preserved that it contained a genuine surprise—internal gills. No other amphibian possesses internal gills, and the structures preserved within the fossil make it clear that *Acanthostega* could breathe with its gills under water, just like a fish, and could also breathe on land, using lungs.[6]

Ichthyostega: A well-known fossil—dated from about 360 million years ago—possessed legs and forelimbs. These creatures were well developed.

Coelacanth: Coelacanth lobe-finned fish were common hundreds of millions of years ago and were thought to be extinct. A living variety, similar but larger, was discovered in 1938.

The order in time of the above 'fishibians' is: Panderichthyids → Tiktaalik → Acanthostega, → Ichthyostega.

Question 3. Anti-evolutionists often argue that the absence of 'missing links' in the fossil record demonstrates that evolution is not a likely explanation of the progress of life. Does the 'fishibian' sequence weaken their position?

In summary, over millions of years, fins from the lobe-finned variety of fish became stronger. They were employed to walk across the bottom, and for some from one pool to another. They would then emerge from the sea to dwell mostly on the land. A double circulatory system developed for the movement to land.

> The first amphibian animals hop and lumber along on ever more muscular fins while trading in their gill slits for air-breathing lungs. Eventually their fins transform into stubby legs, and a second pair is added to make them four-footed creatures, the first in long lines of amphibians, reptiles, birds and mammals.[7]

5. Extinction events influence the course of evolution

There have been five major extinction events in the history of life—events in which well over half known species perished. There have been many other minor extinction events.

5. http://amos.indiana.edu/library/scripts/acanthostega.html. Accessed 18th April 2009
6. Kenneth R Miller, *Finding Darwin's God* (New York: Harper Collins, 1999), 124–125.
7. Brian Swimme, *A Walk Through Time* (Mill Valley, California: The Book Laboratory Inc, 1998), 135.

THE 5 MAJOR EXTINCTIONS

(1) Ordovician

(2) Devonian

(3) End-Permian

(4) Late-Triassic

(5) Cretaceous-Tertiary [K/T]

(.) Minor extinctions

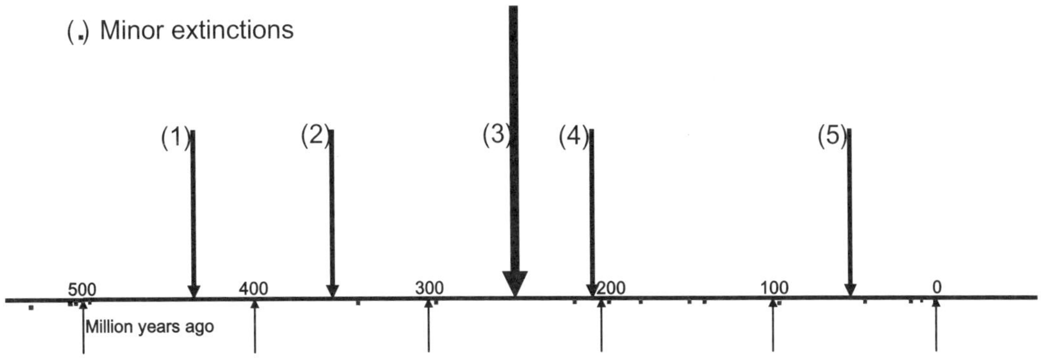

5.1 Causes of major extinctions

Major extinctions can be due to a number of causes.

- ice ages,
- continental drifts placing continents in new positions and hence species in new climatic conditions to which they cannot adapt,
- climate changes involving millennial length droughts or floods,
- asteroid collisions with earth,
- volcanic activity.

5.2 Four extinctions

Considered here are the Devonian, the Permian, the Triassic, and the K/T.

5.2.1 Devonian[8] extinction 370 million years ago (mya)

A series of extinctions over about 10 million years from 370 mya saw eighty-two per cent of species become extinct: species of invertebrates, armoured fish, corals, sponges, sea lilies; the trilobites suffered greatly, and reefs disappeared. There were severe asteroid impacts 368, 360 and 357 million years ago;[9] the crater from 368, the *Siljan* crater in Sweden, was fifty-two km in diameter. Some or all of these impact events could have triggered extinctions, as so much material was lifted into the atmosphere. This prevented the penetration of sunlight for an extended period, meaning death to many plants and algae, and as a consequence the collapse of food chains.

5.2.2 End-Permian extinction[10] 245 mya.

The extinction consisted of two extinction events, separated by up ten million years. There are many suggested causes for this extinction of over ninety per cent of all living species:

- There were successions of ice ages punctuated by greenhouse events. A particularly extensive and frigid sequence of ice ages occurred about 250 million years ago, which

8. Southwood, *The Story of Life*, 65.
9. Ian Plimer, *A Short History of Planet Earth* (Sydney, ABC Books, 2001),109
10. Michael J Benton, *When Life Nearly Died* (London: Thames and Hudson, 2003), 262–283.

ceased suddenly—geologically speaking—248 million years ago. Cooling and warming with associated reduction and deepening of ocean levels would have put pressure on many species. There were variations in oceans depths of hundreds of metres.

- The impact of an asteroid twenty kilometre in diameter. There is one large crater as evidence. But there should be more, as a succession of such events seems necessary to have had such catastrophic results.
- Enormous volcanic activity in Siberia poured out lava during a period of 600,000 years.[11]
- At the end of the Permian, 251 million years ago, giant volcanic eruptions took place in Siberia, spewing out some 2-3 cubic kilometres of basalt lava covering 3.9 million square kilometres of eastern Russia to a depth of 400 to 3000 metres.[12]
- A nearby supernova explosion could have stripped the upper atmosphere of its ozone layer, exposing life forms to harmful ultra-violet radiation.

5.2.3 Triassic extinction 214 mya.

This was made up of two events, one centring on 225 mya and the second 206 mya. Taken together they make up the fourth major extinction, the 'Late Triassic'. This time, about eighty percent of all species perished. Many non-dinosaur reptile groups became extinct, signifying a change from the dominance of life by non-dinosaur reptiles to dominance by dinosaurs. Many other groups particularly marine organisms suffered diminution or extinction.

5.2.4 K/T Extinction 65 mya.

There was another mass extinction about sixty-five mya. Approximately seventy per cent of species perished. It is thought of generally in terms of the extinction of the dinosaurs. They were so huge—some of them—so dominant, had ruled the earth for 150 million years, that the extinction of all of them over a geological minute is a remarkable event in the history of life. However, many other types of sea and land organisms also perished.

For millions of years after a major extinction the number and variety of animals is much reduced, but there is always a resurgence based on those who survived.

EXTINCTIONS & their survivors

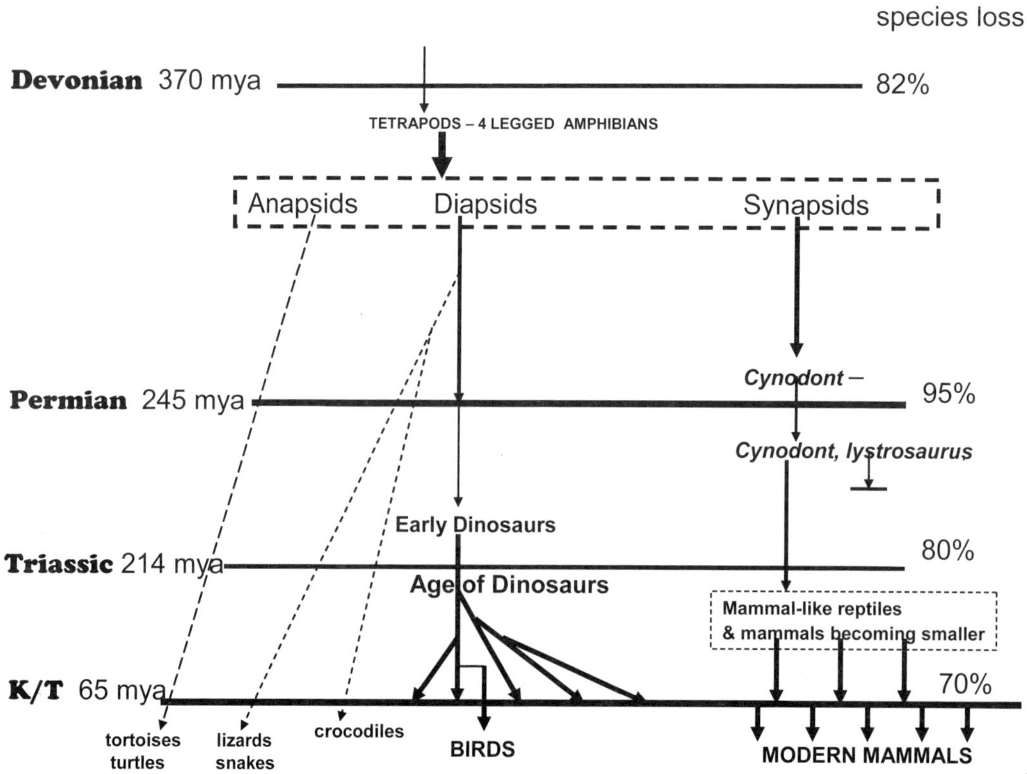

11. *Ibid.*
12. *Ibid*, 262.

<u>Question 4</u>. **Despite catastrophic extinction events matter continued to progress. Were the extinctions needed to cull the prevailing number of species and ready life for further advances?**

6. Evolution after the Devonian Extinction

6.1 Animals

6.1.1 Amphibians.

The lobe-finned fish having developed into fishy amphibians, then evolved into a variety of land-based tetrapods (four legged animals). They spent much time in the water also. Reproduction took place in the water for two reasons. Firstly, their eggs were not protected by shells, and needed the surrounds of moisture. Secondly, the young first went through the tadpole stage, swimmers with a tail, taking in oxygen via gills. The tadpole underwent metamorphosis, losing its gills and developing lungs and limbs. Tadpoles emerged from this process tetrapods: four-legged vertebrates who had developed strong legs. They were of varying sizes, small and mouse-like even up to about 4.5 metres long (Eogyrinus).

Eogyrinus

6.1.2 Reptiles

An evolutionary development, which gave vertebrates the power to become truly land animals was the evolution of the egg. Like all organisms, land animals needed water to survive, but became more independent of a constant watery environment. This was especially so in the case of reproduction. As within the egg was a watery environment, they were now free of water dependence for reproduction, and their young did not spend their first months as water dwellers.

> This egg contains fluid as well as enough food to sustain the embryo until birth. The embryo with its food is encased in a tough protecting membrane or shell from which it can break free to hatch on land.[13]

EGG

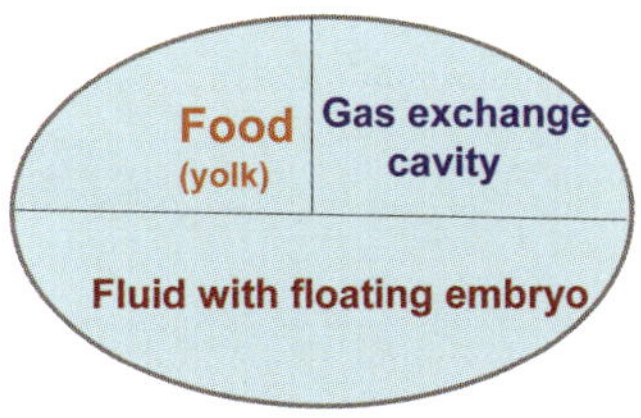

13. Swimme, *A Walk through Time*, 137.

The skin of a reptile is tougher so water could not easily escape, making reptiles again less water-dependent. Water was easily lost through the skin of amphibians, but not so through the skin of reptiles. From 290 million years ago many species, genera, orders of reptiles developed, and spread far and wide.

6.1.3 Three major tetrapod groups

Three major early post-Devonian vertebrate groups were

- the *anapsids*, giving rise to eventually to turtles, and tortoises.
- the *synapsids* giving rise to now extinct reptiles which had evolved into mammals,
- the *diapsids*, which evolved to *thecodonts* which gave rise to crocodiles, snakes, lizards and to dinosaurs. Finally birds.

From about 280 mya the three reptilian groups had evolved. There are now today 6700 species of reptiles living.[14]

6.2 Plants[15]

6.2.1 Forests increase greatly.

Although trees had evolved earlier, from 360 mya onwards there was an unprecedented increase in areas of forests.

Ultimately the forests had a significant influence on evolution:

- They greatly increased the space available for habitation.
  - Organisms could live on trunks, branches, leaves
- They increased the types of habitats available.
- They were the occasion of the evolution
  - Of flight
  - Of bipedalism.

Trees were hosts to plants, fungi, animals, insects.

Firstly trees grew tall, but had shallow roots and no horizontal branches, which evolved in later species. Spores with a short life span evolved to seeds which have an inner food supply and can await suitable conditions before germinating. Ferns appeared and proliferated.

Early trees. Species of *Archaeopteris*

14. Alan Tobin and Jennie Dusheck, *Asking About Life* (Philadelphia: Harcourt College Publishers, 2001), 53.
15. Southwood, *The Story of Life*, 91.

6.2.2 Plants become food. The sight of an animal grazing is commonplace, but animals did not eat plants until 50 million years after they had become land-dwellers. The plants did not have much protein and the cellulose which formed the cell walls was difficult to digest. Bacteria dwelling in the gut of animals—'symbiotic' bacteria—came to the rescue; inhabiting the gut they broke down the cellulose into more readily digestible forms. Once the plant digestion problem was solved, the practice spread widely and quickly among vertebrates.

7. After the Permian extinction towards the Late-Triassic

The Late Permian had claimed all the trilobites, most marine species, many reptiles and mammal-like reptiles; the highly successful *gorgonopsids* perished as most of their prey perished. But millions of years after this devastating extinction, the biosphere had recovered and many species of reptiles and mammal-like reptiles roamed the lands.

Gorgonopsids

The *cynodont,*[16] lived through the Permian extinction. The *cynodont* is the ancestor of all modern mammals. Cynodonts already had many of the characteristics of mammals, well before the age of dinosaurs.

Rhynchosaurus[17] was dominant for a long period after 230 mya, but became extinct. This was a reptile but not a dinosaur.

The dinosaurs are present in the fossil record from 234 million years ago, well before their dominant period after the Triassic extinction. This was a period for other species of reptile, but the Triassic Extinction brought about the extinction of many of these leaving the biospace vacant.

> The fossil record of the Late Triassic reveals several types of reptile that can be regarded as true dinosaurs. The groups to which the many dinosaurs of the Jurassic and Cretaceous belong appear in the late Triassic, but do not seem to have been dominant or abundant.[18]

8. Dinosaurs progress after the Triassic Extinction

8.1 Dinosaurs become dominant

The Triassic extinction—a prolonged process over 20 million years—saw the end of about 20 families of tetrapods, leading to the dominant dinosaur era which is said to have emerged as dominant about 206 million years ago. Their ancestors were insignificant species living during an earlier era. A possible ancestor was a type such as *euparkerion,* which was about half a metre long, and was a fast runner, either on two legs or all fours (so a good survivor). It fed on small animals and insects, and had sharp teeth. There is a multi-million year fossil gap between this and an early dinosaur (234 → 227), but it is thought to be an ancestor of an earlier dinosaur—the coelophysis.

16. See this chapter, section 10.1.2
17. Southwood, *The Story of Life,* 128.
18. *Ibid,* 128.

After the Triassic Extinction there was a continual succession of dinosaur species each of which had an average life-span of about ten million years. The dinosaurs dominated the biosphere for 150 million years. Their era of dominance lasted till about sixty-five million years ago, but then over a very short geological time, they all departed from the fossil record. The species we are familiar with through popular books and television programmes probably lived during vastly different times, or they may have lived at the same time separated by oceans, as tigers and kangaroos are separate today.

8.2 Examples of dinosaurs

Many types of dinosaurs have been identified, small, large, huge, armour-plated, duck-billed, herbivores, carnivores – some with horns, others with tusks, some were bipedal, others quadripedal.[19]

There were so many varieties, and they dominated for so long that many generalisations are not possible.

- Argentinosaurus: had a body length of thirty-five metres, weighed 90 tonnes, and disappeared about ninety-five million years ago (mya). Like very many, it was a plant eater, a herbivore. But dinosaur species as small as 5 cm long have been found in the fossil record.

- Coelophysis: lived in the period 227 to 210 mya. It was less than three metres long and one metre tall, so was a small dinosaur. It was a meat eater, fast runner, could grasp with its front legs, and run on all fours. Its brain was larger than previous reptilian brains. These early dinosaurs were liable to eat their young when food was scarce. In 1947 a herd of hundreds was found, with young inside them. The gruesome discovery was made that these had not jumped evolutionary hurdles to produce their young within, but had actually eaten many of their offspring.

- Plateosaurus: who lived from 221 mya to about 210, was about 8 metres long, fed luxuriantly on vegetation including tree tops, reached by standing on hind legs. Huge numbers of this early dinosaur's fossil remains have been found.

- Tyrannosaurus: a victim of the final extinction sixty-five mya—probably could not run fast. T Rex was fourteen metres long and like most large animals, would have moved slowly. Prolonged running would not have been possible with a limited heart/lung system, and any running at all may have placed too much strain on leg bones. T Rex had large jaws, sharp teeth—could crush bones—but could not chew, so had to swallow prey whole.

- Beipiaosaurus: about 125 million years ago. It measured 2.2 meters in length, and is among the largest known feathered dinosaurs.

19. *Ibid*, 138–145.

There is evidence many dinosaurs lived in herds.

> In some places great numbers of fossils have been found showing that an entire herd had perished in some calamity. The most spectacular example is of an estimated 10,000 duck-billed dinosaurs[20]
> 'Fossils have been discovered of an entire herd of young dinosaurs that died together when they became trapped in mud 90 million years ago'.
>
> 'We found what you would call palaeontological gold', said Paul Sereno, at the University of Chicago in the U.S. and a co-author of a study detailing the find. 'It's the first real population of dinosaurs caught in a snapshot—a death trap—that has ever been discovered.'
>
> 'The remains of more than 25 dinosaurs, all juveniles of the same species, are incredibly well-preserved, even down to the gouges made in the mud as they tried to escape'.[21]

8.3 Reptiles in the sea and the air.
During the same long time, reptiles were inhabiting the sea. *Ichthyosaurs* had to surface to breathe, and one was as long as twenty-three metres. Also reptiles took to the air. *Pterosaurs* were not birds, but had wings, some with extended wingspans. Birds were inconspicuous, but whereas dinosaurs, ichthyosaurs, pterosaurs perished at the K/T extinction, birds survived, and then expanded.

Question 5. Describe life in a dinosaur dominated continent 100 million years ago.

Ichthyohsaur

Pterosaur

9. The K/T Extinction

There was a mass extinction around 65 million years ago. It is thought of generally as the extinction of the dinosaurs. So many different species had prospered and had ruled the earth for 150 million years that the extinction of all of them over a geological minute was a remarkable event in the history of life. However, it was not only the dinosaurs that suffered family death. Ammonites, Pterosaurs, Plesiosaurs, Ichthyosaurs, and Fresh-water Sharks disappeared; and many other groups showed large decreases in species. Insects, tortoises and birds survived well, but mammals lost thirty-five percent of their number of species. The smaller mammalian organisms which were in no way comparable in dominance with the strong species of the land, sea and air, had within themselves the advantage of temperature control and they did not have to lay eggs to reproduce. Once the

20. *Ibid*, 148.
21. Kath Lee, '"Death trap" yields herd of juvenile dinosaurs', found at http://www.cosmosmagazine.com/features/online. Accessed 18/3/2009.

environment was freed up, these organisms could then emerge from the trees, or from nocturnal habits and habitats, and radiate, increase and multiply, not only in numbers, but also in species.

Survivals of K/T extinction

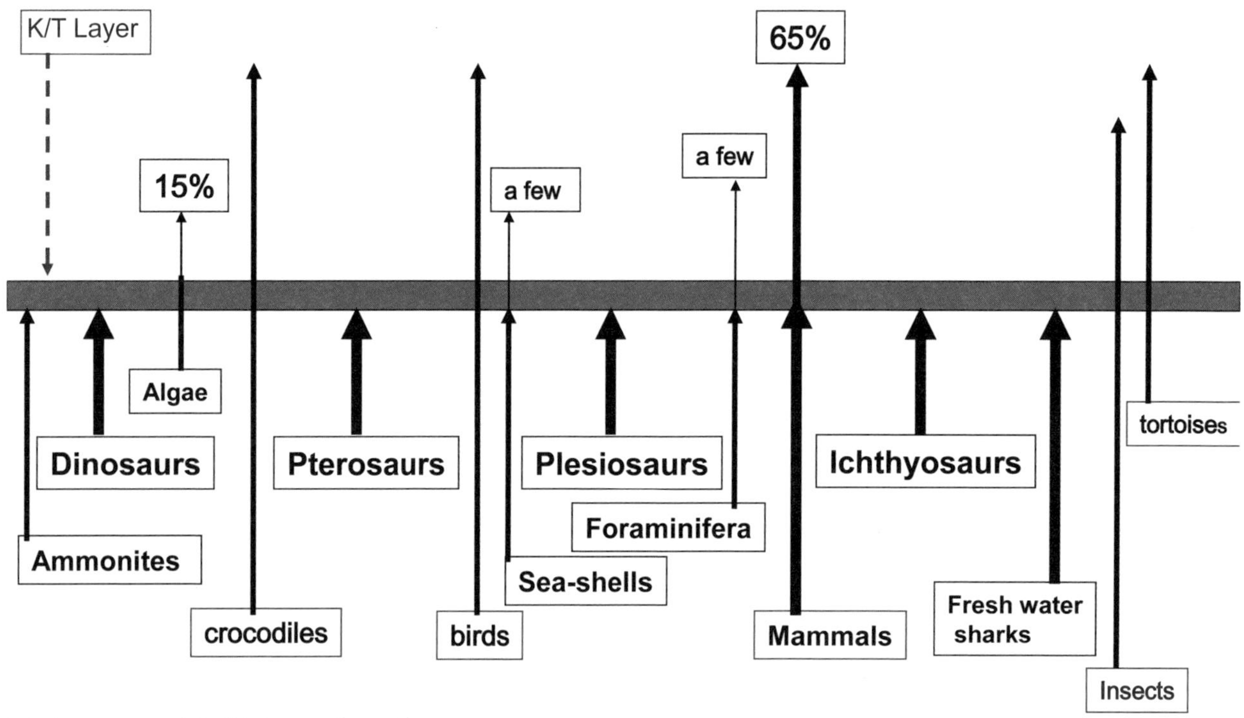

9.1 An Asteroid Collision with earth

The reason for the KT extinction, and the enormous change that followed is widely believed to be as a result of an asteroid colliding with the earth. Michael J Benton summed up this theory as follows:

> A giant rock 10 kilometre in diameter had hit the earth 65 million years ago, punching a vast hole in the atmosphere, slamming into the earth's crust, instantly vaporizing, excavating a huge crater 100 to 150 kilometres across, and flinging millions of tonnes of rocks and dust into the atmosphere.[22]

The residual dust would have blocked out the sun, severely inhibiting the process of photosynthesis so that much vegetation died. This was the basic food for living organisms, so they then died. When herbivores—the vast majority—died, those that preyed on them would also starve.

This fitted the facts, but evidence was needed.

Question 6. Write a composition describing the asteroid collision with the earth, the resulting immense clouds of rock and dust that filled the skies, the withering away of vegetation, the interruption of the food chain and the agonies of the dinosaurs as they starved.

9.2 Evidence for an asteroid collision

9.2.1 *First piece of evidence*

The first piece of evidence was an enhanced concentration of the metal iridium found in many parts of the world in the layer of earth dated back sixty-five million years, put down at the time of the K/T mass extinction—the Cretaceous-Tertiary boundary interval. In this layer there was an abundance of iridium. Iridium is scarce on earth, but is notably more abundant in asteroids and meteors. Normally, iridium is found on earth occurs at twenty-six parts per billion; in this layer and only in this layer it

22. Benton, *The Day the Earth Nearly Died*, 100.

registered forty parts per billion.[23]. Wherever this layer is analysed all over the world, the iridium number is higher than elsewhere. The vaporised iridium from the asteroid remained with the dust blocking out the sun, and eventually fell to earth mixed with terrestrial vaporised rock. This settled in many parts of the earth, being then built upon by millions of years of rock, detritus and soil.

9.2.2 Second piece of evidence.
The second piece of evidence is a huge crater under the sea in the Gulf of Mexico—near the Yucatan Peninsula and close to the village of Chicxulub—which has been dated to sixty-five million years ago. The K/T iridium-rich boundary layer in this region is a metre thick as opposed to one centimetre elsewhere. The remains of the crater is filled with post-impact sediment, ranging from 100 to 130 kilometres across its breadth.[24] Unusual debris is found in the surrounding area.

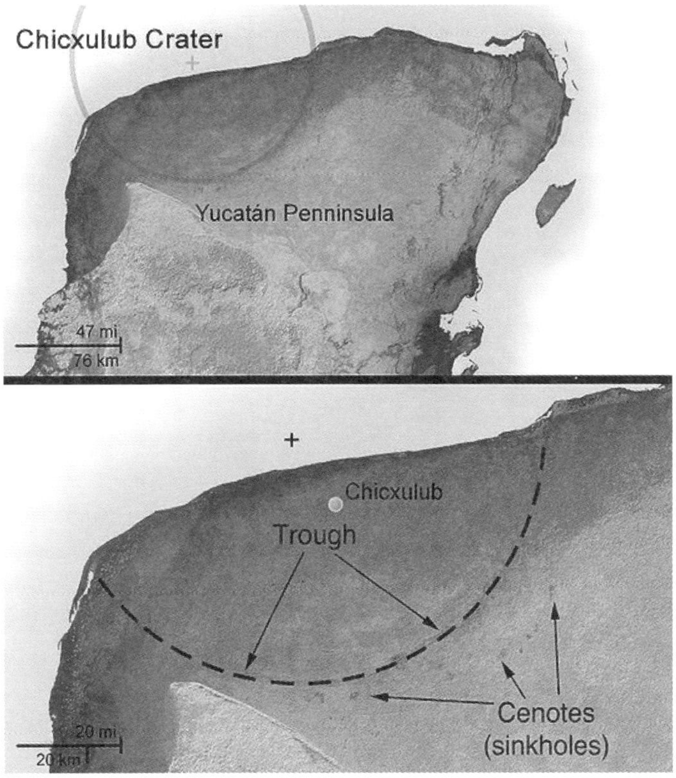

10. The coming of the mammals

10.1 Early mammal-like animals
10.1.1 Lystrosaurus
After the End-Permian extinction very many reptile species had become extinct. One group, *therapsids*, gradually became dominant. Therapsid means mammal-like, so these animals had some mammalian features, even in this era long before the dinosaurs. One theraspid species, *Lystrosaurus*, was very successful. These animals were found in most regions of the earth. They formed large herds, and were herbivores, feeding on leaves, roots, seeds. *Lystrosaurus* was only about as big as a pig. The species seemed to have represented half the large animals on the earth.

23. *Ibid*, 97–98.
24. *Ibid*, 118-120.

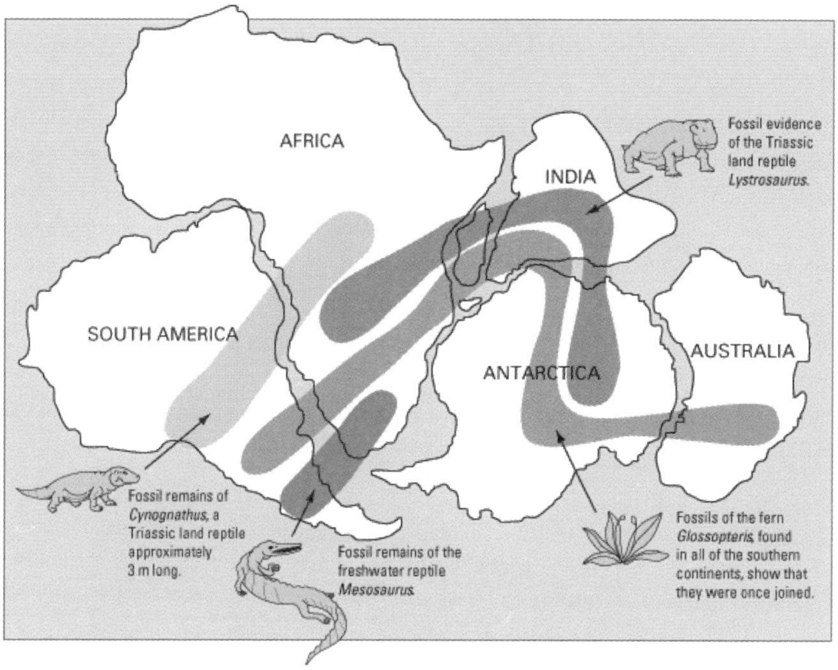

Geographical distribution of Lystorsaurus – mammal-like reptile

10.1.2 Cynodonts.

The *cynodonts* may have evolved from a group known as *Therocephalia* before the End-Permian extinction. *Cynodonts* evolved mammal-like legs which are more efficient than reptilian legs, and mammalian-type teeth.

Cynodont

An interesting cynodont was *thrinaxodon*. Cat-sized, it had a reptilian skeleton, laid eggs, but after hatching, the young enjoyed mother's milk. It fed on insects and small animals, and is thought to be a link with mammals. Having mammary glands was a big advantage, as the mother did not have to leave the young to go out to forage for food.

Thrinaxodon Wiki

10.2 Mammals' advantages

Warm-blooded animals have advantages over the reptiles.[25]

- A more complex brain can develop, giving an increase in intelligence. A spin-off is greater parental care.
- They can answer situations of danger immediately without having to allow time to warm up. Therefore, they can respond immediately in a wide variety of conditions. There is less mortality and so populations grow more quickly.
- Having interior warming also allows the young to develop more quickly, so that parents are not involved for long in educating the young.

10.3 Mammals were small and nocturnal

The mammals were there in increasing numbers soon after the latter half of the Triassic extinction 214 million years ago. They were small, and evolutionary development was impeded by the presence of increasing numbers of therapsid reptiles, some of large sizes for whom they were easy prey.

These early mouse-like mammals probably went out at night to avoid predators.

> The need for small animals to remain fully alert and active whatever the environmental conditions would have provided the main evolutionary driving force for the development of warm-blooded physiology on land. [26]

Megazostrodon, early mammal.

25. Southwood, *The Story of Life*, 126-127.
26. *Ibid*, 127.

Megazostrodon. 200 mya. Final stage of transition from *cynodont* to mammal: it was warm-blooded, did not lay eggs, and had a larger brain/body ratio.

> 'There were placental mammals on earth at the time of the great extinction of dinosaurs about 65 million years ago, Falkowski says. They were, however, tiny, limited creatures; the extinction event itself, while eliminating the dinosaurs, did little to further the mammalian domination of the planet. It was the subsequent spreading of shallow seas, the increase in plant life—and photosynthesis—in addition to the consequent increase in oxygen content that gave the mammals the boost they needed'.[27]

Question 7. Does the universe's behaviour suggest meaninglessness?

11. Evolutionary tree (Non-extinct groups are boxed).

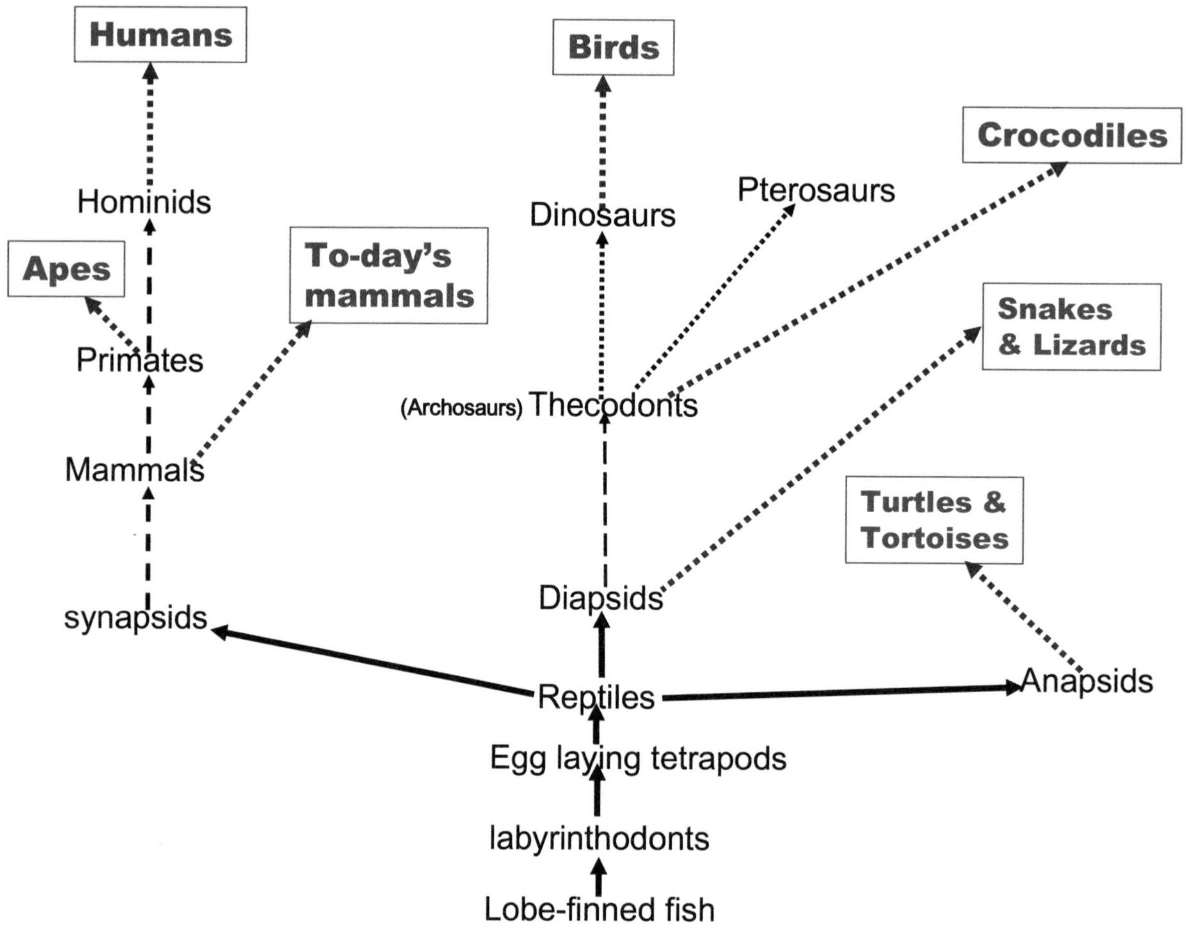

The evolutionary tree is not the complete story of evolution. There are many sideways branches, reversals, interactions between groups. But it does attempt to show the progressive element in the story of evolution.

27. Paul G. Falkowski, *The Rise of Oxygen over the Past 205 Million Years and the Evolution of Large Placental Mammals*, Science 30 Sept 2005, 2202-2204. http://www.sciencedaily.com/releases/2005/10/051003080102.htm Accessed 18th April 2009

Further Reading

Armand Delsemme, *Our Cosmic Origins: From the Big Bang to the Emergence of Life and Intelligence* (Cambridge: Cambridge University Press, 1998).

Chapter 5
Homonisation:
the Speedy Process to Homo Sapiens

Chapter overview

- Hominids on the way to Homo Sapiens
    - * Australopithecus Afarensis
    - * Homo Habilis
    - * Homo Erectus
    - * Archaic Homo Sapiens
- Neanderthal Man
- Homo Sapiens physically
- Homo Sapiens intellectually

1. Australopithecus Afarensis

Over the course of the last eight million years, a very rapid evolution has taken place. From primates swinging in the trees, have evolved intelligent creative beings—*homo sapiens.* Prior to this, our primate ancestors dwelled in the trees, this being the only option as all of Africa was covered in forest. Their arms were not used in painting, constructing, tool-making, but to climb trees and swing from branch to branch.

1.1 Climate change and Australopithecus Afarensis
A great change of a few million years in the making was brewing, as the great southern continent on top of a tectonic plate, was moving towards Asia.

8 million years ago

ALL AFRICA WAS FOREST

Apes lived in the trees:
"arms" used fir swinging between trees
Lived ape-like existence

BUT
Movement of southern continent towards Asia began.
As slow as the growth of a fingernail

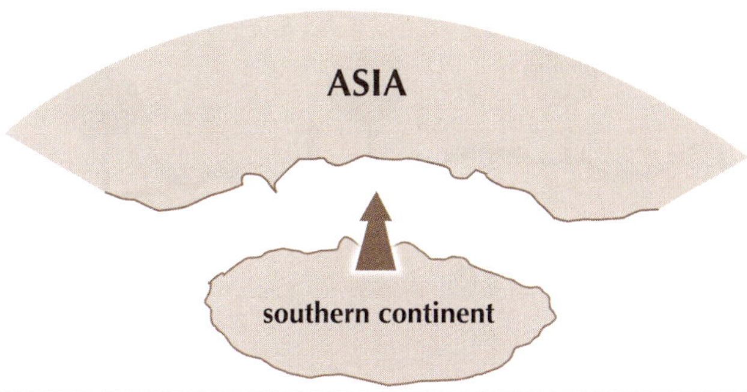

The speed of this movement could be compared to a growing fingernail, which may seem insignificant. At this rate Australia is moving north at two centimetres per year. After a century, this will be 200 cm—2 metres. After a millennium, the distance will be twenty metres. After a million years, the displacement will be 20,000 metres—20 kilometres. After ten million years, it will be 200 kilometres; and ten million years is a slow blink of a geological eye. So in the course of geological time, these movements are significant. The movement of the great southern continent eventually brought it up against Asia. The earth's crust was no obstacle to the islands of rock, so the struck land was uplifted by the tectonic plate which could no longer move northwards; it uplifted ultra-gradually, but remorselessly, resulting in the Himalayas. They are still rising at millimetres per year. The vast increase in altitude of the continent forced the moist air currents upwards into the cooler air. Here the vapour condensed, and became monsoonal rain. The consequence was that the moisture, which had been previously driven to Africa in great quantities for millennia no longer reached there. The result was that the African forests did not receive sufficient rainfall to preserve them.

Question 1. Try to get the feel of geological time. If the Cambrian Explosion is approximated at 500 million years ago, represent that by one year. If the period is thus compressed to one year, how long would one year today be in that compressed time scale?

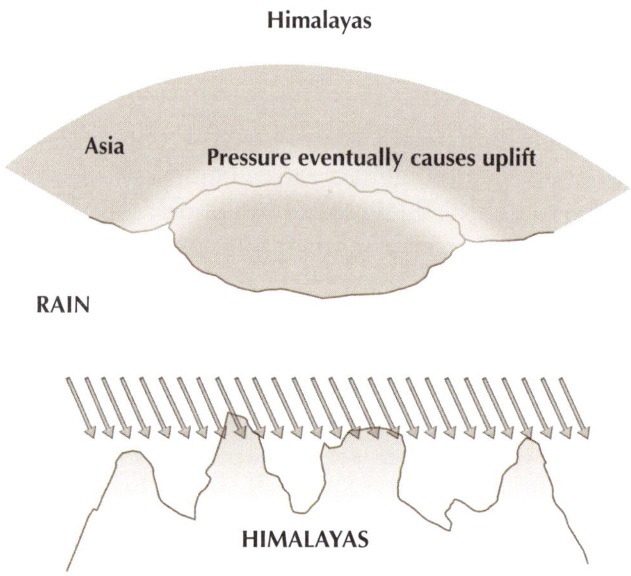

Over many years, the African forests became woodlands – grassy country with some trees. The primates could no longer swing between the trees. They came down during the course of thousands of years where some primates developed a mutation for bipedal walking.

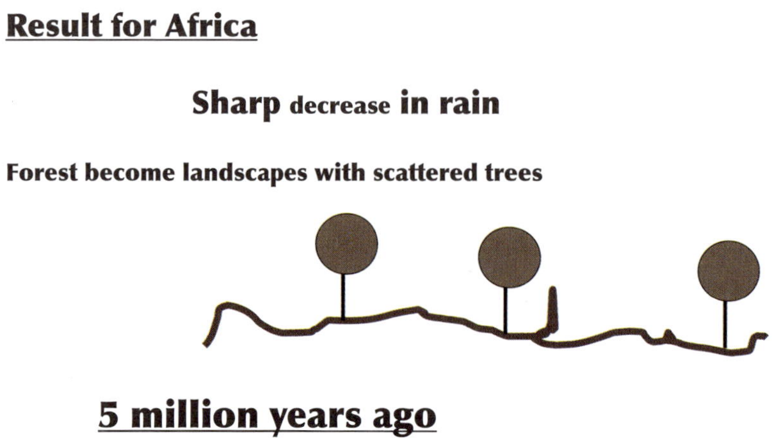

1.2 The bipedal hominid

300,000 generations ago, *Australopithecus Afarensis* lived in Africa.

Australopithecus Afarensis was the name applied to many similar hominids of about three to four million years ago. This apelike hominid could walk upright and also could climb trees. Upright walking involves a number of skeletal changes in the spine, the hips, the pelvis, the toes.[1]

Why is walking on two legs an advantage? The bipedal *Australopithecenes* could see further in this way; this made it helpful firstly in gaining early warnings about predators, and secondly in seeking out what might be advantageous. Walking on two legs was also slightly more energy efficient. Thus, a woman would recover more quickly from childbirth, enabling her to raise one extra child over her lifetime. This would be crucial for the survival of the species. Another result from walking on two legs was that the hands were freed; but *Australopithecenes* did not use tools with later hominids finding uses for the hands.

What sets this human forbear apart from the other apes at the time was walking on two legs; there was nothing else remarkable.

Question 2. Climate change is a continual feature of planet earth given the presence of tectonic plates. Was bipedal walking an inevitable evolutionary development as at some point in time conditions would necessitate descending from the trees?

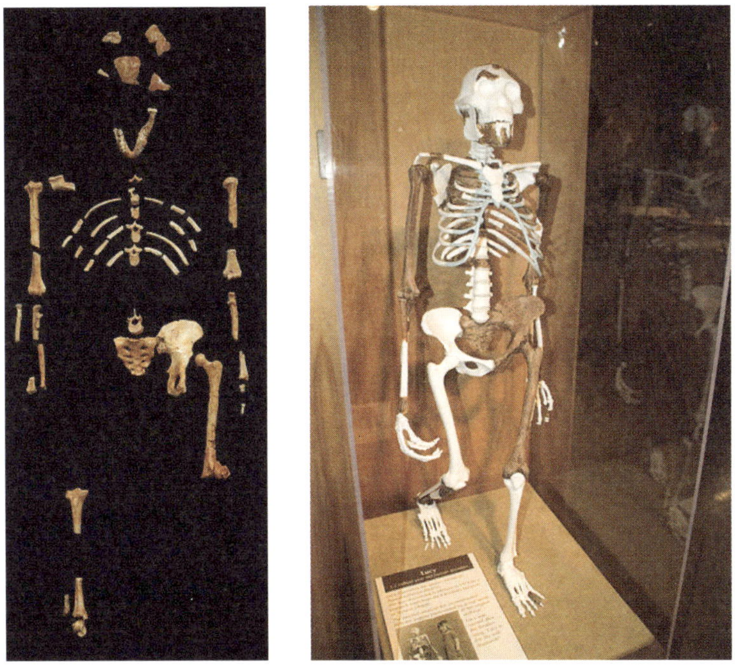

Lucy's bones and a reconstruction

2. Multiple species of hominids. 2.5 — 3 million years ago

2.1 Climate change

A change in the earth's tilt brought about an ice age. Water froze, became ice, with a significant volume of the ocean being stacked up at the poles. This resulted in shallower oceans, less water, and a further decrease in rain. The trees disappeared, leaving woodlands and any remaining forests to become grasslands.

1. Melvin Bolton, *The Road to Now* (Crows Nest: Allen and Unwin, 2001), 95.

3 million years ago: THINGS START TO HAPPEN

Earth's tilt changes

Earth becomes colder

Much of the ocean becomes ice at the upper latitudes

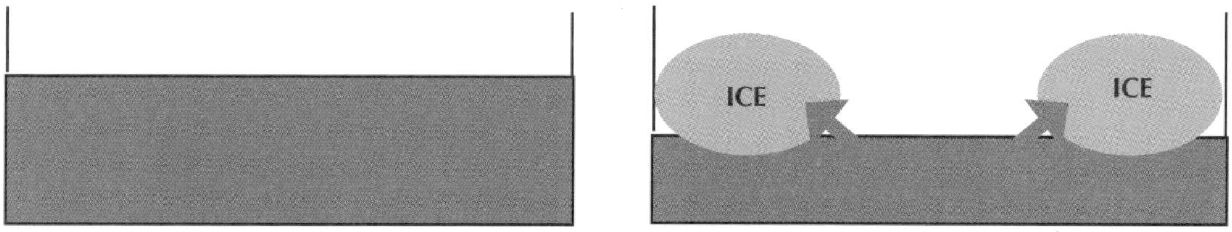

The earth dries out and remaining forests die

So at 2 million years ago:

Because the Earth had become colder
Year by year the polar ice-caps increased.
Thus Earth dries out and forests die.

The ice-caps grew by mopping up much of the water
Resulting in the long dry. 100s of 1000s of years
The areas of woodland died leaving grass

grass grass

Grasses and shrubs meant: *new foods,*
New foods → new animals
New animals → variety of new hominids

All because 3 million years ago
the tilt was getting larger and
also the sun growing colder
Moisture was becoming frozen
and so water was becoming
scarce.

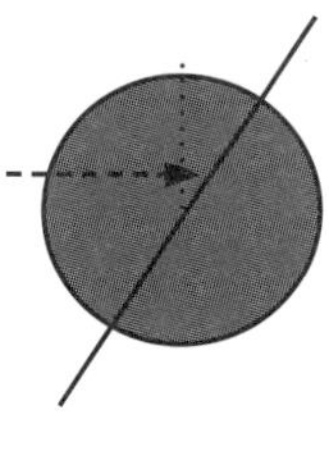

Question 3. Estimate the relevance of climate change and Milankovitch Cycles[2] to human evolution.

2.2 New hominid species

Over thousands of years new species of plants and animals evolved in the drier grassier African lands, and three million years ago a number of forms of hominids were present in Africa. Two important species were Homo Boisei and Homo Habilis

Boisei

Habilis

2.2.1 Homo Boisei

These hominids survived on bamboo, which was plentiful in the dry conditions, and they achieved protein through feeding on termites. Such food was in abundance, enabling the members to have the leisure and energy to breed and survive as a race.

2.2.2 Homo habilis

2.5 million years ago *homo habilis* abounded in Africa. *Habilis* was the first tool-maker, the first of the species *homo*. The intellectual capacity of this species was significantly advanced. At last after a few million years, the free hands were put to use. Today's primates use rocks to crush nuts, but do not fashion tools. The members of this group were the first to fashion tools out of stone. This use of tools meant the hominids could scavenge, could cut up dead carcases, eat the meat, and enjoy the nutritional bone marrow. This diet led to an increase of brain size.

2.2.3 Survival of habilis, extinction of boisei

The weather was now changing constantly, not every day but in millennial cycles of warming and cooling (ice ages and inter-glacials). The changeable circumstances put pressure on species so that the more specialised became extinct; they had evolved adaptations for particular circumstances, but those circumstances had changed. Thus *Boisei* who was perfectly suited to a dry climate and its prevalence of edible bamboo did not survive. The breaking of the million year drought was bad news for *boisei,* whose range of abilities was restricted to survival in dry times and who could not build shelters.

Homo habilis had more dietary options, and was not dependent on one food source. With more dietary options, and the resulting bigger brains, *Habilis* gained in intelligence and became quick-witted, investigative, and scavenging, well able to survive even the next climatic stage, the breaking of the long drought.

2.2.4. Fate of the australopithecines

Some *australopithecines* had co-existed with *habiles;* but they gradually disappeared during the long drought. The drought conditions deprived the savannah land of trees, and the *australopithecines* needed trees for defence against wild animals such as lions.

2. Chapter 1 section 6.2

> They 'had no weapons such as horns or powerful canines, nor the strength to wrestle successfully with any of their potential enemies. Presumably most australopithecines perished in the hundreds of thousands of years of this vegetational turnover'.[3]

3. Breaking of the drought and *Homo Erectus*

About two million years ago various more advanced species of *homo* emerged, all of which are conveniently gathered under the title *homo erectus*.

The brain was significantly larger with an average volume of about 1000 cc. Corresponding with this, the range and complexity of tools was an advance of those fashioned by *homo habilis*. *Erectus* had lost thick body fur, this being replaced by fine short hair, and importantly, there were sweat glands under the skin. This meant that the species had an advanced cooling system, and thus could travel and work in the heat. The better tools allowed these *homines* to secure more meat, chiefly by scavenging, enabling them to travel widely, which they did. Thus over thousands of years *homo erectus* was present all over Europe, in China, and in Java. There is good evidence a group in China in a particularly cold environment maintained fires, and used them for cooking.[4] As brain size increased, more developmental time had to be spent outside the womb. Thus mothers had to look after the young while the brain was being completed, and a sense of family grew.

Homo Erectus wiki

Shaanxi History Museum in Xi'an, China

3. Ernst Mayr, *What Makes Biology Unique* (Cambridge: Cambridge University Press, 2007), 199.
4. Steve Parker, *The Dawn of Man*, (London: New Burlington Books, 1992), 98.

4. Archaic Homo Sapiens[5]

EVOLUTION OF HOMO

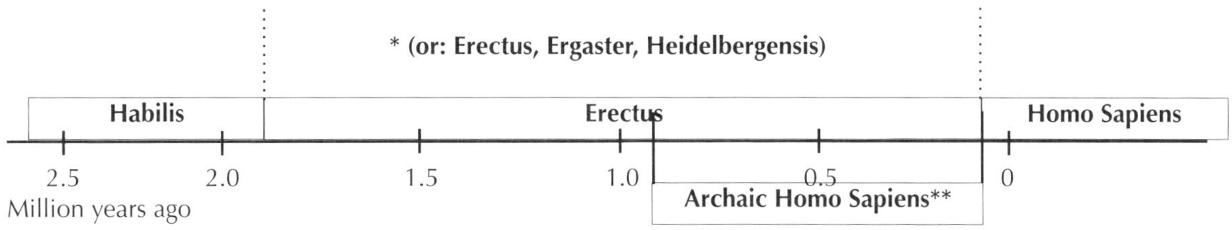

***Erectus, Ergaster, Heidelbergensis. There are slight differences in various groups. Some classify them all as *Homo Erectus*. Others distinguish them.**

****Archaic Homo Sapiens. Some classify all these as *Homo Erectus*.
Some see Erectus as gradually evolving greater and greater capability.
Some classify the significantly more capable as *Archaic Homo Sapiens*.**

Question 4. For a million years there was no advance in the range of tools use by *homo*. What prompted the end of this stagnation?

4.1 A gradual transition from Erectus to Sapiens

> There are various fossil forms that are intermediate in appearance between H. erectus and 'anatomically modern humans. Those intermediate types that are judged to be closer to H. erectus than to *H. sapiens* are collectively referred to as 'archic moderns'. Sorting out the possible relationships through this level is another highly contentious business[6]

The next advances were seen in the design of tools and spears for throwing. This facilitated the hunting of large animals, and using more sophisticated means of dismantling carcases. Hunting involved planning, which seemed to demand some kind of speech. Fossils date back 500,000 years—others 400,000 and 300,000 years ago. Their brains were significantly larger, though not as big as today's average size. Climate was still undergoing oscillations between icehouse and greenhouse events. In fact these events were becoming more intense. This tested survival skills, and natural selection was in the direction of greater intelligence to cope with the changes. They were able to survive harsh conditions and successfully hunt large animals, so that they survived and advanced.

Some fossils seeming to share features of *homo erectus* and *homo sapiens* dating about 150,000 to 130,000 years ago have been found [7] in China, Africa, and at many sites in Europe.

It is difficult to classify species during this evolutionary advance which occurred at different rates in different places. Some classify the more advanced of the in-betweens as *archaic homo sapiens*; some find a place for *homo heidelbergensis*; some make all the varieties equivalent.

> The evolutionary dividing line between *homo erectus* and modern humans was not sharp. It extended over several hundred thousand years. Adding to the confusion about this important transitional period is the fact that some regions were ahead of others in the process of evolving into our species.[8]

5. R. Southwood, *The Story of Life* (New York: Oxford University Press, 2004), 224.
6. Bolton 99.
7. Parker 104
8. http://anthro.palomar.edu/homo2/mod¬_homo¬_1.htm Accessed February 9th 2009.

5. Homo Sapiens and Neanderthal Man

5.1 Early Modern Humans.

Between 300,000 and 400,000 years ago *homo erectus* was gradually developing features of *homo sapiens*. The gradual transition from *erectus* to *sapiens* seems to have begun from even as far back as 800,000 years.

Homo sapiens seemed to have appeared more than 100,000 years ago. Some fossil evidence indicates anatomically modern humans, *homo sapiens*, existed even earlier[9]. The species had the same brain size and anatomy as ourselves, but there is little evidence of advanced intellectual ability as is found in the human race today. *Homo sapiens* arose in Africa and spread to Asia, Indonesia, Australia, North America, South America, gradually replacing *homo erectus/archaic homo sapiens*.

A significant group dates back 40,000 to 30,000 years ago. Their remains from about this time have been found in many places in Europe–France, Italy, Czechoslovakia—and in the Middle East and in Northern Africa.

5.2 Neanderthal man and homo sapiens develop separately

The origin of *homo sapiens* is thought to have taken place because of weather conditions—not just a few years' drought—but over thousands of years. 400,000 years ago, during the present ice epoch, *homo erectus/archaic homo sapiens* split into two separate groups—the precursors of the Neanderthals in the cold north, and the precursors of *homo sapiens* in the warm dry south.

150,000 years ago there was a severe ice age. Ice spread down from the poles over much of Europe. Neanderthals in the north were subject to the icy conditions, the southerners to the pains of prolonged drought.

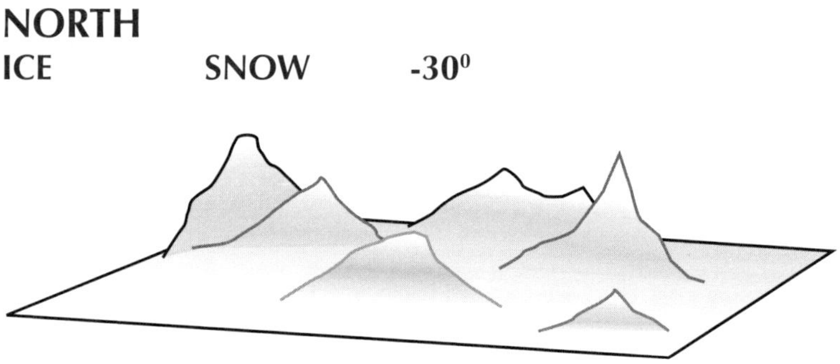

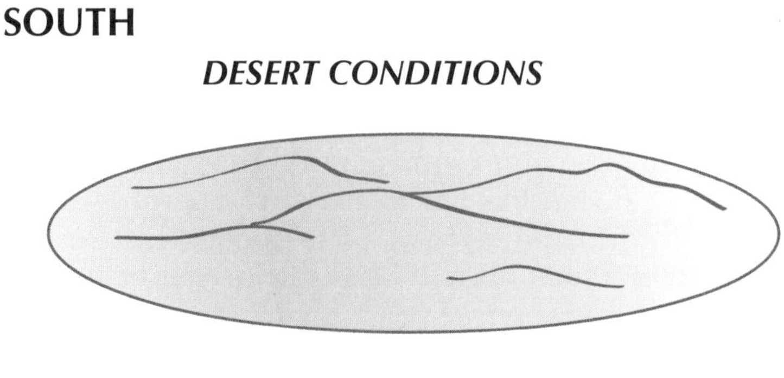

5.3 Homo Sapiens develops in the hot south

The group that remained in the south underwent arid, hot desert-like conditions. Such conditions favoured those who developed intelligence rather than physical prowess.

Anatomically modern *homo sapiens* seems to have emerged between 100 and 150 thousand years ago, and this advanced group spread out into all the regions occupied by *homo erectus* and beyond—except, seemingly into Europe and the cold Neanderthals' territory. After 40,000 years ago, they

9. Robin McKie, 'Origin of a Species', *Cosmos Magazine*, Issue 26 Apr/May 2009: 75–82.

also migrated into Europe, and by 30,000 years ago had outbred the Neanderthal occupiers who could not compete. The usurpers had developed imagination; because their drought conditions for thousands of years had been harsher, they had evolved in intelligence to meet the challenges. Had they not evolved in this way, they would not have survived. The two groups did not seem to interbreed, the DNA of one being markedly different from the other.

SOUTH **arid**

1000s of years living in vast tracts of desert.
He is physically like us
but taller and slimmer than Neanderthal.

<u>140,000 years ago all at brink of extinction</u>

Only a very special group survives
There is something inside their minds
Imagination

They can think ahead

Foresight, planning

5.4 Neanderthal Man develops in the cold north
The *archaic homo sapiens* group in the icy climate of the north developed a strong physique to cope with the harsh conditions, shorter bodies to conserve heat, and in the face of the conditions developed a considerable intelligence. 250,000 years ago they developed these features, together with brains slightly larger than those of *homo sapiens*. They flourished in Europe, Wales, Russia, and the Middle East. They lived together, used fire, survived by hunting, even hunting big game. They looked after the aged and the sick, practised burial rituals, and produced art work. They became extinct ten thousand years after *cro-magnon* man spread to Europe—30,000 years ago. They had advanced in physical prowess to deal with the cold, but their cognitive advance did not equal that of the southerners.

<u>Question 5</u>. Explain how different conditions produced different species of *homo*

6. *Cro-magnon* man—an intellectual advance

Cro-magnon man, *homo sapiens sapiens*, originally found at Cro-Magnon in France, has left remains 40,000 years old in some places. The oldest remains in other places are not so old, some being only from 20,000 years ago. *Cro-magnon* flourished in southern Europe during the last glacial age. They looked just like modern humans and the average brain size was about the same as today.

6.1 General development
There is development in many ways. They were meat eaters—reindeer and horse, but they also probably ate a wide range of plant materials. They were hunters and gatherers; they followed the animals during the seasons, but built semi-permanent huts. They hunted mainly with spears. They used a variety of more highly developed tools, which improved with the passing millennia. They were technologically superior to anything seen before. Anatomically it seems as if they had the physical capacity to speak.

6.2 Cultural development

But the major development was an intellectual one.

They constructed artistic Venus figures, and they made many drawings on the walls of caves, and used colours of red, black and others from different berries. The artistic exploits suggested an advance in intelligence—they constructed a world in their minds based on the world out there, but expressed symbolically. It seemed as if a cultural/intellectual advance had taken place—perhaps some brain mutation which saw this species maintaining the same brain size and anatomy, but progressing in art and associated symbolic and abstract thought.

Art has been found in many places on cave walls.

> the Cro-Magnon people who painted the caves at Lascaux and Altamira some 15,000 years ago are us—and one look at the incredible richness and beauty of this work convinces us, in the most immediate and visceral way that Picasso held no edge in mental sophistication over these ancestors with identical brains.[10]

10. Stephen Jay Gould, *Life's Grandeur* (London: Jonathan Cape, 1996) 220

'The remains of modern humans . . . are dated around 100,000 years ago. However, at least another 50,000 years passed before the tools and other artefacts associated with modern man appeared. This was a very key time, the time when biological evolution virtually stopped and cultural evolution took over.'[11]

Question 6. A person born 50,000 years ago would have been capable of surviving well in today's society. What have been the steps in progress over the 30,000 years? Why has the process accelerated exponentially in the last 100 years?

11. Southwood, 229.

Further Reading

Doublas Palmer, *Seven Million Years: The Story of Human Evolution* (London: Phoenix, 2006)

Richard Leakey, *The Origin of Humankind* (London: Weidenfeld & Nicolson, 1994).

Merlin Donald, *A Mind So Rare: The Evolution of Human Consciousness* (New York: WW Norton & Company, 2002).

Roger Penrose, *The Large, the Small and the Human Mind* (Cambridge: Cambridge University Press, 1997).

John R. Searle, *Mind: a brief introduction* (Oxford: Oxford University Press, 2004).

Roger Penrose, *The Emperor's New Mind* (Oxford: Oxford University Press, 1990).

David J Linden, *The Accidental Mind: How Brain Evolution Has Given Us Love, Memory, Dreams, and God* (Cambridge, Massachusetts: The Belnap Press of Harvard University Press, 2007).

Becoming Human: Evolution and the Rise of Intelligence, *Scientific American*, Volume 16, Number 2, Special Edition, 2006.

Chapter 6
Laws of Nature Plus Change Guide Evolution

Chapter overview

- The special laws of nature have guided cosmic and biological evolution
  - * To construct the universe
  - * From matter to mind
- The law of gravity
- Chance
  - * Varieties of chance
  - * Chance a factor in evolution
- Questions at the interface
- Are the scientific models what is in reality?
- Extensions
  - * More about mutations
  - * More about the specialness of nature's laws

1. The history of the universe is a history of ordering

Evolution began at the very first micro micro trillionth of a second of the existence of the universe. Encased in this ultra tiny entity of space-time-energy were the laws that would guide firstly the evolution of the cosmos, and then the evolution of life. Life has begun in at least one location. Some say this is a rare event,[1] even unique; others say life probably abounds.[2] The number of stars in the universe is greater than all the grains of sand on the earth's beaches. This question so far is unresolved.

The initial entity progressed from energy to protons, neutrons and electrons, to atoms, to hydrogen-helium gas clouds, to stars. Inside the stars, laws of nature brought about the manufacture of the elements. The laws engineered a gigantic explosion which then sent the ninety-two elements into space where eventually they were captured by other hydrogen-helium gas clouds which in turn became stars. These later generation stars were thus laced with all the elements of the periodic table. As the new star contracted, it shed successive rings of these ninety-two elements, which through the action of gravity became planets.[3]

On one of these planets, a suitable distance from the star and blessed with ample water, primitive life forms emerged. Thus began a development in life forms from single cells to multi-celled organisms, finally to intelligence.

Question 1. Why has matter evolved to such a state as intelligent consciousness? Why has it evolved at all?

2. The ultra-specialness of the Laws of Nature[4]

2.1 Special laws

All this occurred because of the laws of nature. The 'definite series of outcomes is coded into the laws of nature'.[5] The laws guided the results of the initial event to water, rock, carbon, and future

1. Simon Conway Morris, *Life's Solution: Inevitable Humans in a Lonely Cosmos* (Cambridge: Cambridge University Press, 2005).
2. Paul. Davies, *The Goldilocks Enigma* (London: Allen Lane, 2006), 150
3. Chapter 1, sections 2.4 and 2.5
4.. See Extension (2), this chapter, section 9
5. W Stoeger, 'The Immanent Directionality of the Evolutionary Process, and its Relationship to Teleology', in *Evolutionary*

ingredients for life. These laws are not any old laws, but are exceedingly special. There does not seem to be an *a priori* reason why they are as they are. The laws are mathematically describable. The force laws relating gravity and electric repulsion in stars, and nuclear force and electric repulsion in nuclei and the mass ratios are exquisitely suitable to generate a universe hospitable to life.

- Gravity: if a bit stronger the universe would have collapsed in a big crunch; a bit weaker, and matter would never have coalesced into stars and galaxies. That 'bit' is very tiny.

- Smoothness of Big Bang: The Big Bang was not entirely smooth; it contained fluctuations vital for the later formation of structure. If the initial fluctuations were a bit smaller, the universe would be dark and featureless. If a bit larger, the universe would have been dominated by black holes.

- Masses of particles: The neutron is slightly heavier than proton and this makes hydrogen possible. If protons were slightly heavier than the neutrons, they would decay into neutrons, so there would be no stable elements and so no stars.

- Strong nuclear binding force: Positive particles are kept together in the nucleus by this force. If the strong nuclear force were a bit weaker there would be no nuclei, the universe would have only hydrogen. If it were a bit stronger protons would pair up so hydrogen could not exist, and so stars as we know them would not be possible[6].

Question 2. A definite series of outcomes is coded into the laws of nature. Is this the correct explanation for cosmic and animal evolution?

Was the universe designed by a pure mathematician? Martin Rees describes six of these numbers[7]—constants regulating strengths of various physical process, laws, masses—to highlight the specialness of the universe. Paul Davies asks two questions: Why are there any laws of nature at all? Why are they so suited to producing a fruitful universe?

Davies[8] declares there are thirty constants of nature, many of which have to be almost exactly what they are so that the laws can engineer a productive and fruitful universe.

For instance, the gravitational constant G has to be 6.67×10^{-11} SI units within a very narrow range for the universe to have emerged as it has: the formation of stars, the manufacturing of higher elements, the distribution of these to space, the existence of a long-life star suitable for the evolution of life.

Lee Smolin[9] estimates the chance of the emergence of intelligence from the Big Bang to modern humans is $1/10^{229}$. As the number of particles in the universe is estimated as about 10^{80}, this alleged chance is inconceivably small.[10]

Question 3. Could $1/10^{229}$ sensibly be regarded as zero?

The constants of nature have to have very specific values for the universe to be fruitful—for any type of meaningful structures to eventuate, and more so for life to come about.

---

and Molecular Biology (Notre Dame Ind: University of Notre Dame Press, 1998), 163–190.

6. Paul Davies, *The Goldiloocks Enigma* 151–170
7. Martin Rees, *Just 6 Numbers: The Deep Forces that Shape the Universe* (London: Weidenfeld & Nicolson, 1999).
8. Paul Davies, 15–17, 166.
9. Lee Smolin, *The Life of the Cosmos* (London: The Orion Publishing Group, 1997), 45.
10. He proposes an evolution of universes theory, so that the emergence of one universe with correct laws is the result of a natural selection process.

> The universe is fit for life and had some of the laws of physics or the initial condition of the universe differed by even a tiny amount, then life—at least as we know it—would almost certainly be impossible.[11]

2.2 Special Laws of Nature have sponsored evolution
The evolutionary process depends on having very special laws of nature. These laws are seemingly extraordinarily unlikely. They are present somehow from the first stages of the Big Bang. They were part of the Creation event. Creation was destined to create itself by the action of the laws on successive stages. As new stages came about, new realities were present within the stages, which were guided by the old laws and new laws appropriate to the new realities; new stages were guided to further stages, culminating as it has turned out in intelligence.

Question 4. Could the suitability of the laws of nature for evolution be described as 'a packet of marvels that happens to be', or 'not requiring explanation'?

3. From matter to mind

3.1 A long process.
On planet earth, evolution by natural selection has over billions of years led to increasing biological complexity. The laws of nature were not content with having constructed a universe of stars, galaxies, comets, planets, moons. Once the conditions for further ordering were there in at least one place in the universe, they set about constructing mind in a long series of processes.

The initial one-celled organism developed a nucleus. Living cells joined up to form multi-celled ocean dwellers, out of which suddenly emerged a host of different body forms in what is known as the Cambrian Explosion. In these are represented the basic structures of all living animals today. After the appearance of plants on the land, fish developed the ability to walk, breathe air, and from these emerged tribes of amphibians. Thus some of the post-Cambrian species left the water and became land-based, though needing to return to water for breeding. The development of the ability to lay eggs enabled more evolved species—reptiles—to be entirely land based. Some developed heat control and the ability to spawn young within themselves—the mammals. Many forms with this added advantage of heat control spread over the land, and some returned to the sea. Controlled body heat and development of the young within the mother are features of the mammals. Mammals advanced to primates, hominids, and finally *homo sapiens* The development of bipedalism, the incremental increase in brain size, eventually gave rise to *homo sapiens* who can look back now over the whole process.

Biological Evolution

Non-life → one cell → multi-celled

→ more developed forms → Fish

→ To land: Amphibians → Reptiles

→ Mammals

Mammals → Hominids

Hominids → ***homo sapiens***

11. Paul Davies, *Science and Theology News*, April 2006

3.2 Fertility of the universe

Associated with the increasing complexity was the emergence of new properties each of which seemed to transcend the properties of the preceding state and all of which seemed to transcend the physical-chemical properties of the matter from which it originally arose.

Biological organisms exemplify the dictum that 'the whole is greater than the sum of its parts'. At each new level of complexity in biology new and unexpected qualities appear, qualities which apparently cannot be reduced to the properties of the component parts.[12]

The fertility of the universe[13] was a pre-condition for life to emerge from non-life, giving to an organism a property not reducible to the properties of the atoms/molecules involved in its construction.

The laws of nature could not do it on their own, but they needed fertile matter to act upon and they needed the help of chance to accomplish this feat.

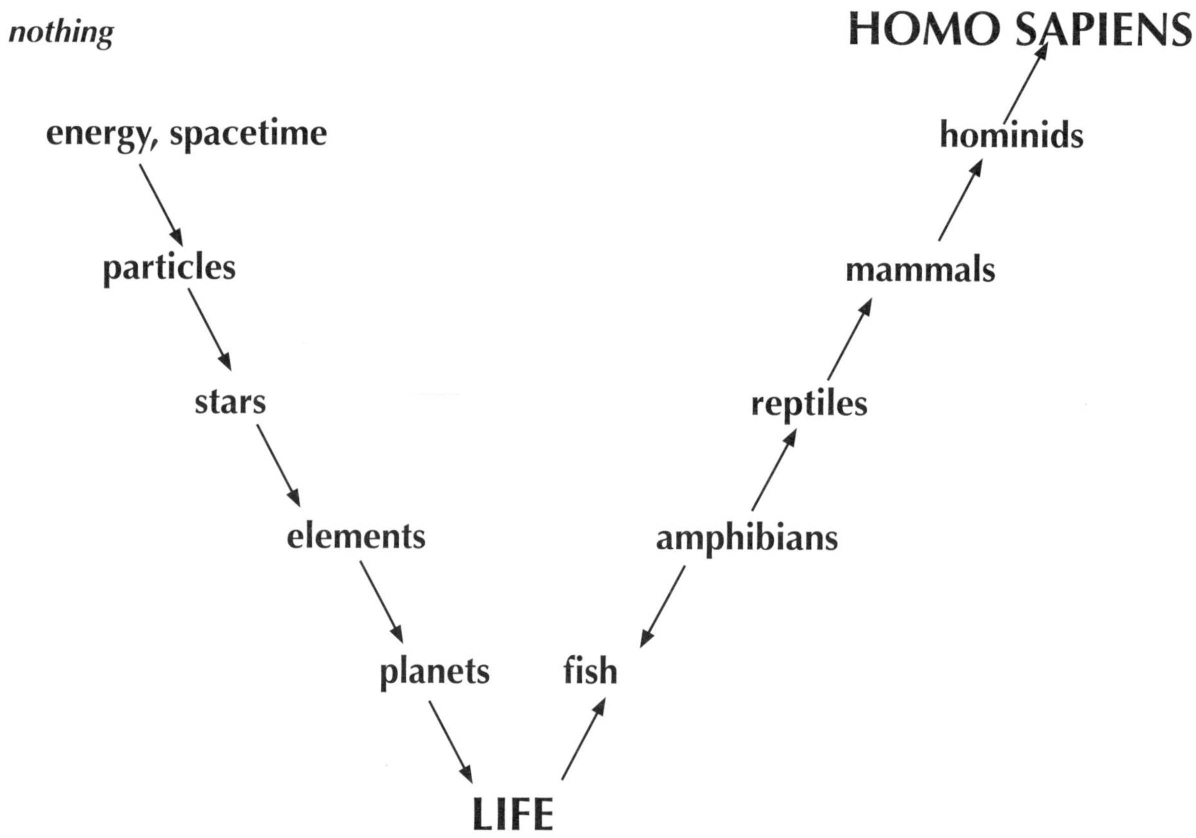

4. The law of gravity as an example of a law of nature

The laws of nature are firstly statements about how material reality operates. One aspect of reality is singled out, and tested, prescinding from whatever else is going on at the same time. Take for example, gravity. It was observed obviously that everything falls, then less obviously, that everything falls at the same rate with an acceleration of 9.8 ms^{-2}. Before Galileo, it was assumed heavier things fell faster than lighter things. However, if you discount the action of air resistance, a feather will fall at the same rate as a lump of lead (demonstrated in the 1960s on the moon). But things fall at different rates on different planets, moons or stars. Things fall with an acceleration of 1.6 ms^{-2} on the moon, and at 3.7 ms^{-2} on Mars. If you drop something from 6000 km above the earth's surface, its acceleration will be only 2.45ms^{-2}. On the basis of all this Newton worked out the general mathematical law of gravity.

12. Paul Davies, *The Cosmic Blueprint* (London: William Heinemann Ltd, 1987), 94.

13. George Coyne, 'God's Chance Creation', at <http://www.thetablet.co.uk/article/1027>, accessed 17 January 2009.

4.1 Newton's law of gravity

All things with mass attract each other with a force directly proportional to the amount of mass of each and inversely proportional to the square of the distance between the masses. Thus the earth pulls on the moon with a giant force causing it to keep curving in its trajectory; in the same way and with a similar result the sun tugs on the earth. Even lumps of lead in the laboratory were found to exert tiny forces of attraction on each other.

The force F is given by the equation: $\mathbf{F = [GM_1M_2]/d^2}$

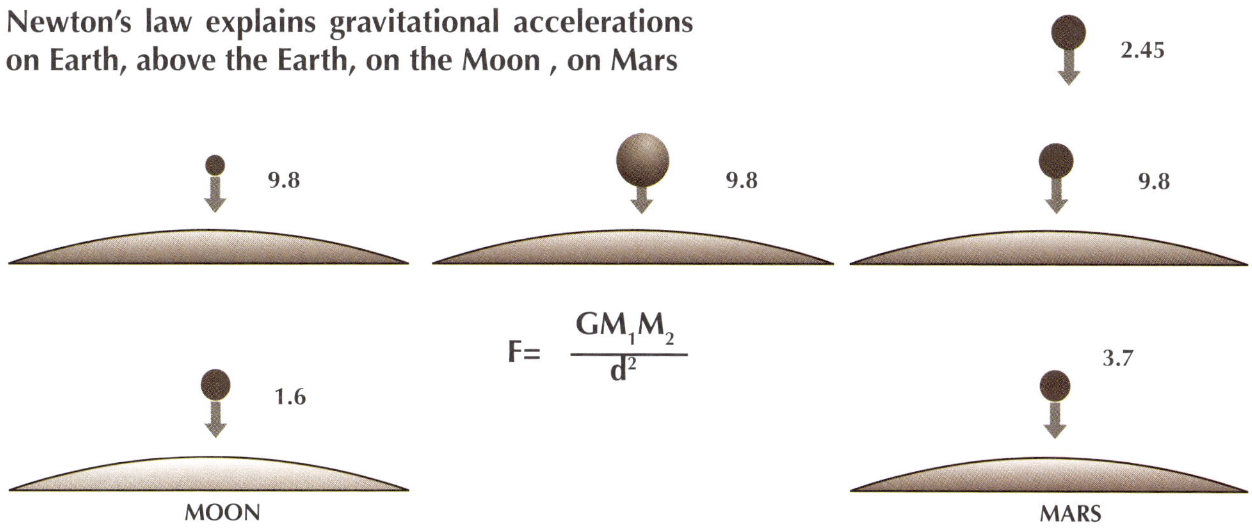

But why is Newton's Law like this?

4.2 The broad scope of the law of gravity

This law was instrumental in enabling hydrogen clouds to clump together to form stars, and now keeps the sun's matter all together despite the fact there are enormous explosions happening there all the time to give us light and heat, food and oxygen. (The sun shining on plants causes photosynthesis and this gives us food and oxygen). The sun does not blow itself to pieces, but all the pieces from the explosions keep falling back to the sun because of its gravity.

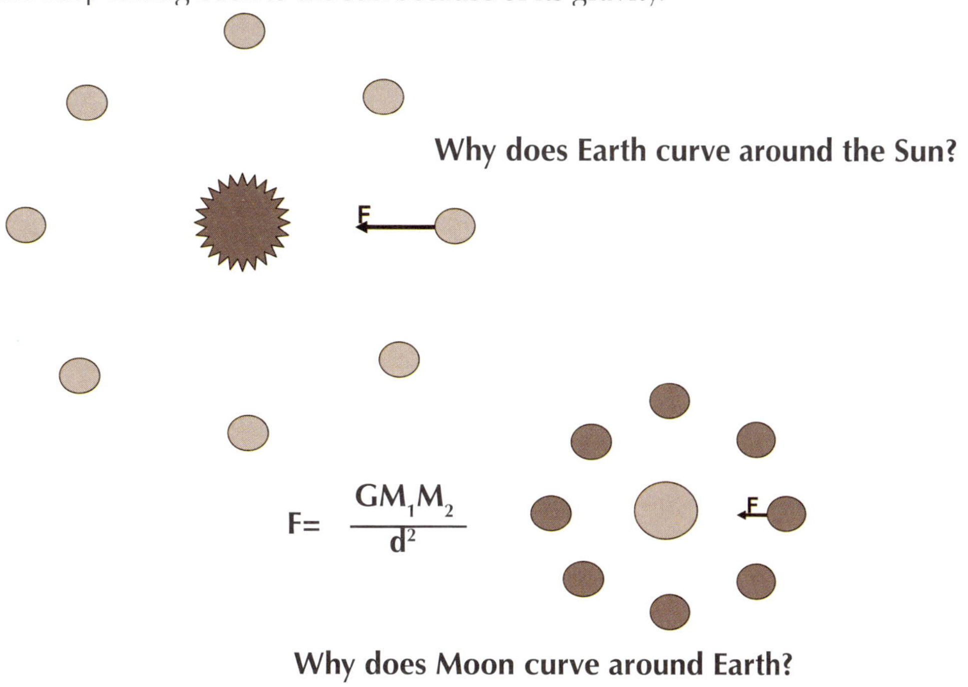

This beautifully simple law was found to be not the ultimate answer. Extreme situations exist where it fails (Neutron Stars, Black Holes).

4.3 The radical change in our knowledge of the law of gravity
There is the further refinement; this law has been found to be not the ultimate law. In extreme situations that we shall never meet, it doesn't work; black holes and pulsars do not follow Newton's Law; and strangely it has been demonstrated gravity actually affects the rate of time. For these extreme situations, there is a more fundamental law, general relativity, which advances counter-intuitive ideas such as curved space, space-time, large masses curving space-time. In everyday situations, this reduces to Newton's law. But once again, the question arises, why general relativity? Is curved space-time real, or just a convenient means of calculating?

Question 6. Theory of gravity evolved from the geocentric universe[14] theory, to Newton's law of forces, to general relativity. Do we ever reach the truth in science, or is each theory awaiting its own demise?

Since we have had to revise the model of reality behind the laws from interacting masses to general relativity, is this the final statement? And even if it is, do we really know what is in reality that makes giant masses curve space?

4.4 What is in reality that makes gravity act the way it does?
But what is there in reality that demands, proscribes that material reality acts in this way? We do not know. The law of gravity keeps us on earth, keeps the earth in orbit, keeps the Sun together by bringing the exploded bits of the sun back, has fashioned the galaxy, has built the stars, has brought about the rise in temperature inside stars that enables them to give light and heat, and also in some, brings about the conditions necessary for the synthesising of all the elements, but does not act strongly enough to keep the manufactured elements in the grip of the star when it explodes as a supernova. It is a wonderful law, strong enough, but not too strong. But what is the underlying reality that causes it to behave like this? We do not know. We can describe what it does, but we don't know the hidden reality itself, or why it acts the way it does.

Cosmologist-theologian William Stoeger sees this as a difficult question to answer.

> Why do two masses attract? The law of gravity. And why does the law of gravity operate?
> It operates because material objects determine a space-time manifold; the amount of mass-energy within a certain volume of space curves the spatial slices of the manifold in that region and objects subject to no forces will follow geodesics in that space-time. All this is given by Einstein's field equations. Why does mass-energy curve space? Why do objects in space-time follow geodesics? An infinite regress beckons.[15]

4.5 Many other laws of nature
The law of gravity is supremely important, but it is only one law of nature. There is the atomic theory which gives an account of how matter itself is structured, how matter reacts with itself, and the theory provides an excellent description of how particles behave. Why this theory exists is not answerable by science. And they lead us to counter-intuitive models. The laws involving the build up of matter seem common-sense enough until we try to go deeper than atoms themselves. We are then confronted by electrons which sometimes behave as waves sometimes as point-like particles, quarks which combine together to constitute protons and neutrons, and which combine together through the strong nuclear force which suddenly turns repulsive if they get too close. Forces between quarks

14. Earth is the centre of creation. Things naturally fall to the centre.
15. William Stoeger, 'Contemporary Physics and the Ontological Status of the Laws of Nature', in *Quantum Cosmology and the Laws of Nature*, edited by Robert John Russell *et al* (Notre Dame: University of Notre Dame Press, 1999), 227.

are mediated either by ghostly fields, or shared photons ('gluons'), all being subjected to their other nature—the wave-function. Reality ultimately is fields.

Question 7. Do laws of nature merely give a description of what's happening, without really telling us what is in reality and why it behaves as it does?

Today, on the brink of the twenty-first century, we can see that Ryle was right to dismiss the notion of the ghost in the machine[16]—not because there is no ghost, but because there is no machine.[17]

5. Realities behind the laws.

5.1 Are scientific models what really exists?

There arise descriptions of theoretical entities which then are related by mathematical laws which enable us to describe what is happening. They are descriptions, but they are not the final answer; they may not even be real, but if they are real, they do not explain themselves.

William Stoeger[18] talks about mentally constructed entities essential for describing reality:

> . . . the wave-function, fundamental particle spin, superstrings . . . space-time . . . fundamental constants. These entities "exist" at most only in the sense that they indicate relationships between theoretical entities which model the complex of physical phenomena and the idealized events which model the interactions and transitions . . . There is a tendency to reify these entities . . .

The models have changed radically over the years. For example, the model describing the universe has undergone many 'revolutionary' changes, and given the startling revelation that over 90% of the matter/energy in the universe has never been encountered signalling that another 'paradigm change' (Thomas Kuhn's philosophy of science) may be needed.

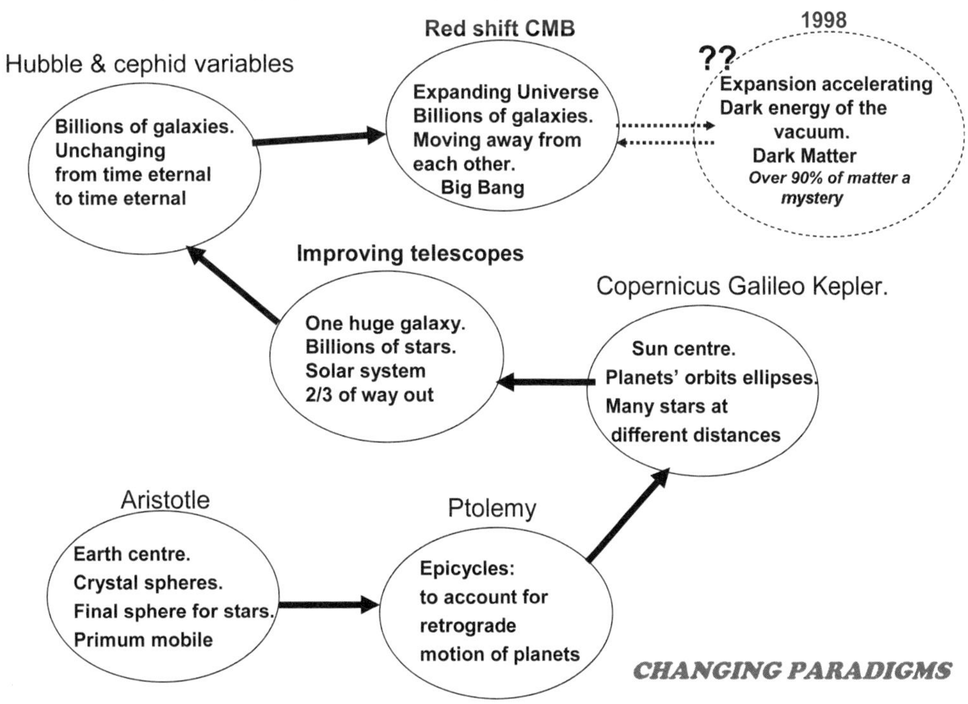

CHANGING PARADIGMS

16. Philosopher Gilbert Ryle in deriding Descartes' notion of the soul inhabiting the body, reduced it to nothing—'the ghost in the machine'
17. Paul Davies and John Gribben, *The Matter Myth* (London: Viking, Penguin Books Ltd, 1991), 301.
18. Stoeger, *Laws of Nature*, 217.

Can they be considered sources of physical necessity? We can end up giving them an independent status.

We don't really know the reality behind the laws which arise out of the reality.

We do know reality behaves in a predictable way, and it is this determined lawfulness which has directed material reality along the path of cosmic evolution, and which has combined with chance to direct reality further along the path of biological evolution.

5.2 Where do these laws of nature come from?

Paul Davies summarises views about the laws[19]

Do the laws pre-exist the universe? Either

* as an abstract necessity,
* or in the mind of God,
* or in some subsistent world of mathematical ideas?

<u>Question 8.</u> What is your answer?

Roger Penrose proposes the third possibility:

> According to the Platonic viewpoint, mathematical ideas have an existence of their own, which is accessible via the intellect only. When one sees a mathematical truth, one's consciousness breaks through into this world of ideas, and makes direct contact with it.[20]

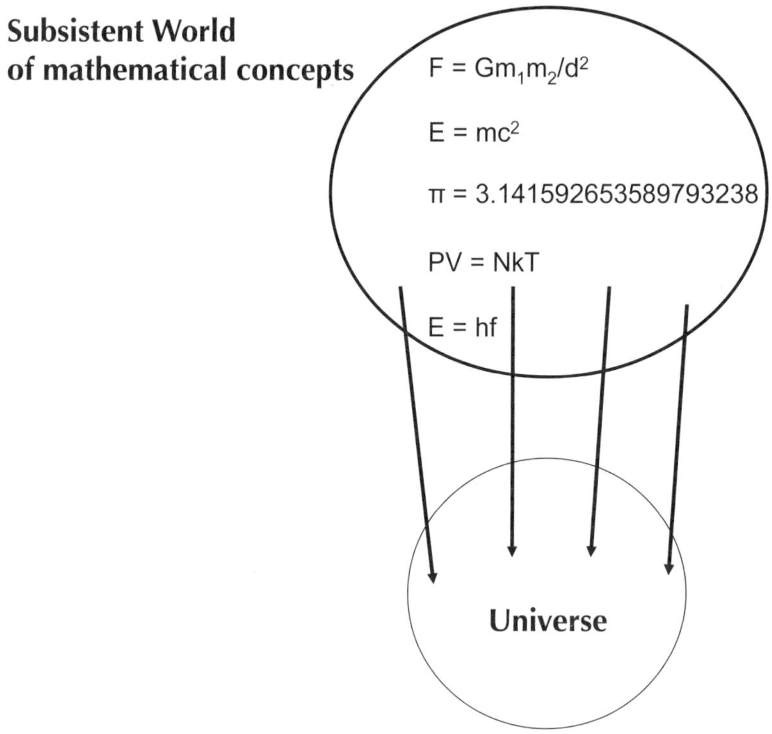

6. Chance

Clearly there has been a complexification process, an acquiring of more and more specialized and advanced abilities. There is the enigma of the absolute necessity of the involvement of chance in the process. Each stage progressed through slight incremental changes through a combination of gene mutations, natural selection, changes in climate and/or geological conditions.

---

19. P Davies, *The Goldilocks Enigma*, 13–14.
20. R. Penrose, *The Emperor's New Mind*, (London: Oxford: Oxford University Press, 1990) 428.

6.1 Varieties of chance

[1] Event without a cause: Sometimes things seem to happen spontaneously, a road bridge collapses, a blind suddenly goes up—seemingly without a cause. But a cause can be discovered by close examination. In the macro world everything that happens has a cause. Not so in the micro world:

(a) *Radioactive decay:* A carbon fourteen nucleus will decay into a nitrogen nucleus. Carbon atom decays to a nitrogen atom plus two small particles.

${}_{6}C^{14} \rightarrow {}_{7}N^{14} + {}_{-1}e^{o} + {}_{0}v^{o}$.

All billions of Carbon 14s in a sample are likely to do this. One specific one does. Nothing tips it over the edge. It just happens. It may never do so, it may do so in the next second. Yet there is predictability for a large number: half the nuclei in a large sample will have decayed in about 5,500 years.

A mutation could possibly be located here.

(b) *Virtual particles:* Every second millions of electron-positron pairs pop into existence, and pop out again within about 10^{-20} of a second. They come from nothing, but mutually annihilate almost immediately—their presence has been detected. This 'chance' happening is governed by the Heizenberg uncertainty principle, so arguably is not chance at all.

[2] Two totally independent causal chains.

Family camps under tree in central Victoria. There's a thunderstorm, and the tree is struck by lightning. One person in the car is killed by a falling branch.

Rock dislodged from cliff by heavy rain crushes passing vehicle and its occupants.

A person is hit by a meteor. Earth is hit by an asteroid.

This is too infrequent or unlikely to be applied to mutations.

[3] Very slim chance in an event someone must win.

Raffle. Even if there are a million tickets, someone must win, though the chances for each ticket-holder are minimal. River takes one particular course through a valley. River must take one course. The course it eventually takes was possible from the beginning.

A one-off style of chance does not fit the mutation phenomenon.

[4] Very slim chance in an event in which there is not necessarily a winner.

Lotto events demand certain numbers out of a selection of numbers must be predicted to win the prize. In Tatslotto, six numbers have to selected out of forty. Thousands of entries may be made, but there may not be a winner.

[5] Order emerging from a random process. All the molecules in a closed box move in one direction at the same time—upwards—and the box jumps upwards. All the molecules are moving, chaotically. If they all moved in the same direction at the same time, the box would jump upwards. The chance of this is effectively zero.

Throw pieces of jig-saw up in the air, and on coming down they have linked together by chance to form the picture.

Shuffle cards and they are all in order of number and suits.

This sort of thing seems to happen in the construction of proteins which happen upon the one structure in billions that will fit them for a specific purpose.

[6] Chaos. Given the initial state of a system in which determined laws are operating, you cannot predict its situation some time later. Two systems which are seemingly the same at the start will evolve differently in the long term. Their situations some time later will be very different. The future histories of the systems are acutely sensitive to seemingly immeasurable differences in initial conditions. The laws operating on a system are deterministic laws but their activity is so dependent on the initial conditions that their subsequent histories in individual situations are *de facto* unpredictable. Thus it is difficult to predict the weather over more than a few days. True causes are there, but the presence of so many particles moving in so many different ways makes knowing them impossible. The

development and progress of a cyclone, the patterns on a flowing river depend on the interactions of trillions of causes. What happens is inevitable, determined, but for us unpredictable.
The way one gene may mutate does not resemble the behaviour of systems consisting of billions of particles.
[7] One small event triggers an event out of all proportion. A ruler balanced on its end falls over, but in which direction? Butterfly flapping its wings in Las Vegas causes a tornado in China. Pebble dislodged by a hiker in The Andes knocks a slightly larger pebble in its downward roll, and the process is repeated many times causing a mudslide and a village is buried.

Question 9. What variety of chance accompanied evolution?

6.2 Chance events and evolution

6.2.1 Questions.

'Did the universe happen by chance?' can have many meanings.

1) Did it pop into existence without a cause ? without pre-existing laws ?
2) Did it just happen to have that set of constants, and strength of "Big Bang" so that stars could form, burn for a long time, structures could form, elements could create themselves in supernovae, and life emerge ?
3) Did the molecules which form life arrange themselves by chance, or were life's pathways biased in their favour?
4) Was the fact of chance mutations the overwhelming originator of evolution?

6.2.2 Favourable chance occurrences are selected.

Chance has played a crucial role in evolution. Instructions for all aspects of the animal are encoded in the DNA, which resides in the nucleus of every cell. Different regions of the DNA strands contain these instructions. The instructions are passed on to descendents. Changes occur in these instructions at a constant rate over time. The individual changes are random events. Most are not helpful, but every now and then one happens randomly that imparts a favourable phenotypic characteristic to the organism. If the change results in instructions for some betterment factor such as sharper claws, greater speed, better resistance to cold or heat, the recipient of such a change in the next and succeeding generations will be favoured so that after thousands of years, the possessors of this variant will have outbred the ones without the change. Hundreds of millions of years are available for such processes, which then build on each other. At the same time there are retrogressions or sideways developments, but it is undeniable there has been progressive development such that mammals replaced most of the reptiles, who had replaced most of the amphibians. Yet early stage life forms, bacteria, outnumber all other organisms. The viability of mammals and *homo sapiens* depends on the continued existence of prokaryotes.

6.2.3 Mutations—the chance feature for evolution

The nucleus of the cell contains DNA. DNA is the blueprint for life. A strand of DNA contains a long array of chemicals known as bases. There are only four units (bases) involved in the long strand: A, C, G and T. The order in which these occur determines the properties and functioning of the organism. Chance events, chance DNA mutations, are factored into the nature of DNA. Particular chance happenings in the DNA are not prescribed. They are all random events. Chance involved with the mutations could be factored into some intrinsic brittleness of DNA. DNA is very stable, but not entirely. Codons have a certain freedom to relocate. Or perhaps chance could be occurring at a quantum level.

For example: Mutation for thicker fur (not the actual base sequence)

MUTATION

Base order for fur thickness

← **TCGTAGCGGCCATCACGCCCCGAATTGAACCGT** →

Two bases swap places:

TCGTAGCGGCCATCACGCCCCGAATTGAACCGT

TCGTACGGGCCATCACGCCCCGAATTGAACCGT

OR

Three bases migrate to a new position:

TCGTAGCGGCCATCACGCCCCGAATTGAACCGT

TCGCGGCCATCACGCCCCGAATTGAACTAGCGT

Such a random change could cause thicker fur

All characteristics are determined by the DNA.[21] For example, the part of the strand determining the thickness of fur may be arranged as above. Thus all animals have a definite fur-thickness. But changes in these orderings of bases occur spontaneously and randomly. Three letters may move to a different place, or one of the letters may change, or letters swap places. The resulting strand—the gene for fur-thickness—may cause thicker fur. If the animal is in a cold climate, this individual would prosper more. The offspring would possess this mutated gene, and have thicker fur. So would its offspring. These favoured individuals would survive better than the non-mutated; they would be less affected by the cold, could hunt for longer periods, would be more active in the hunt. Eventually over many generations, the population would consist of those with thicker fur.

MUTATION

- Slight change in DNA
- Causes a different life-chemical to form
- DNA Mutations occur by chance regularly
- Usually they are deleterious
- Occasionally they provide advantage
  - * Strength
  - * Speed
  - * Eyesight
  - * Cope with climate change
- The ones with this advantage
  - * Survive over time
    - {1000s of years}
- Survival of the fittest

For life's evolution, the earth's biosphere is so huge and time is so vast that enough chance mutations occur to facilitate the progress of life from single prokaryotic cells to intelligence. The vastness of time is not itself a cause, but it is a situation in which natural selection can achieve what it has with the appropriate laws and the inbuilt fertility of matter.

21. Chapter 2 Section 2 (most of questions/answers in section 2)

6.2.4 Was it merely chance?

Three things operate together:

- laws of nature, seeded into the big bang, which suggest consciousness was implanted (planned?) in the big bang,
- blind chance, which suggests the ultimate end point was a fluke, not planned,
- the fertility of the Cosmos.

Question 10. The whole evolutionary process was meaningful? The whole evolutionary process was nothing more than chance? What is your decision and why?

7. The issue comes down to this

Despite the evolutionary bush, with species going sideways, backwards and forwards, more advanced species have emerged in the course of time on some twigs. There has been a directionality in evolution in so far as a being with reflective consciousness has emerged from mindless matter in a series of progressive stages from cell, to multi-cell, to fish, to amphibian, to reptile, to mammal, to primate, to hominids, to *homo sapiens*. Was this prewritten into the laws of nature? And what is the origin of these laws? And the catch is that this whole process at every stage was guided by natural selection which has as an absolute requirement chance events, chance mutations happening in the DNA. On the other hand, the world of matter seems an exceedingly fertile scenario on which the laws and chance operate.

8. Extension (1): DNA and mutations.

A mutation is fundamentally a change in the DNA. It may be as small as a change in one letter, or two letters swapping positions, or a three-letter 'word' (codon) migrating further down the chain. If a letter is changed, the codon is changed and this codon will now attract a different amino acid. A different protein is thus formed. It could be the protein responsible for the thickness of fur. If this changed protein confers an advantage—thicker fur in an ice age—the fur will grow thicker, and the animal will have an advantage which will change the population in numbers of generations.

Each word attracts a particular amino acid in order to synthesize a protein, for a particular function, need.
The acids are numbered 1 to 11

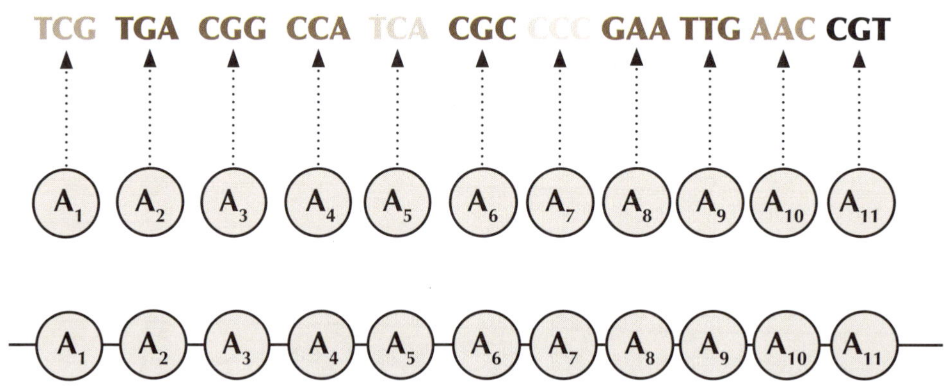

If the letters below are swapped, this change means two new amino acids are in the chain.
Acids 12 and 13 have replaced 2 and 3.
New protein: probably harmful, but could be an advantage

← TCG TAG CGG CCA TCA CGC CCC GAA TTG AAC CGT →
← TCG TAC GGG CCA TCA CGC CCC GAA TTG AAC CGT →
The changed words (triplets) attract different amino acids

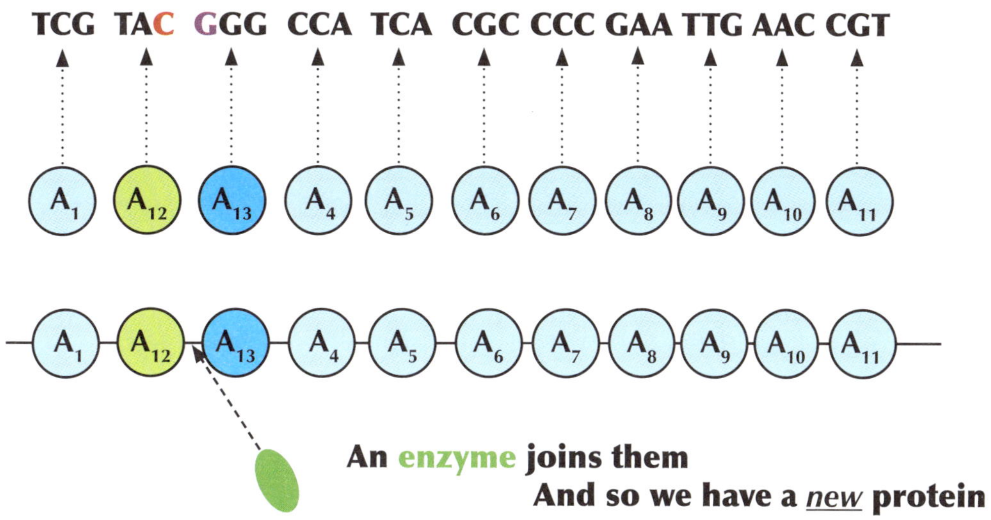

9. Extension (2) Cosmic coincidences

(1) *Stars are flukes:* A star like the sun is necessary for life. A star is a continuous nuclear fusion explosion.

Why doesn't the sun's continuous nuclear explosion blow it to bits and scatter its remains into space? Because its strong gravity pulls back the debris from the explosion. Why then doesn't the strong gravity cause the star to implode to insignificance or even nothingness? Because the electrical repulsive forces between atoms are strong enough to resist gravity. The ratio between the gravitational forces—just right to prevent blowing itself to bits—and the electrical forces is a delicate one—it has to be just as it is. Change one slightly without changing the other and stars would either not exist or would not live long enough or shine brightly enough to allow life to form. There does not seem to be a reason why the two laws are exactly as they are. There is an immeasurable number of other strengths these laws could have. Is this chance, or were these laws designed?

(2) *A nucleus is unlikely*

(i) *Balance of forces:* Matter is formed of atoms, and atoms have at their centres a nucleus. It is the nucleus which determines the nature of the material. Iron is iron because of the particular nucleus of the iron atom. Carbon is carbon because of its nucleus. A stable nucleus depends a harmonious relationship between the nuclear force and electrical repulsion. Tweak one of these forces slightly and nuclei would not be possible.

(ii) *Balance of masses:* Nuclei are composed of protons and neutrons. For a nucleus to be stable, it needs the proton to neutron mass ratio to be what it is. Neutron mass/proton mass = 1.00137841870. The neutron is 0.1% heavier than the proton. If the heaviness were very slightly less, necessary nuclear reactions could not take place. If it were 0.1% lighter than the proton, matter could not exist for longer than ten minutes. Are these force and mass ratios necessarily so? Is this necessity? Is this chance? Or were these laws designed?

(3) *Carbon formation mysteries:* Carbon is essential for life. All life is built on carbon, on its extraordinary property of being able to form endless chains. Human DNA is three billion carbon atoms in a chain—to start with—and enzymes, proteins, are all based on carbon. Carbon was generated inside large stars.

There are three coincidences involved in the fact of carbon. Carbon was formed. Carbon was then not destroyed. Carbon was then released into space

- *Carbon was formed:* Its synthesis depends on its having a particular energy level. This energy level had to have a particular relationship to a level in the synthesised material, helium. If the level were slightly above or slightly below what it actually is, carbon would not have made it. If the levels were slightly out of sync, no carbon.

- *Carbon was not destroyed:* The carbon formed would have been immediately destroyed if a reaction with another helium nucleus were possible. Calculations show this destructive event just does not work.

- *Carbon was then released into space:* this carbon had to escape into space to be taken up into a new cloud and become part of a potential life-generating star such as our sun. An extraordinary value of the so called 'weak nuclear force' enabled carbon to escape from the remnant of the large star in which it was hatched. In a gigantic explosion—supernova—the first generation star exploded and delivered all of its elements into space. Calculations show that given any other value of the 'weak force' the carbons would have only got so far out from the remnant, and then been sucked back to be forever buried and unavailable.

Astronomer Fred Hoyle researched the question of the synthesis of elements inside stars. His discovery of an energy level in carbon coincidentally just right for its formation in a very unlikely particle collision, and the fact that it just avoided subsequent destruction in a likely collision led him to conclude there was a Designer

> Some super-calculating intellect must have designed the properties of the carbon atom, otherwise the chance of my finding such an atom through the blind forces of nature would be utterly minuscule. A common sense interpretation of the facts suggests that a superintellect has monkeyed with physics, as well as with chemistry and biology, and that there are no blind forces worth speaking about in nature. The numbers one calculates from the facts seem to me so overwhelming as to put this conclusion almost beyond question[22]

(4) *The big bang coincidence*
The Big Bang was not any old big bang. Its explosive power had to be orchestrated very precisely otherwise the particles would have been forced back to where they had come from, or would have travelled out so fast that they could never had formed stars.

Materialist science, even in principle, cannot tell us why the universe of matter is structured in a way that prevents us from understanding it fully.[23] Absolute materialism does not triumph because it cannot fully explain the nature of reality.

22. Fred Hoyle, 'The Universe: Past and Present Reflections', *Engineering and Science*, November, 1981, 8–12 From Wikipedia *Sir Fred Hoyle*, accessed 30/4/2009.
23. Kenneth R. Miller *Finding Darwin's God* (New York: Harper Perennial, 2007), 219.

Further Reading

Keith Ward, *The Big Questions in Science and Religion* (West Conshohocken PA: Templeton Foundation Press, 2008).

Charles Birch, *On Purpose: A New Way of Thinking for the New millennium* (Kensington NSW: New South Wales University Press, 1990).

Richard Dawkins, *River out of Eden* (London: Weidenfeld & Nicolson, 1995).

Robert John Russell *et al* (editors), *Quantum Cosmology and the Laws of Nature: Scientific Perspectives on Divine Action* (Vatican City State: Vatican Observatory, 1999).

John D Barrow, *New Theories of Everything* (Oxford: Oxford University Press, 2007).

John D Barrow, *The Constants of Nature: from Alpha to Omega* (London: Vintage, Jonathan Cape, 2002).

Chapter 7
Darwin's Evolution: a Theory for Today

Chapter overview

- Charles Darwin
- The 5-year voyage on the '*Beagle*'
    - Charting the coast of South America
    - Tortoises and finches on the Galapagos Islands
- 20 years of research after the voyage
- Publication of '*On The Origin of Species*'
    - Darwin's theory
    - Natural selection
- Convergence in evolution
- The question of teleology

Darwin at 50

1. Darwin

Charles was the son of a doctor, Erasmus Darwin. As a boy he was fascinated by anything to do with animals—fishing, hunting, collecting insects. He was slow to choose a career; so his father put him into a medical course. He could not interest himself here, and his father once wrote to him saying 'you care for nothing but shooting, dogs and rat-catching, and you will be a disgrace to yourself and all your family'.[1] His father then sent him to Cambridge to study to become a clergyman. He found he was more interested in phenomena of life, became active in biological circles and eventually retired from his theological studies.

1. A Tobin and J Dusheck, *Asking about Life* (Philadelphia: Harcourt College Publishers, 2001), 325.

2. The *Beagle*

In 1831 Darwin successfully sought a place on HMS *Beagle* embarking on a world cruise whose function was to survey the South American coast.

The *Beagle* was twenty-seven metres long, and its captain was Robert FitzRoy who offered Darwin a place on the ship so that he would have someone to talk to on his level.

> FitzRoy proposed to the hydrographer 'that some well-educated and scientific person be sought who would willingly share such accommodations as I could offer, in order to profit by the opportunity of visiting distant countries yet little known.'[2]

Darwin's official duty was to collect specimens of plant life, animal and bird life, and fossils. Although he had no biological qualifications, he was recognized in the field as he had spent many hours of his theological studies in the company of naturalists, and was a member of the *Royal Society*. The voyage was no holiday cruise, as he was almost perpetually sea-sick.

2.1 Geological gradualism: Evidence from the voyage

He spent time on the voyage studying a geological history of the earth, which was proposing the earth was very old. The prevailing generally accepted theory was 'catastrophism': the earth had existed for a short time, during which major catastrophes such as floods shaped the land and caused extinctions. For biblical fundamentalists, the defining flood was the flood that saved Noah. At a stopover at Cape Verde islands, Darwin noticed a long layer of rock in a cliff contained seashells despite its being thirteen metres above the sea, and realised it had been formed thousands of years previously at the bottom of the sea.

> The entire formation rose to its present height gradually enough to maintain its shape.[3]

Evidence in the Andes of similar rock layers high above sea level convinced him of mountain uplift slow enough to preserve the layer intact, and hence of geological gradualism: geological change occurs slowly over long periods of time. He transferred this concept in his later thinking to the history of life.

The findings everywhere, especially those on the Galapagos Islands, gave him matter to think upon for life evolution rather than for geological evolution.

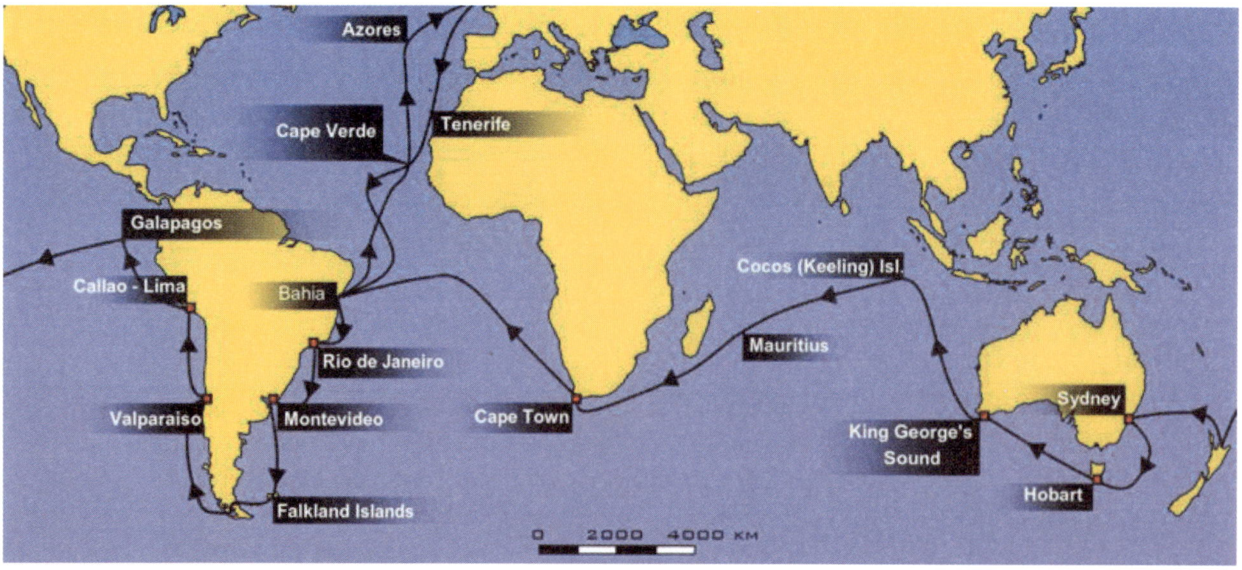

2. Tony Rice, *Voyages of Discovery* (Crows Nest, NSW: Allen & Unwin, 2008), 231.
3. Edward J Larsen, *Evolution* (New York: The Modern Library, 2004), 59.

2.2 Three and a half years along the coast of South America

The *Beagle* took over two years to chart the east coast of South America. The ship often stayed in places for some time, at one time remaining three months in Rio de Janeiro. During these intervals, Darwin spent the time on land. He undertook two journeys of 960 kilometres, one from El Carmen to Buenos Aires, the other up the Parana River to Santa Fe and back. He used these occasions to observe the geology, and to gather specimens of organisms from extinct large mammals to living beetles. After unearthing the bones of giant mammals he sent them back to England while he continued his land and sea expeditions.

The ship then progressed slowly up the west coast; this leg of the sailing occupied 15 months, much of which time, Darwin again involved himself in trips into the country including two expeditions up the Andes.

> Everywhere the living organisms he observed showed wonderful adaptations to exploit the vagaries of their often harsh environment.[4]

2.3 Westward to the Galapagos Islands.

The ship then turned westward and stopped at the Galapagos Islands. Here he observed that tortoises differed slightly according to which island they inhabited, indicating they had adapted to the conditions of each island. If a tortoise was on an arid island, one which had less feed, it had a gap in its shell near the neck so that it could reach higher for food. Tortoises on fertile islands had no such gaps in their shells.

> . . . remarkably, several of the islands had their own unique forms, distinct from those on neighbouring islands only a few tens of kilometres away.[5]

4. Rice, *Voyages of Discovery*, 234.
5. *Ibid*, 235.

Finches

Similarly finches' beaks varied from island to island to island. If edible seeds and/or nuts had hard shells, the beaks were tougher; if the edible nuts had soft shells, the beaks were not made of such firm material.

Fuel for a theory: A blue-footed booby on San Cristobal Island, part of the Galapagos Archipelago. Slightly different species of tortoises, finches and other groups gave Darwin the idea that species might evolve by a process of natural selection.

3. Research and thinking after the voyage

3.1 Extensive research

Once back in England, Darwin worked on the many specimens he had brought back with him, helped by experts at the Zoological Society of London. The common knowledge that fossils represented animals no longer existing, and the extensive variety of specimens he collected led him to doubt whether God had created all existing species directly. One of the experts was the distinguished artist-ornithologist John Gould who explained to Darwin the finches were not different species, but adapted versions of the same species.

> Within six days of receiving them, Gould was able to announce that despite their totally different beaks they were all, in fact, finches.[6]

He investigated aspects of evolution by experimenting in a rural setting on plants and animals; he wrote many articles, and became well known as somewhat of an authority. But he did not publish; instead he allowed the evolutionary ideas to consolidate within his mind.

3.2 The conclusions after two decades research

Darwin was persuaded by four features of the natural world:[7]

1) The forms of certain living creatures seemed adapted to their needs . . .
2) Some species were known to have become extinct . . .
3) He was impressed by the peculiarities of island populations.
4) Many creatures possessed 'rudimentary structures' with no apparent function—wings on flightless birds.

6. *Ibid,* 236.
7. Alister McGrath, 'Darwinism', in *The Oxford Handbook of Religion and Science*, Philip Clayton, editor (Oxford: Oxford University Press, 2008), 684.

3.3 Publication of 'On The Origin of Species'

Having returned to England in 1836, he did not publish *'On The Origin of Species, by Natural Selection'* till 1859, twenty-three years later. He may have delayed publication still further had he not realised Alfred Russel Wallace had developed the same theory. He and Wallace corresponded.

He published *'The origin of species'* in 1859, and it was a best seller. The first edition of his book consisting of over 1,000 copies sold out in one day.

Chilean Mockingbird

3.4 The revolutionary idea

The idea of evolution was not new at the time, but Darwin's revolutionary addition was to provide a mechanism for the process. The mechanism was natural selection. Changes occurred randomly in populations. Some individuals are thus better adapted to surroundings and have a better chance of surviving and producing offspring. Some may have an advantage—for example greater speed—and in the existing conditions and over a long time, outbreed the others. Others may lie in wait for a climate change—an ice age for example—and be better adapted to new conditions and eventually become the only members of the species. The evolutionary mechanism, natural selection, distanced the Designer God from the natural order.

4. Darwin's theory

4.1 Multi-pronged theory

Ernst Mayr[8] separates Darwin's theory into five different parts:

1) Evolution as such: *organisms change with time* with some degree of directionality. The biosphere is not static.
2) *Common descent*: All organisms have come from other more ancient species.
    a. Embryos of more advanced species contain features of more ancient species – for example, gills: these features disappear during embryonic development.
    b. DNA of later species can be seen to be related to the DNA of earlier extinct species.

> The affinities of all the beings of the same class have sometimes been represented by a great tree . . . The green and budding twigs may represent existing species; those produced during each former year may represent the long succession of extinct species[9]

8. Ernst Mayr, *What Makes Biology Unique* (Cambridge: Cambridge University Press, 2007), 97–114.
9. Charles Darwin, *On The Origin of Species,* in *Darwin, The Indelible Stamp,* edited by James D Watson (Philadelphia: Running Press, 2005), 408–409, 414

> The incredible variety of living things made Darwin's conclusion of descent with modification from a common ancestor seem completely counterintuitive.[10]

3) Gradualism versus saltationism: *Changing in organisms proceeds gradually* and never in sudden large events (saltationism).

> . . . natural selection will always act with extreme slowness . . . Nothing can be effected, unless favourable variations occur and variation itself is apparently always a very slow process .[11]

4) *The multiplication of species:* There are up to 10 million species of animals and two million plant species known today. Darwin found an abundance of species during his voyage—nowhere near as many as this—but concluded the number of species in the world was large.

5) *Natural selection:* deals with the mechanism of evolutionary change. By this time the idea of evolution itself was commonplace. His disturbing addition to this idea was natural selection.

> Living things vary among themselves. These variations arise randomly, that is without regard to whether a given variation would be beneficial or not. Those living things with advantageous variations tend to stick around a bit longer than others, and give rise to more like themselves. Hence their numbers increase.[12]

As molecular biology did not exist at the time, and Darwin made no reference to the work of Gregor Mendel on inheritance, he could not answer two questions: (1) how the chance variations arose; (2) how these were then transmitted to successive generations.[13] These questions have been answered by gene mutations, and the existence and role of the human genome.

As the weaker were constantly giving way to the stronger, the theory was disturbing. How could such a Creator-Designer be compassionate? And what need was there now for a Designer-God at all as it was a chance directed process?

4.2 Group selection—a difficulty

In species of social insects—ants, termites, bees—there exist individuals who cannot reproduce and who seemingly work not for themselves but for the good of the community. How could such variations be produced by natural selection, when natural selection's clear intention was to produce fitter individuals in a given situation? Darwin recognised this difficulty.

> No amount of exercise, or habit, or volition, in the utterly sterile members of a community could possibly have affected the structure or instincts of the fertile members, which alone leave descendants.[14]

Darwin solved this by saying the fertile individuals had developed the ability to produce a certain proportion of infertile offspring for their own benefit.

> Fertile males and females of the same community flourished and transmitted to their fertile offspring a tendency to produce sterile members.[15]

10. Ted Peters and Martinez Hewlett, *Evolution from Creation to New Creation* (Nashville: Abingdon Press, 2003), 168.
11. Origin, 402.
12. Timothy Shanahan, *The Evolution of Darwinism* (Cambridge: Cambridge University Press, 2004), 2
13. James Watson, Foreword to *Origin*, viii.
14. Origin, 471.
15. *Ibid.*

There are many other examples of non-self-interested behaviour:[16] one baboon attacks a leopard to defend the troupe; adult musks form a defensive circle around vulnerable females and juveniles; bees kill themselves to defend the hive.

> A bear rips apart a beehive with its powerful claws; hundreds of bees boil from the hive in defence and retaliation, driving their stingers into the intruder and then pulling away, leaving their barbed weapons in the bear; the attached poison sacs continuing to pump venom into the wounds. The bear is deterred but at terrible cost to the defenders. The bees, their viscera ripped from their bodies, fly off a short distance to die.[17]

Despite tensions arising, Darwin extended his idea to group selection.[18] As we would express it today, the evolved genotype has encoded within it a mutation favouring some sort of sacrifice, and this ultimately favours the survival of every individual. Every individual could be called upon to sacrifice, but ultimately it itself has *a priori* a higher chance of survival because of the species characteristic.

5. Evolution of Darwinism?

Has Darwin's theory changed since it was originally enunciated in 1859? The simple answer is 'No'. Its acceptance by scientists has waxed and waned, until today it is universally accepted by scientists: evolution through natural selection of random variations (today, in response to mutations). It has survived challenges. It has been vindicated by the findings of cell biology, by DNA structure and its associated mutations, by the study of gene sequences of organisms, and comparing these sequences with those of known ancestors.

5.1 Natural selection in action

Darwin's theory, is well illustrated by the observation of natural selection in action in the behaviour of bacterial populations resisting the action of anti-biotics. In summary this can be dsecribed as the following:

> After World War 2, a new drug, penicillin, became available, and was found to be an effective cure for many bacterial diseases. After some time, many bacteria became resistant, and were unharmed by penicillin. The resistant bacteria had undergone a mutation which delivered immunity to the drug. This population increased. Many other anti-biotics have been developed. Many are still effective, but drug-resistant populations have continued to arise. The 'golden staph' is even resistant to the strongest antibiotic, vancomycin. This is explainable by mutations in the bacterial DNA. The mutations are statistically unlikely, but there are so many organisms in one sample that a one in a million mutation brings resistance to a few, and these survive while the others in a particular sample may be wiped out.[19]

5.2 A rival theory: Lamarckism

Jean-Baptiste de Lamarck in 1809 proposed that characteristics acquired during life could be passed on to the next generation. If a person genetically disposed to obesity dieted strictly and acquired a thinner body appearance, the offspring would inherit this acquired characteristic.

Some elements of Lamarckism

- Once life was established it inexorably improved. Animal life had within itself an inherent power of increasing its complexity and hence its powers.
- That there were species in all stages of complexity meant that life had begun many times.

16. Shanahan, 64.
17. *Ibid.*
18. Shanahan, 37–39.
19. Summary of the well-known phenomenon in in the *Advertiser Review* 3 January 2009, 2.

- The human species being the most highly developed came from the earliest event of life formation.
- Organisms interacted with their environment during which vital fluids within the organism caused changes, which enabled the organism to cope better with the environment. The resulting changes—enhancements—were then inherited by the offspring. Hence the mantra associated with Lamarkism is 'inheritance of acquired characteristics'. Before Darwin this was very popular, and maintained many adherents after 1859.

5.3 Lamarckism and Darwin fight it out for a century[20]

Neo-Lamarckism, acceptable Lamarckism after Darwin, allowed for natural selection. Natural selection could function as a negative force to eliminate the unfit, but could not cause new characteristics. There seemed a good case for the acquiring or losing of characteristics through use and misuse.

For twenty years after the acceptance of Darwin's general idea of evolution, Darwin's natural selection mechanism remained a minority view. This was still the situation for a further twenty years, except for a gradual loss of faith in the inheritance of acquired characteristics. After the discovery of Gregor Mendel's work in 1900, a significant number of evolutionists opted for occasional major changes through mutations—a saltationist view, a sudden great leap forward. Many not opting in this way, remained with Lamarck.

By the 1930s no consensus had emerged; most opted for natural selection for change *within* species, but the question of the origin *of* species was not agreed upon.

Lamarckian inheritance remained the view of many. After 1947 agreement had been reached regarding the operation of natural selection for speciation, biodiversity.

5.4 Darwin vindicated

From 1950 onwards, the discovery of the double helix and subsequent progress in molecular biology confirmed the origin of species through random mutation and natural selection.

Thus it can be said that the essence of Darwin's theory is the same today as it was in 1859; it has won through after more than a century's waxing and waning; been confirmed as the well-substantiated theory of evolution. It has been singularly endorsed by molecular biology.

A recent book revives the cause of Jean-Baptiste de Lamarck.[21] Assessment of this will no doubt be forthcoming.

> With the dawn of the twenty-first century, Lamarck's widely discredited work began its ascendancy, and some of the muddiness cleared. Evidence supporting Lamarck continues to build with an increasing number of reports of Lamarckian inheritance at work.[22]

6. Natural selection: the object of selection

On what does natural selection operate, the gene or the phenotype? Does the 'survival of the fittest force' select to enhance/protect the genes or to enhance/protect the animal?

6.1 Gene selectionism

In the struggle for existence, natural selection operates to give a slight advantage to the individual animal. Is this for the animal or for the genes? If it operates also for the good of the group as in dangerous calls for the warning of others or for the production of slave classes within the nest, selection seems to be occurring to favour the gene, not the individual possessing the gene. The bird calls a warning, exposing itself to possible death but enabling a whole group to fly to safety. The genes of the group are protected at the expense of an individual. The slave ants in the nest assist not for themselves but for the sake of the genes. The theory of gene selectionism[23], argues in this way:

20. Ernst Mayr, *What makes Biology Unique* (Cambridge: Cambridge University Press, 2007), 117–126.
21. Ross Honeywill, *Lamarck's Evolution* (Miller's Point: Murdoch's Books Australia, 2008).
22. Honeywill, 186–187.
23. Richard Dawkins, *River out of Eden* (London: Weidenfeld & Nicolson, 1995), 105–106.

Only genes are passed on from generation to generation; genes are the only true units of selection.

The selected animal eventually dies, and its species may become extinct, but the genes have survived, and built themselves more sturdy receptacles.

6.2 Phenotype selectionism

The argument that only genes get preserved therefore they are the units of selection is not universally accepted. Selection itself results in the preservation of former and enhanced genes, but the actual selection operates on the animal's qualities. It has greater speed, so will escape former predators, and will outrun new prey.

The genes are not magic, their chemistry is not all-powerful, but what is crucial is the information they contain, information about qualities and abilities, which is passed on.

> I strongly disagree with Dawkins, since I feel he has confused bookkeeping (which may be done efficiently in terms of genes) with causality.[24]

Seemingly in favour of the hypothesis that the gene is the primary object of selection is the discovery of many DNA sequences that carry information about their own replication, and nothing of benefit to the animal. These sequences replicate themselves and are then found in other parts of the genome as well.

Thus the particular sequence replicates at a higher rate, conferring an advantage upon itself. But this says nothing about the acquiring of genes that favour the phenotype.

However, the ultimate beneficiaries may be the genes but the actual selection operates on the organism.

Question 1. Is the gene, DNA, the driving force of evolution, as it continually seeks to better itself ? Or is the DNA only a record of the changes mutations and external conditions have forced upon the organism?

6.3 Adaptation vs adaptive trait

An adaptation is a quality that has arisen because of natural selection. An historical adaptation is one that conferred an advantage on a creature in the past. It was not developed by the present possessor, for example, the wings of an eagle. Because it emerged through natural selection, it is called an adaptation.

The eye is an adaptation. The ability to read is not an adaptation. The eye did not evolve to give this specific ability. The ability to read is referred to as an adaptive trait. More generally, an adaptation is a term applied to a quality that enables its possessor to survive and thrive.

7. Convergence in Evolution

Various stages on the upward path have evolved independently many times.

In his book 'Life's Solutions' Simon Conway Morris[25] lists and discusses many, even ubiquitous, examples of evolutionary convergence. There are many pathways, and many have been trodden, but they all lead to the same destinations. The evidence for convergence is indisputable.

7.1 Evolution of the camera eye

The camera eye has muscles to control the size of the pupil, a lens containing fluid, a mechanism to change the focal length of the lens, a retina in which sight sensitive rods are embedded, and nerves leading to appropriate regions of the brain.

---

24. Stephen Gould *the Richness of Life,* edited by P McGarr and S Rose (London: Random House, 2006), 226.

25. Simon Conway Morris, *Life's Solution* (Cambridge: University Press, 2003).

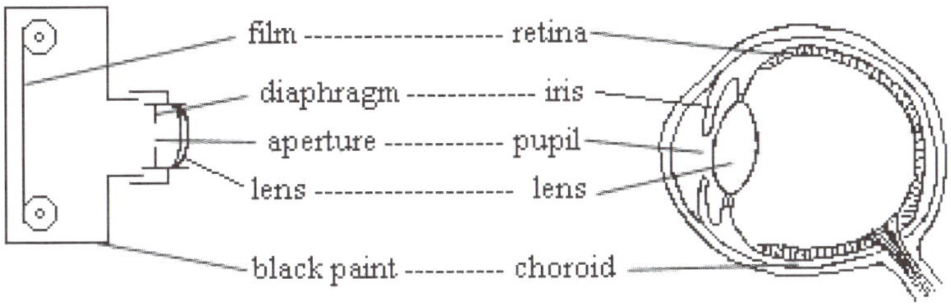

The camera eye[26] has evolved over hundreds of millions of years. Flat light sensitive patches developed into sensitive spots. These did not cause images, but merely allowed the possessor to be aware of light and its intensity, an advantage. The next step introduced a pinhole, and finally an eye with a lens.

These evolutionary stages exist in different organisms today.

The *Euglena* is a one-celled organism with a flat light sensitive patch; the *planaria* is a multi-celled organism has the cup-shaped sensitive spot, which enables it to monitor the intensity of light, and ascertain from which direction it is coming.

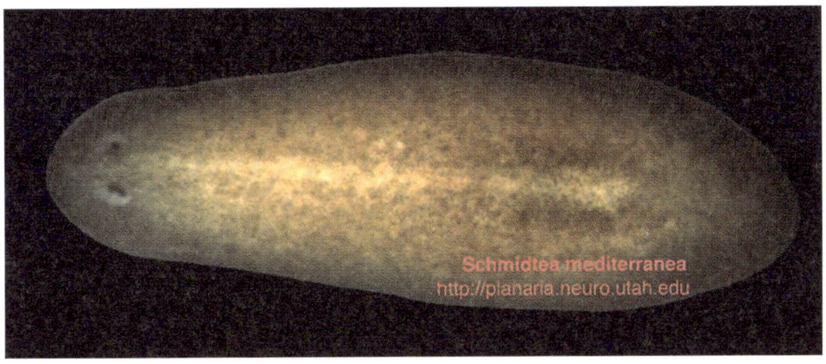

Planaria

Nautilus

The *Nautilus* lives on the bottom of the ocean, and has a pinhole eye, with no lens. This enables an image, but one that has poor resolution, but the Nautilus does not need anything more developed.

7.2 Multiple evolution of the eye

The eye is a complex structure. The resulting structure has been reached along different paths. It has evolved separately[27] in vertebrates, cephalopods, snails (three times), some deep-sea fish, *mysid* shrimps, the scallop, annelids, some spiders. Various jellyfish have camera eyes but no brain—the northern Australian *box jellyfish* ('stinger') has eight eyes. The retina, optic nerve, other features, are common to all camera eyes, but are arranged differently in the different evolutionary results. Light sensitive patches and spots have evolved separately many times, and the chemical, rhodopsin,[28] widespread in application to many forms of seeing and light sensitivity, evolved much earlier in single-celled organisms, in storage for eventual application to seeing, hinting that the evolution of seeing is an evolutionary imperative.

26. See http://library.thinkquest.org/28030/eyeevo.htm. accessed 18th April 2009
27. Morris, *Life's solution*, 151–158.
28. *Ibid*, 170.

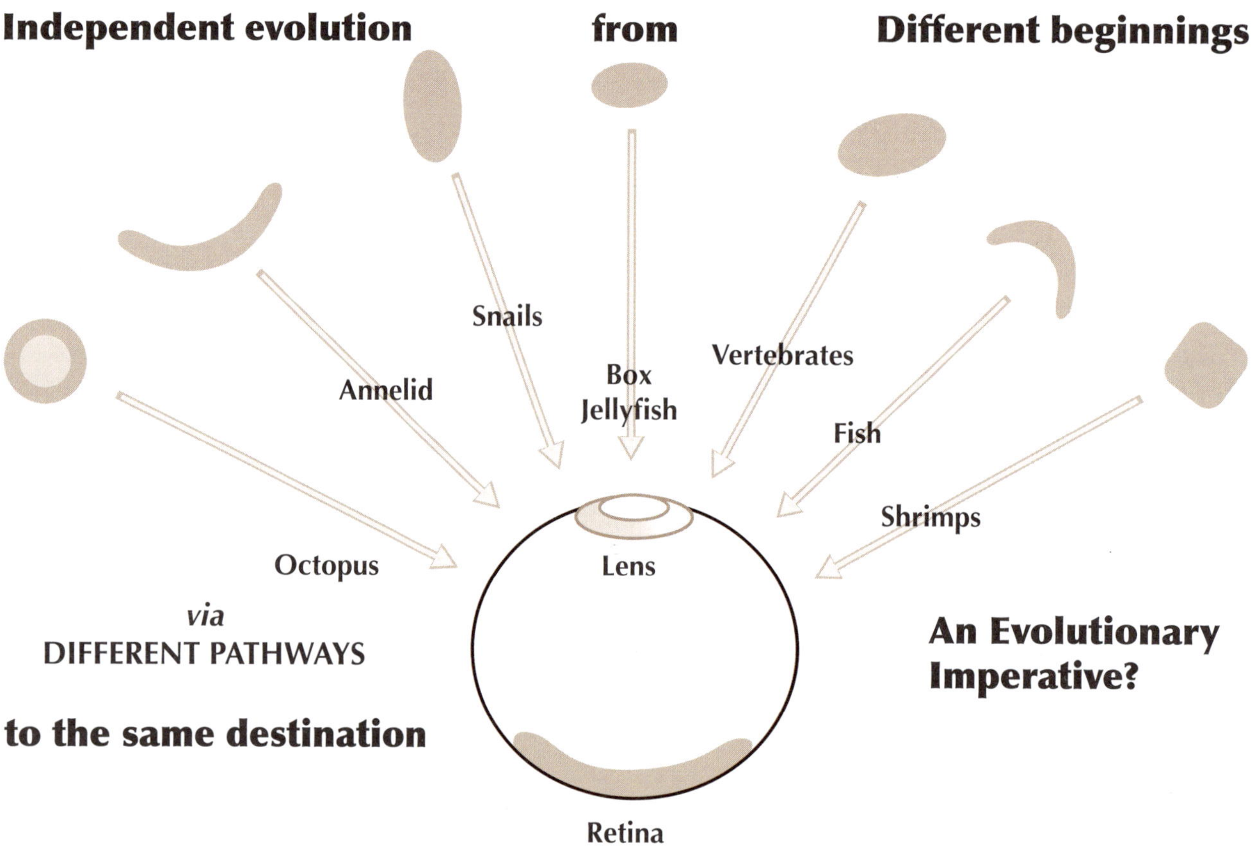

The Camera Eye

7.3 Various other examples of convergence

The evolution of the camera eye many times is only the beginning of the convergence story.

Hearing in vertebrates[29] has evolved independently to similar solutions a number of times. Hearing has also evolved independently in insects. Crickets don't make noise for no reason: they emit their noise as mating calls, which have to be heard. Their hearing organs are found on their legs. Spiders have hairs which vibrate in response to sound waves, and the vibrations are transferred and interpreted.

Electric ability: Some fish emit and receive communicating signals electrically.[30] This ability has evolved separately at least six times.

Echolocation is an ability to find one's way around dark places, and to locate other members of the species or other species in the dark. Echolocation has evolved in bats, in some cave-dwelling birds, and also in dolphins for exploitation of the watery environment.

Ant farming: A type of ant[31] has developed an efficient form of farming; some collect leaves, some transport them, others cut them up, still others supervise the conversion of leaves to fungus, some tend the fungus, others harvest it. Such ant colonies have evolved separately five times. Similar beetle colonies have evolved seven times.

Dual circulation: Cephalopods[32] (for example, the octopus) and vertebrates have separately developed dual circulatory systems – one for the body, the other for the lungs or gills.

Anti-freeze: Arctic and Antarctic fish produce the same anti-freeze for their bloodstreams, albeit by different genes.

---

29. *Ibid*, 190–194.
30. *Ibid*, 182–187.
31. *Ibid*, 205–207.
32. *Ibid*, 216–222.

And more: The ability to develop offspring within has evolved over 100 times. Endothermy (inner heat control) has evolved five times.

7.4 Cognitive convergence
New world and old world monkeys evolved separately, and both developed tool-making skills. Whales and elephants acquired communication by sounds separately. Hominids acquired tool-making a number of times. Dolphins have different whistle sounds, and communicate by means of learned signals. Present day dolphins' brains are larger than those of fossilized dolphins. Is the march towards intelligence relentless such that if *homo sapiens* had not emerged from Africa, rational intelligence would inevitably have emerged somewhere?

> If we hadn't walked out of Africa then probably sooner rather than later, our analogues would have strolled out of S. America holding tools and enjoying the taste of meat.[33]

7.5 The path is predetermined
All the steps that have culminated in humanness have been repeated so many times suggesting that the end product—intelligence—is inevitable. Some see evolution as haphazard, at the whim of chance, finally yielding intelligence very accidentally. There are so many possible ways for evolution to go, yet it stumbles upon the functional solutions.

> When convergence is the rule, you can rerun the tape of life as often as you like and the outcome will be much the same. Life has a direction.[34]

<u>Question 2</u>. When convergence is the rule, you can rerun the tape of life as often as you like and the outcome will be much the same. Does this mean life has a direction?

This sentiment is not universally embraced by biologists. Many think that if the tape were re-run something entirely different would happen.

8. Is evolution a progressive process?

8.1 Progressive evolution
The story of evolution looked at in one way is one of extraordinary progress.

Non-life → prokaryotic cell → eukaryotic cell → multi-celled organisms → Cambrian explosion → amphibians → reptiles → mammals → primates → australopithecines → homo erectus → homo sapiens; seemingly inert matter has given rise to living matter, which in turn has led to the animal senses of seeing, hearing, memory, and finally to intelligence. Natural selection brought about this process; random mutations plus felicitous laws of nature plus the right conditions enabled this remarkable story.

Underlying each of these successive stages is greater biological/chemical complexity. Each stage confers a greater ability to survive in environments and to organize and harness whatever is found in the environment.

8.2 Non-progressive evolution
By no means all species developments are progressive.

- There is a large number of primitive life forms remaining on earth—bacteria far outnumber all the other organisms at the present time. From this angle, Evolution is not progressive.
- Nor is at progressive in every feature. *Homo sapiens* can read, but cannot fly like an eagle, swim like a shark, manage the dark like a bat, or grow as large as *Argentosaurus*.
- There are many examples of regression; cave fish have lost the ability to see, whales the ability to walk on land.

33. *Ibid*, 268.
34. S Conway Morris, 'We Were Meant to Be', *New Scientist*, 16/11/2002.

- Many organisms that have evolved are dead ends, for example *draculoides bramstokeri*: this half-centimetre long invertebrate lives in the soil in caves on Barrow Island, North West Australia.

> The small arachnid, *draculoides bramstokeri,* uses large fang-like pedipalps or pincers to grasp invertebrate prey and crunch it into pieces before sucking out its juices. Named for this method of dispatching victims and for the author of *Dracula,* this creature dwells in dark caves in Australia. Often mistaken for a spider, it is a schizomid: a small soil-dwelling invertebrate that walks on six legs and uses two modified front legs as feelers.[35]

Or *selenochlamys ysbryda,* a slug with no eyes that lives underground and squeezes its body into cracks to get at worms which it kills with its blade-like teeth.

Some organisms cannot be compared. Is a seagull better than a trout?

8.3 Darwin and progress

Although Darwin's theory today is often taken as not advocating the idea of evolutionary progress, Darwin himself was not so definite. In fact, his attraction to progress seemed to reveal itself in later editions of *The Origin.* He advocated evolved species to be higher than their predecessors in the first edition, but that might have been in a feature pertaining to a new particular environmental condition. In later editions he admitted evolved species had organs more specialised for different functions. An increased specialisation of parts led to 'higher' organisms; evolutionary progress is a result of natural selection, but not a necessary one.

8.4 Two contrary views on progress

The ability to survive, to adapt to changing circumstances, reproduce, exploit the environment has certainly progressed, as has self-awareness. Some hesitate to attribute progress to evolution considering the previous section (8.2).

- Richard Dawkins firmly associates progress with evolution.

> . . . evolution is not just incidentally progressive, it is fundamentally necessary that it should be progressive if Darwinian natural selection is to perform the explanatory role in our world view that we require of it, and that it alone can perform.[36]

> Directionalist common sense surely wins on the very long time scale: once there was only blue-green slime and now there are sharp-eyed metazoa.[37]

- Stephen Jay Gould on the other hand denies any such association.

> Claims for progress represent a quintessential example of conventional thinking about trends as entities on the move. From life's infinite variety we extract some 'essential' measure like 'average complexity' or 'most complex creature'—and we trace the supposed increase of this entity through time. We label this trend to increase as 'progress'—and we are locked into the view that such progress must be the thrust of the entire evolutionary movement . . . no pervasive or predictable thrust towards progress permeates the history of life.[38]

<u>Question 3</u>. Is Richard Dawkins speaking soundly when he asserts evolution is progressive:

35. See http://nationalzoo.si.edu/Animals/Invertebrates/whataname.cfm. Accessed 18th April 2009
36. R Dawkins in Review of *Full House* by Stephen Jay Gould, in *Evolution,* 51/3 (June 1997).
37. Shanahan, 218 quoting Dawkins.
38. SJ Gould, *Life's Grandeur* (London: Johnathan Cape, 1996), 146.

'Directionalist common sense surely wins on the very long time scale: once there was only blue-green slime and now there are sharp-eyed metazoa.' (also see quote for note 38)

8.5 In what sense can direction mean also progress?
8.5.1 Some particular cases of progress:

- Bony skeleton → jaws → specialised teeth.
- Prokaryotic cells → eukaryotic cells → multi-cellularity → Cambrian explosion.
- Light patches → camera eye → hawk eye.
- Wings of archaeopteryx → highly specialised wings of modern birds.
- 3 chambered heart of reptile. → 4-chambered heart of mammals
- Amphibian → egg-laying reptile → inner heat control of mammal
- Brain of Australopithecus → of Homo Habilis → Homo Erectus → Homo Sapiens

8.5.2 More general measures of progress:

- Being more successful in surviving and reproducing.
- Being more efficient in acquiring energy.
- Possessing complex nervous systems which enable organisms to better adapt to changing environments.
- Advances in the ability to know and to will.

8.5.3 Other observations concerning progress:[39]

[1] The fact that evolution has featured some progress does not imply that one allegedly more advanced animal be the best in every way. Rather, has there been an advantageous change in some property in the history of life.

[2] One can affirm one organism having an advantage over another in one particular property; a rabbit is more intelligent than a jelly fish.

[3] There are occasions when one organism can be thought of as more advanced overall than another: *homo sapiens* is superior to a sponge (although you could not run a human through a sieve and have the human reform afterwards).

[4] Species acquire advantageous qualities in a number of areas as time goes on. One would expect them to become altogether more advanced as a general rule.

9. Does the scientific picture show a teleology? Was evolution intended?

Teleology means goal-directedness. Teleology means not only progress, but raises the question of goal-directedness—was the end result of evolution intended?

Goal-directedness can be intended or unintended. A teleological process can mean one which has simply resulted in some end-point, or can mean one which is the result of an intended end point. Ernst Mayr[40] would call the first sense a *teleomatic* process. He distinguishes this from an intended process which he calls *teleonomic*. The key point: is evolution to intelligence a true teleological (teleonomic) process, one which has produced an intended end-point, or is it a teleomatic process—one which has ended up producing intelligence, but which was in no way an intended goal? In other words:

> Does having a teleology or purposiveness inherent in nature require a definite predetermined goal or target?[41]

Question 4. Is there an inbuilt goal in the evolutionary process?

39. Shanahan, 242.
40. Ernst Mayr, 49–51.
41. W Stoeger, 'The Immanent Directionality of the Evolutionary Process, and its Relationship to Teleology', in *Evolutionary and Molecular Biology* (Notre Dame Ind: University of Notre Dame Press, Notre Dame, 1998), 182.

Further Reading

Michael Ruse, *The Evolution-Creation Struggle* (Cambridge, Massachusetts: Harvard University Press, 2006).

John R Searle, *Mind: A Brief Introduction* (Oxford: Oxford University Press, 2004).

Peter Macinnis *Mr Darwin's Incredible Shrinking World: Science and Technology in 1859* (London: Murdoch Books UK Limited, 2008).

Steven Johnson, *Emergence: The Connected Lives of Ants, Brains, Cities and Software* (London: Penguin 2002).

Harold J Morowitz, *The Emergence of Everything: How the World became Complex* (Oxford: Oxford University Press, 2002).

John F Haught, *Science and Religion: From Conflict to Conversation* (New Jersey: Paulist Press, 1995)

Chapter 8
The God of Evolution: Dawinism and the Contemporary Believer

Chapter overview

- Does chance do away with the need for a Designer?
- Laws of nature are conducive to the emergence of life
- Does the theory of evolution imply an intended purpose?
  - * The question of the detection of purpose
  - * Beyond the powers of science
  - * The philosophic principle of sufficient reason applied to the findings of science
- The views of some non-agnostic scientists
- Reasons for a theistic response
- The questions proposed by the emergence of *homo sapiens*
- Questions proposed by some scientists and philosophers
- Extensions
  - * (1) Is DNA's survival urge the force driving evolution?
  - * (2) A criticism of 'The God Delusion'.

1. Evolution's achievements—progress, dead-ends, regression

The scientific enterprise of evolution has unearthed ample evidence, which leads to an almost unanimously agreed theory. The evidence is a succession of forms over long stretches of time producing organisms incrementally of superior nature with regard to degrees of consciousness, brain size, complexity, range of functions, ability to adapt to different environments, reflective ability.

This is not the only facet of evolution. Creatures have evolved to fill every possible bit of biospace; intelligent beings are only one of many finished products. Rudimentary prokaryotes (bacteria) far outweigh all others in biomass; there are cases of regression, and many organisms have evolved which are dead ends.[1]

What leads to deeper questions is the successive appearance in time of more complex organisms, better able to handle the environments. This happened through natural selection. Evolution is not 'only a theory', but is a compelling explanation for the fossil evidence.

2. Does the influence of chance imply no designer, no purpose?

Darwinian Evolution

Darwinian Evolution involves four phenomena:
- Particular laws of nature.
- Chance mutations occurring in DNA
- Survival of the fittest
- Fertility of matter

2.1 Atheistic response

2.1.1 Particular questions suggesting an atheistic response:
- *Randomness:* How can you reconcile the divine will with a random chance process like evolution? Doesn't the very randomness of evolution rule out any notion of divine purpose?
- *Deterministic Laws:* Isn't the deterministic invariance of laws of physics or the inexorable filtering of DNA by mindless natural selection a sign of an ultimately impersonal universe?

1. See section 7, this chapter.

- *General:* Is such a universe as ours ruled only by blind necessity and blind chance and so is pointless?

2.1.2 Atheistic reasoning

The evolutionary process is intrinsically linked to chance—chance mutations. If it is by nature dependent on chance, evolution to higher forms is promoted by chance. Hence it need not have happened. The fact that it took the path that it did is so dependent on chance events that it could not happen in the same way again. Thus the emergence of *homo sapiens* was a chance event of indescribable unlikeliness.

If it depended on chance it could not have been planned. There is no designer of evolution. Evolution's progress to *homo sapiens* has been fully explained by natural selection operating on chance events. No further explanation is necessary. There is no Designer God.

> By coupling undirected, purposeless variation to the blind, uncaring process of natural selection, Darwin made theological or spiritual explanations of the life processes superfluous.[2]
>
> The universe that we observe has precisely the properties we should expect if there is, at bottom, no purpose, no evil, no good, nothing but blind pitiless indifference.[3]

Francisco Ayala disputes that evolution depends entirely on chance:

> Arguments stating incredible improbability of chance events to account for adaptations are irrelevant. Rather there is a natural process (natural selection) that is not random, but oriented and able to generate order.[4]

Question 1. How can there be an inbuilt goal if the process is intrinsically bound up with chance?

2.2 Theistic response

Particular questions suggesting a theistic response

- *Special laws:* Why are the laws of nature so conducive to the emergence, continuance and explosion of life?
- *Progression:* How do you account for the progressive element in the story of evolution? Why is matter fertile?
- *Mind:* How can a remarkable property like intelligence emerge from lifeless matter?
- *Against chance:* Why doesn't contingency or chance so prominent in evolution prevent order from emerging?
- *General:* Why is natural selection so rigorously lawful and yet open to new creation?

3. Theistic reasoning

3.1 Why are the laws of nature so conducive to the emergence of life?

- *Life chemicals preferentially formed:*

  There seems to be an inbuilt tendency in matter to form compounds; among these compounds are chemicals that can perform vital functions in a living organism, chemicals that lie on an upward pathway on the way to increasing levels of consciousness. Similar chemicals have been formed along different pathways.

2. Futuyma, *Evolution*, Sunderland (MA: Sinauer Associates, 1986), 2, quoted in Miller (footnote 16), 168.
3. R Dawkins, *River out of Eden* (New York: HarperCollins, 1995), 132–133.
4. Francisco Ayala, *Darwin's Gift to Science and Religion* (Washington: National Academy Press, 2007), 77.

- *Arrangement of units in life chemicals very unlikely:*
  The worker chemicals in the drama of life are proteins.[5] They are anti-bodies, digestive juices, hormones associated with emotions. The ways in which a hundred or more (up to a 1000) components of a one protein can be arranged are legion. Then the number of potential shapes of the protein once the elements are arranged in the correct order is even more astronomical, beyond astronomical. Random experimentation to arrive at the right protein that can fold into the right shape so that it can perform its function would seem to take the age of many universes. Yet the trick has been done many many times.

> Life has a peculiar propensity to 'navigate' to rather precise solutions in response to adaptive challenges . . .
>
> The current consensus is that any such zone of occupation has been arrived at by chance, and there is a very large number of alternatives, probably well in excess of the number of habitable planets in the galaxy.[6]

Life-causing chemicals are preferentially formed. There is a purposiveness in nature.

3.2 Progression

Nature inexorably has travelled down a path of increasing complexification, resulting in increasing awareness. The progress dynamic is present in matter and the laws. Matter is continually transcending itself and advancing to new stages with new laws. The philosopher asks for a reason—a designer. The theologian has a reason. This has been set up in a creation event—perhaps the Big Bang—by God, and is being sustained by the God of creation, whose primary creative action was not exhausted in a single moment. The progress suggests an inbuilt purpose.

If there is purpose, there is a God.

There is purpose, so there is a God.

Question 2. Do laws conducive to life's emergence and the consequent story of evolution indicate purpose and hence a designer?

3.3 The question of emergence—new realities

Associated with increased complexification is the appearance of new realities accompanied by new laws. The behaviour of new levels is dependent on the laws of previous levels, but adds new laws to the behaviour specific to the new level. For example, the working of a cell depends on the laws of physics and chemistry, but also new descriptions of behaviour appear, which are not reducible to the laws of physics and chemistry.

One can go up the scale of entities:

1) quarks, gluons, electrons, neutrinos
2) Protons, & neutrons & electrons
3) Atoms
4) Molecules
5) Macromolecules
6) DNA
7) Cells
8) Groups of cells coordinated together
9) Sensation
10) Mind, Thought etc

5. Chapter 2, section 3.4
6. Simon Conway Morris, *Life's Solutions* (Cambridge: Cambridge University Press, 2003), 308, 309.

Each new level of complexity needs specific laws and theories, and while dependent on laws of simpler levels the new laws are not reducible to them. Nuclear physics does not explain how an octopus can do some rudimentary learning, even though the nuclei of the octopus are obeying the laws of nuclear physics.

The new concepts at higher levels of complexity refer to new realities—dog, cat, oak tree; if you boil them down you will only find quarks, electrons and gluons whose properties fail to explain the higher entities. There is a reality attaching to person not discoverable by dissection.

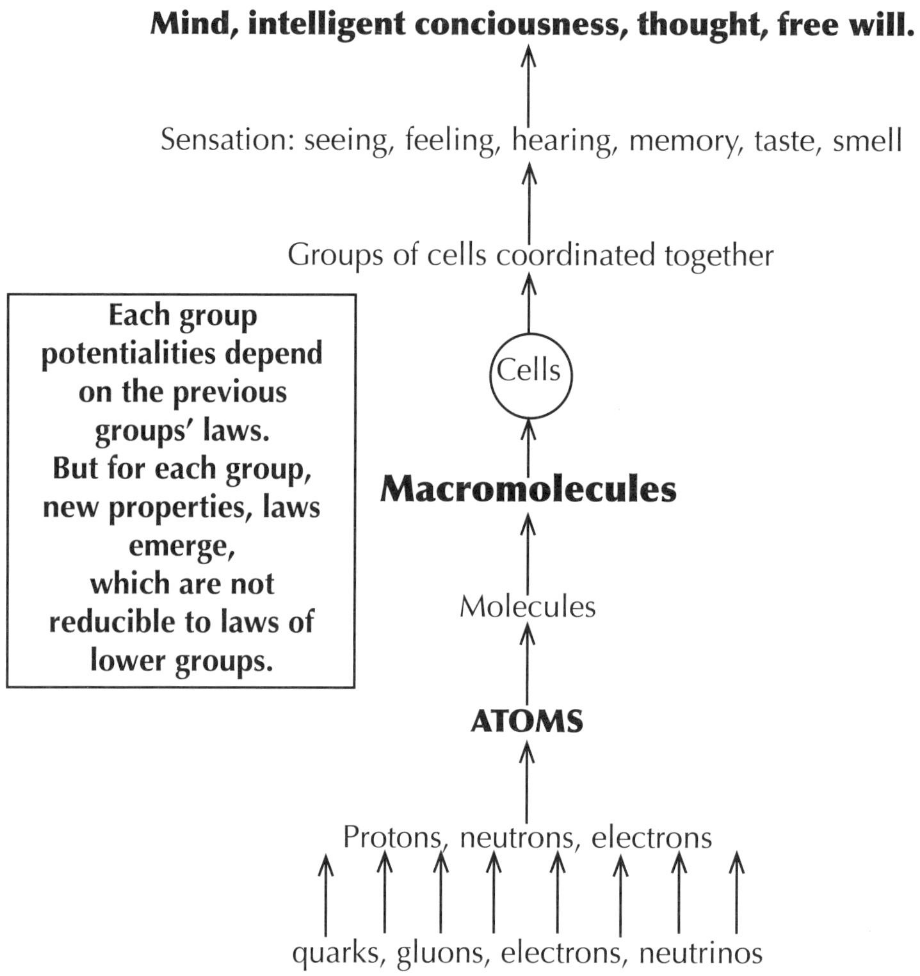

ladder of increasing complexity/ascending awareness

<u>Question 3</u>. Can the behaviour of living matter – cells, awareness – be completely explained by the properties of atoms and molecules?

3.4 The fertility of matter

New realities are generated from within; matter is fertile. One cannot say atoms are more real than cells. Emergent properties are emergent realities without addition of new realities *ab extra*. As matter goes up from stage to stage, more of its potentialities are being revealed which seem to be part and parcel of matter itself, and not explainable fully by the process by which the new realities are revealed—natural selection.

The universe's matter is fertile—its secrets lying in wait to be revealed by the action of the laws and accompanied by chance and natural selection.

> Analysis . . . does not claim that 'the smallest parts' give all the answers. Analysis differs from reduction by not claiming that the components provide complete information on all the properties of a system[7]

4. Purpose

4.1 Evolution has produced a result, but was it intended?
Does the universe show goal-directedness? Does the universe show a teleology? (Teleology means goal directedness). Ernst Mayr[8] has distinguished two types of teleology:

- *Teleomatic process:* one which has simply resulted in some end-point; for example, a rock rolls down a hill, a tornado uproots a tree.
- *Teleonomic process:* one which is the result of an intended end point; for example, a company structures its inputs, its overheads, its prices so that it will record a profit: a government builds a dam to provide town water.

The key point: is evolution to intelligence a true teleological process, one which has produced an intended end-point? Is it a teleonomic process? Or is it a teleomatic process—one which has ended up producing intelligence, but which was in no way an intended goal? In other words:

> Does having a teleology or purposiveness inherent in nature require a definite predetermined goal or target?[9]

4.2 Science and the detection of purpose
4.2.1 Questions.
From examining the evolutionary conclusion arrived at by the scientific method, three questions can be asked:

1) Can Science conclude that evolution to higher forms was intended? (Teleonomic)
2) Does Science say evolution just happened to end up with mind? (Teleomatic)
3) Is Science open to either conclusion?

<u>Question 4</u>. Can the scientist devise an experiment to answer the question 'does nature have a purpose'?

In other words can science declare whether the process was intended, just happened, or is the answer beyond science?

4.2.2 Answer is beyond science:
The answer to these questions is found by inspecting the nature of the scientific method.

Science proceeds by experiment, coming to a law or theory as a result of empirical (experimental) testing. If one says science has precluded purpose, one can ask what was the experiment, and the consequent experimental result which precluded purpose? This is not possible. Similarly, if one says 'Science has shown there is a purpose', one can ask what was the experiment, and the consequent experimental result which demonstrated purpose? Since science cannot devise a test whose conclusion is 'there has been a purpose', conclusion 1) is beyond the powers of Science. And equally conclusion 2) is beyond the powers of Science. No experiment can be set up which can verify or falsify the hypothesis 'there is a purpose'. Science can merely lay out what has happened and propose a cause involving material entities—natural selection. It is beyond Science to invest the laws, chance, the fertility of matter with purpose, or to conclude there is no purpose. The statement that it is beyond the powers of science to decide on the question of purpose does not lead to the conclusion there is no purpose as if science is the only path to truth.

---

7. Ernst Mayr, *What Makes Biology Unique* (New York: Cambridge University Press, 2007), 70–71.
8. *Ibid,* 49-51.
9. Bill Stoeger, 'The Immanent Directionality of the Evolutionary Process, and its Relationship to Teleology', in *Evolutionary and Molecular Biology* (Notre Dame Ind: University of Notre Dame Press, 1998), 163–190..

> But do these nested directionalities we have detected in the evolutionary process indicate *consciously* directed intention or purpose? From the point of view of natural sciences, they do *not*—nor do they rule it out.[10]

4.3 Is purpose therefore altogether excluded?
Supposing then one says if science cannot deliver on the question of purpose, then there cannot be a purpose, or the knowledge of whether or not there is a purpose will never be attainable. One can then reply there are many other ways of accessing truth besides the scientific method. An assumption that Science is the only path to truth is a dogmatic statement. It can be stated as an initial starting point, but it cannot be proved. In fact, humans constantly use other ways of reaching conclusions: philosophy, literature, drama, religion, morality, personal reflection. And the justification for the scientific method itself is beyond the scope of the scientific method. You cannot devise an experiment whose conclusion is the legitimation of the scientific method. Science opens up a marvellous vista of things and processes, but the cogency of its methods stems from considerations not verifiable scientifically. In addition, the good things it delivers to us are still at the beck and call of human beings who can use them for good or for ill, indicating another source of understanding reality—morality.

Thus, science takes a step back. Science cannot either rule out nor admit the concept of purpose, but science can bring forward considerations which can be used in finding answers to deeper questions. The history of thought bears eloquent witness that science is not the only road to truth.

Question 5. If Science cannot detect a purpose, does this mean there is no purpose, that reality is ultimately meaningless?

> The metaphysical naturalist is the person who is an atheist, who does deny that there is anything beyond blind law working on inert matter. The *methodological naturalist*, who may well be an ardent Darwinian, is one who states that for the purpose of doing science nothing but law will be entertained, but who recognizes that there might be more, in fact or meaning.[11]

5. Beyond science—the principle of sufficient reason

The principle of sufficient reason is used fruitfully in physics to construct models of what material reality might be. When a phenomenon is unveiled and consequently explained scientifically, it is assumed there must be a cause adequate to account for what is discovered. It has recently been discovered the expansion rate of the universe is actually increasing. So a cause is immediately sought out, and declared by some to be 'the dark energy of the vacuum'. The same principle can be used meta-physically to deal with questions arising from science but unanswerable by the scientific method. What is the sufficient reason for the occurrence of purpose in nature?

> I believe we can construct an argument for a primordial initiating cause on the basis of both the existence and order of the universe. From there it is possible to argue to the conclusion the order has been consciously intended.
>
> We would need for example the principle of sufficient reason, applied to ultimate questions.[12]

5.1 Reason itself—metaphysics applied to physics
Philosophically in line with the principle of sufficient reason, we can say there has to be a reason why the laws encoded into the reality emerging from the Big Bang resulted in an unlikely cosmic

10. *Ibid*, 185.
11. Michael Ruse, *Can a Darwinian be a Christian?* (New York: Cambridge University Press, 2007), 99.
12. Bill Stoeger, *Immanent Directionality*, 186.

evolution, and then promoted biological evolution whose end-point has been a creature who can work out what has happened. This reason is the designer God.

There has to be a reason why matter has been endowed with potentialities that seem beyond its initial state: each new state reveals something that cannot be traced back to the previous state. Matter carries within it a purpose. There is an overriding intelligence.

Such conclusions are compatible with what science has shown us.

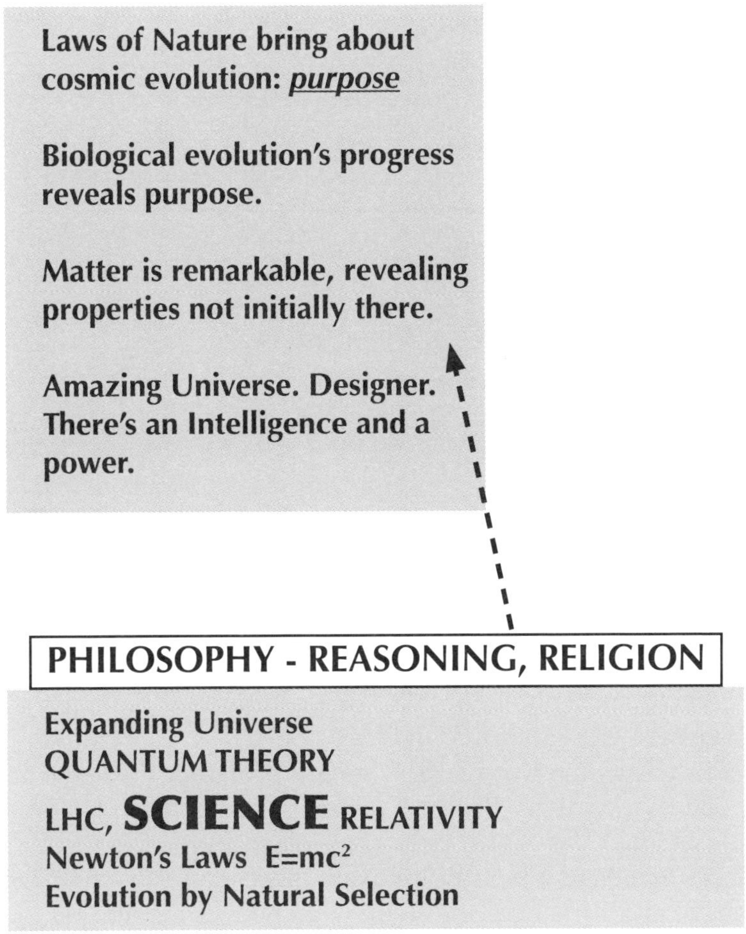

> Emergence of intelligent life is not an accident: the laws of physics the nature of the physical environment and the physical constraints of replication and mutation ensure that in a universe with the basic physical constants and laws of this one, carbon-based life forms with opposable digits eyes in their heads and large brains are bound to come into existence.[13].

5.2 Non-theistic reply

But philosophy has led others to the opposite conclusion, either because philosophy gives no empirically verifiable conclusions, or for other non-theistic arguments.

Many who understand science see the scientific enterprise yielding further speculations leading to a theodicy, and consonant with Christian faith.

13. Keith Ward, *The Big Questions in Science and Religion* (West Conshohocken, 2008), 66.

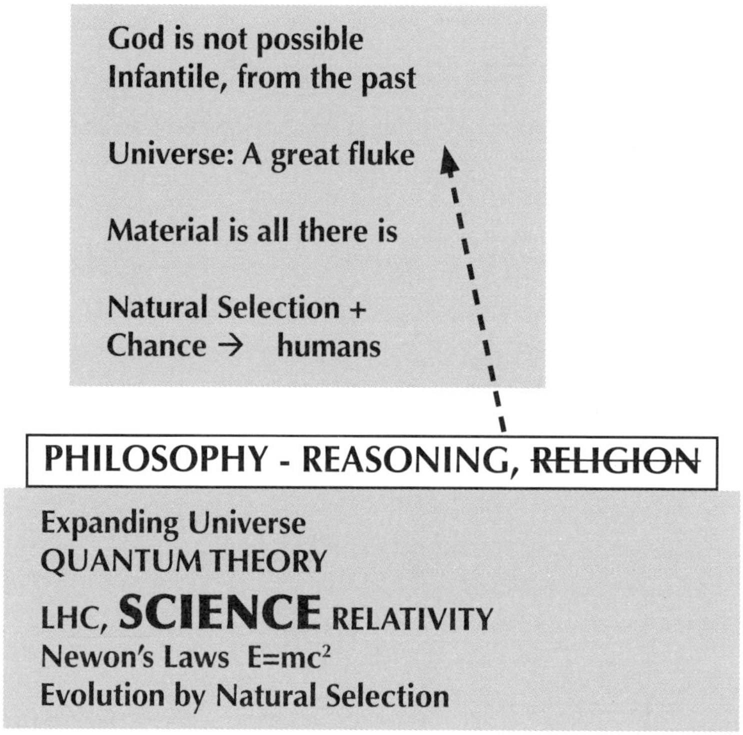

6. Non-agnostic scientists

Religion and science in the popular mind are often presented as in unresolvable conflict. This is particularly the case with regard to evolution. Popular writers such as Richard Dawkins[14]are well known for their outspoken atheism. There is another side to the picture; there are theistic scientific writers who do not receive such public notice. An evolutionary biologist's answer to Dawkins' bestseller 'The God Delusion' is summarised in Extension (2).

Kenneth R Miller has a PhD, in biology. He is now a professor in the Department of Molecular Biology, Cell Biology and Biochemistry, Brown University, Rhode Island, USA.

> Given evolution's ability to adapt, to innovate, to test and to experiment, sooner or later it would have given the creator exactly what he was looking for.
>
> . . . an accurate and complete understanding of that world, even in purely material terms, should deepen and strengthen the faith of any religious person.[15]

Stephen Barr has a PhD in Physics. He is a theoretical particle physicist at the Bartol Research Institute of the University of Delaware in Newark.

> Our universe's openness to biological evolution appears to be a consequence of the fact that its laws are indeed very special. A slightly different set of laws would, it seems, have led to a completely lifeless, sterile universe. If this is so then Darwinian evolution, far from disproving the necessity of a cosmic designer, may actually point to it. We now have the problem of explaining not merely a butterfly's wing, but a universe that can produce a butterfly's wing.[16]

14. Richard Dawkins, *The God Delusion* (London: Bantam Press, 2006).
15. K Miller, *Finding Darwin's God* (New York: HarperCollins, 2007), 238, 169.
16. Stephen M Barr, *Modern Physics and Ancient Faith* (Notre Dame: University of Notre Dame Press, 2003), 112.

Francis S Collins, head of the Human Genome project.

> . . . I had reached the conclusion that faith in God was much more compelling than the atheism I had previously embraced . . . The study of genomes . . . an incredibly rich and detailed view of how descent by modification from a common ancestor has occurred. I found this elegant evidence of the relatedness of all living things an occasion of awe, and came to see this as the master plan of the same Almighty who caused the universe to come into being..the God of the Bible is the God of the genome. He can be worshipped in the cathedral or in the laboratory. His creation is majestic, awesome, intricate and beautiful.[17]

Dr Paul Davies, is physicist and cosmologist who now works at the Arizona State University.

> Intelligent Design *of the laws* does not conflict with science because it accepts that the whole universe runs itself according to physical laws. The designer of the laws is *responsible* for the universe. The type of God I am describing comes close, I think, to what many scholarly theologians—and for that matter, quite a few scientists—profess to believe in.[18]
>
> There is no evidence for cosmic determinism, the fact that the laws are the only possible ones; the multiverse is overkill, untestable, and it merely takes design back one step; [the laws are] just a packet of marvels that happens to be? But we use logic all the time, why not about the laws? Having excluded these possibilities the conclusion is intelligent life was intended. I'll leave it to the philosophers and theologians.[19]

Francisco J Ayala, Professor of Biological Sciences, University of California.

> 'The validity of knowledge acquired by non-scientific modes of enquiry can be simply established by pointing out that science dawned in the 16th century, but mankind had for centuries built cities and roads, brought forth political institutions and sophisticated codes of law, advanced profound philosophies and value systems, and created magnificent plastic art as well as music and literature. The crops we harvest and the animals we husband emerged millennia before science's dawn . . . [20]

7. Is there a designer?

7.1 Signs in evolution

- Why has matter evolved to such a state as intelligent consciousness? Why has it evolved at all?
- Why are molecules on the pathway to intelligence preferentially stable?
- Why has evolution by natural selection achieved the same solutions from different starting points, and through different pathways?

Question 6. Consider in detail the three questions above in 5.1

7.2 Directional trends:

There has been a betterment associated with evolution. Shanahan lists betterment features:

1) size of cells, fact of cell aggregations.
2) increase in complexity and specialisation.

17. Francis S Collins, *The Language of God* (New York: Free Press, 2007), 211.
18. Paul Davies, *The Goldilocks Enigma* (London: Allen Lane, 2006), 226.
19. Davies, summary of ABC Lateline 1993.
20. Ayala, 178.

3) increase of harmony between parts.
4) increase of self-regulation: organisms become more independent of changes in the external environment.
5) increase in bringing the past to bear on present problems – greater memory, learning.
6) increase in psychical faculties of knowing, feeling, and willing, and their relative importance in life of individuals[21].

7.3 The question.
Do we accept the process as 'just is' and declare the controller/fashioner to be natural selection? Thus evolution is explained. Or is there purpose, meaning? If so, how do you explain purpose and meaning in the context of evolution?

Despite the evolutionary bush, with species going sideways, backwards and forwards, more advanced species have emerged in the course of time on some twigs. There has been a directionality in evolution in so far as a being with reflective consciousness has emerged from mindless matter in a series of progressive stages from cell, to multi-cell, to fish, to amphibian, to reptile, to mammal, to primate, to hominids, to *homo sapiens*.

So you have two things operating together: laws of nature, seeded into the big bang, which suggest consciousness was implanted (planned?) in the big bang; and blind chance, which suggests the ultimate end point was a fluke, not planned. The whole evolutionary process was meaningful? The whole evolutionary process was nothing more than chance?

8. Theistic response—a designer

The laws of nature are exquisitely fine-tuned to mastermind cosmic evolution, the coming of life from non-life, and within life itself, evolution to higher forms. These laws encompass not only laws of physics but also control an inbuilt mutation rate for DNA. Together, the deterministic laws and the in-built chance variations have catalysed the march from one cell to mind. This can easily be thought of as due an overall intention latent in reality and so suggests a designer.

> I must conclude that it takes a great deal more faith to believe in an accidental universe than to believe in an intelligent creator, or God who crafted such a marvelous universe[22]

The evolution to consciousness has progressed slowly over the aeons. Examples of all the initial and intermediary stages have survived—sea lilies, fish, crustaceans, reptiles, many species of mammals, primates, and single celled organisms which easily outnumber all other organisms. Nevertheless, intelligent consciousness progressed through various species of hominids, and achieved its highest form in one species, *homo sapiens*.

8.1 How random is the chance question?
Mutations must happen. As indicated previously, mutations are built into the nature of DNA. There is a rate of mutations intrinsic to DNA. Changes in the genes, in the DNA will happen as a matter of course. Most of these are deleterious or have no bearing on the offspring. Occasionally one is advantageous. Deleterious changes inhibit the progress of the recipient. Advantageous changes enable the possessor to outbreed other offspring, and after many generations possessors of the advantage will make up the species. The others will be less successful and become extinct.

> Do we have to choose between the absolute empire of accident and a living, immanent ever-working God? God has not just produced a ready made world; he has done something cleverer than that in making a world that could make itself.

21. Timothy Shanahan, *The Evolution of Darwinism* (Cambridge: Cambridge University Press, 2004) 198-203
22. Walter L. Bradley, *Is There Scientific Evidence for The Existence of God? How the Recent Discoveries Support a Designed Universe.* http://www.leaderu.com/real/ri9403/evidence.html (17/4/2009), 27.

> Concentrate not only on the contingency in evolution. Mutations are not directly linked to survival needs, but these are selected by interaction with environmental necessity, in a process of remarkable fertility. Chance is a means for realizing in contingent ways something of the rich potentiality present in the necessity of natural laws.[23]

The selection is not chance. Once mutations have occurred, if they are deleterious the offspring will not be favoured, and the mutation will not persevere. If mutations are favourable, natural selection will ensure they survive preferentially.

> . . . evolution is not the outcome of random processes. There is a 'selecting process' that picks up adaptive combinations because these reproduce more effectively and thus come to prevail in populations.[24]

Question 7. **The randomness of the chance aspect is mitigated in that only those mutations favoured by the laws of nature are selected for the benefit of the organism. Comment on the diagram.**

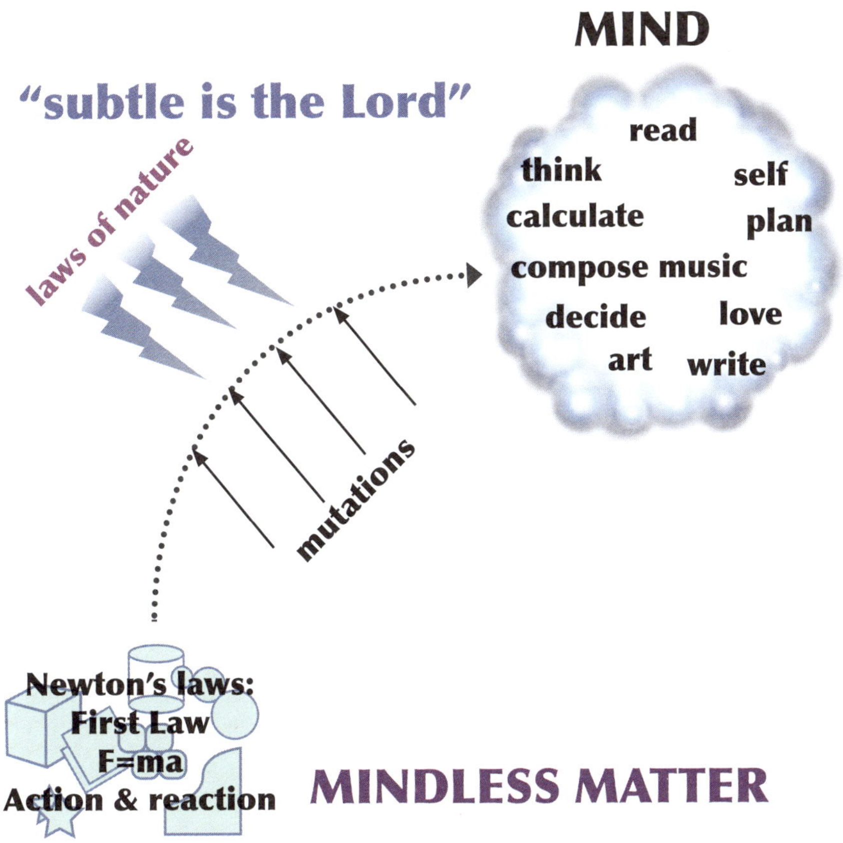

God has given creation freedom. *Homo Sapiens* has been given freedom to develop, to explore creation, to live well or not live well. God has given inanimate creation the freedom to develop itself, to explore many many pathways always with the chance of unleashing the ultimate essence buried within its seeming barren material nature. This is a prelude to the freedom given man and woman.

> Such laws (of nature) may be 'blind', but they result in the possibility of purposeful and intelligent life. They may be 'pitiless' but they permit the possibility of human

23. John Polkinghorne, *Beyond Science*, (Cambridge: Cambridge University Press, 1998), 77.
24. Ayala, 62.

compassion and mutual care. They may be 'indifferent', but they seem inherently fitted to generate life in all its variety and wonder.[25]

8.2 The molecules on the pathway to intelligence are preferentially stable

Genes are composed of many atoms, even up to a million. Why are meaningless combinations of molecules not equally stable, shutting up molecules into fruitless combinations so that they are never available for building genes? Why are the gene molecules exceptionally stable?

This necessary stability of the gene is not a total stability; mutations, slight changes in the order of molecules attached to the DNA have been factored in so that natural selection is now a possibility. This happens only because the stability of gene molecules has an inbuilt slight instability, or changeableness.

In addition the fruitful ordering of units involved in life molecules is unlikely. The order of molecules composing the gene is essential. How come the order of molecules composing the gene has been achieved, and is maintained? The number of possible orderings[26] of a molecule in a functional protein can be shown to be 10^{190}. The shape of the protein molecule is also vital if it is perform its function. If this requirement is also factored in to the number of possible molecules the number is 10^{200}. The observable universe is unimaginably vast. It contains roughly 10^{80} atoms. So how big is the number 10^{200}? Remember 10^{81} is 10 times 10^{80}.

8.3 Implication of convergence

Various stages on the upward path have evolved independently many times.

Why has evolution by natural selection achieved the same solutions from different starting points, and through different pathways?

In 'Life's Solutions' Simon Conway Morris[27] lists and discusses many, even ubiquitous, examples of evolutionary convergence. He then reflects philosophically on the scientific evidence before him and comes to the conclusion that in evolution, matter seeks out the pathways leading to advances in size, ability to handle the environment, physical abilities, cognitive sensitivity, awareness. There is an inner dynamism in matter leading inevitably to new and more able forms, and eventually given the time and the continuance of conditions, leads to intelligence. Paths to seeing, hearing, intelligence etc., are many and varied, but they converge on the same solutions.

8.3.1 The path to mind is predetermined

All the steps that have culminated in humanness have been repeated so many times suggesting that the end product—intelligence—is inevitable. Some see evolution as haphazard, at the whim of chance, finally yielding intelligence very accidentally. Replay the tape, and the result would be very different, they say. But the tape has been played and replayed many times in parallel, always coming to the same conclusions. The eye has evolved forty times[28]. The paths are different, the molecular structure of the conclusions differs in detail, but the functioning of the arrived-at states is similar. Despite the number of species, there are only a few solutions possible to the evolutionary quest. Many more possibilities can be thought up, but they have not occurred.

8.3.2 Mind the intended result

There are so many possible ways for evolution to go, yet it stumbles upon the functional solutions.

> Minds are not accidents of evolution; (note the) repeated emergence of complex processors in the form of brains, which whether insect, lobular brain of octopuses, or the complex vertebrate brain, they provide huge potential for solving problems of survival.

25. K Ward, *The Big Questions in Science and Religion*, 74.
26. WL Bradley, *op cit*, 23
27. Chapter 7, section 7
28. Ayala, 65.

> Dolphin brain differs from primate brain in many significant ways—microstructure, development of particular regions and lobes, so that similarities in the intelligence and social behaviour of dolphins and apes, and humans is remarkable.
>
> Dolphins can recognize themselves in mirrors as can the chimp. They have a sophisticated communication system—recognising 100+ other individual whistles. They can mimic. They form a mix of temporary and stable alliances (as do chimps).
>
> When convergence is the rule, you can rerun the tape of life as often as you like and the outcome will be much the same. Life has a direction.[29]
>
> The vast number of potential blind alleys is so enormous that in principle all the time since the beginning of the universe would be insufficient to find the one in a trillion-trillion solutions that actually work. Darwinian evolution remains central as the agency, but the nodes of occupation are effectively pre-determined from the Big Bang.[30]

Convergence shows life, brain, and ultimately intelligence were factored into the laws, as the same solutions are arrived at from different starting points, along different pathways. There is an intention detectable.

9. Homo sapiens

The fact that mindless matter has spawned from within itself a consciousness that can not only deal with the environment, but also can reflect on itself, and on the process from which it has come is worthy of the deepest consideration.

9.1 Beyond natural selection
Despite the huge variety of species and the variety of developmental characteristics, there has been a directional trend culminating in *homo sapiens* in whom natural selection has ceased; this species can master its own evolution and is not necessarily guided by survival of the fittest. Nursing homes, state sponsored welfare, looking after the poor and infirm, national and international refugee organizations, United Nations assistance after the onset of disasters all fly in the face of the natural selection which has guided the biosphere to reflective consciousness.

Reality is positively disposed to the emergence of spiritualness. The evidence is there especially in the rapid expansion of cranial capacity on the road to *homo sapiens*. This is explained by a mind, a power, a giver of purpose to reality.

9.2 Qualities not needed for survival
Homo Sapiens has developed complex systems of mathematics, has written poetry, has created art works which others can appreciate, performs drama, and has composed many great works of music. The qualities needed for these achievements are not necessary for survival. Many of the end products of natural selection are not in the service of survival.

Question 8. Why have there emerged properties far in excess of those demanded by 'survival of the fittest' ?

29. S Conway Morris, 'We Were Meant to Be', *New Scientist*, 16/11/2002:
30. Morris, *Life's Solutions*, 309–310.

10. Questions asked by non-reductionist biologists and philosophers

10.1 Philosopher/theologian John Haught[31] asks:
Is nature so driven by mindless determinism that a truly new and unpredictably meaningful future is ruled out?

He then asks on the other hand does evolution demand an intelligence and a power?

Does the process by which mind evolves from mindless matter require an intelligence to mastermind such a process, and a power to equip reality with such properties?

And finally with regard to the Christian scenario, Haught enquires:

Is there in this scenario a purposeful universe cared for by a compassionate god?

10.2 Kenneth Miller[32] (Brown University Biology Professor in department of Molecular and Cell Biology).
How can you reconcile the divine will with a random chance process like evolution?

This is often perceived as an insurmountable problem for believers, but Miller then answers this question:

'But does a perceived lack of inevitability translate into something incompatible with the divine will? (This) seriously underestimates the Western God. Is God a puppeteer?'

Then Miller asks a positive question leading to a search:

'For the believer how do such chance events fit into the scheme of things?'

10.3 Jesuit cosmologist Bill Stoeger[33] presents a question on the laws of nature:
'To what extent are these developments coded into the laws of nature?'

His answer to this is:

> Definite series of outcomes is coded into the laws of nature and conditions of earlier times. Conditions and regularities are set for the structures we now have. For example, given stars plus laws of nuclear physics and constants of nature, fabrication of elements heavier than lithium is inevitable.

10.4 Sir Roger Penrose,[34] mathematical physicist, reflects, leaving the reader with an implicit question:

> There is still something mysterious about evolution, with its apparent groping towards some future purpose. Things at least seem to organize themselves somewhat better than they ought to, just on the basis of blind chance and natural selection. It may well be that such appearances are quite deceptive. There seems to be something about the way that the laws of physics work which allows natural selection to be a much more effective process than it would be with just arbitrary laws. The resulting apparently intelligent groping is an interesting issue.

Question 9. Comment on the above reflection of Sir Roger Penrose.

10.5 Timothy Shanahan[35] Marymount University Philosophy professor presents the dilemma arising from our knowledge of evolution:
Are we the special creations of a loving deity, made in his image, or accidental by-products of a blind purposeless process which never had us or anything in mind in the first place?

---

31. John Haught, *God after Darwin* (Boulder, Colorado: Westview Press, 2000), 102.
32. Miller, 234.
33. Stoeger 167, 8.
34. Roger Penrose, *The Emperor's New Mind* (Cambridge University Press, Cambridge, 2000), 301
35. Shanahan, 5.

He further reflects with two philosophical/theological questions about ourselves:

> Do we have immortal souls? Which make possible consciousness, conscience?
> Do we have a glorious future or will each of us at the moment of death simply cease to exist.?

Question 10. How does evolution change our concept of Creator God?

11. Extension (1). Richard Dawkins' proposal concerning the pre-eminent role of DNA in evolution

11.1 Is DNA the cause of evolution?

Biologist Richard Dawkins has proposed a driving force for evolution, human DNA, which above all is dedicated to its own survival. To do this DNA encases itself in more and more sophisticated and specialized phenotypes. It is not so much natural selection but the urge of DNA which brings about better and better protective environments for itself in forcing the biosphere from uni-cells, to multi-cells, all the way to primates and then to *homo sapiens* who goes beyond natural selection and plots and plans his own survival and enhancement all to securing the ultimate survival of DNA. It is not intelligence that is doing this, but rather relentless DNA consistently bettering itself and entrenching itself more and more permanently in existence, beyond the reaches of natural selection.

> . . . the true utility function of life, that which is being maximized in the natural world, is DNA survival. But DNA is not floating free; it is locked up in living bodies and it has to make the most of the levers of power at its disposal. DNA sequences that find themselves in cheetah bodies maximize their survival by causing those bodies to kill gazelles. Sequences that find themselves in gazelle bodies maximize their survival by promoting opposite ends. But it is DNA survival that is being maximized in both cases.[36]

This seems to be a 'false cause' argument, *post hoc ergo propter hoc.* Survival and enhancement of DNA's protective environment occurs, therefore DNA has caused this. In addition, this thesis invests DNA with properties far beyond its own nature. DNA is a code for life and life functions; it is a set of instructions. In the right environment it performs its functions. There is no imperative about it. The imperative comes from natural selection acting on favourable mutations, often aided by external climate or environment changes.

> According to Dawkins, evolution is driven by 'replicators'—genes, and also 'memes,' viruses of the mind that spread and persist in human populations. Those genes and memes that replicate most effectively become dominant, with every consequence for the natural world and for civilization and history. The usefulness of this notion, which does have the virtue of simplicity, is a question obscured by the demands Dawkins has placed on it.[37]

> But DNA alone doesn't make an organism. Organisms also possess many different proteins (each, in turn, made of amino acids), as well as other molecules that help make structures like cell membranes. Moreover, all these parts must be arranged in just the right way: membranes on the outside of the cell and DNA on the inside, and so on.[38]

He places the urge for progress in some sort of inner dynamism ascribed to DNA by which it relentlessly seeks out better and better phenotypes to preserve itself. But DNA is not alive; it is a set of instructions for life. It is not like a soul or a sense of self, or an onward driving force. What it does, is that it gives the instructions for development if the potential organism finds itself in the right situation. The progressive urge finds itself not in the DNA, but rather there is a more basic inner urge in

36. R Dawkins, *River out of Eden* (London: The Orion Publishing Group, 1995), 105–106
37. Marilynne Robinson, Harper's Magazine, July 2006, 20.
38. H Allen Orr, *A Mission to convert,* New York Review of Books, 54/1 2007.

matter to reveal more and more fully its capacity for spiritualisation. This is not survival at all costs, but rather a flowering. Darwin himself, in several places, affirmed evolution as progressive.[39]

12. Extension (2). An evolutionary biologist's criticism of 'The God Delusion'

12.1 Dr H Allen Orr

Dr H Allen Orr is an evolutionary geneticist; he is a professor and at the University of Rochester, New York. Among other awards, he was one of thirteen recipients in 2008 of the Darwin-Wallace Award, which is bestowed every fifty years by the Linnean Society of London. He is critical of 'Intelligent Design' in the American creationist sense (W Dembski, M Behe). He is equally critical of materialist scientific reductionism (EO Wilson, D Dennett, S Pinkner)

Although the author of this criticism praised Richard Dawkins' book *The Selfish Gene,* as the best popular science book he had read, he was not happy with *The God Delusion.* He attacked it on three major counts: his case against religion, the weakness of Dawkins' argument against God's existence, and the general tenor of his argumentation.

12.2. Summary of Orr's criticisms of 'the God Delusion' in 'A mission to Convert'[40]

1) *Dawkins treats all religions as though they are all fundamentalist, as though religious adherents are all biblical literalists.*
   Dawkins maintains that religion is nonsense. Because some forms are fundamentalist and interpret ancient texts literally, he writes as if all forms are of this persuasion, not meeting at all, other forms on their own ground.

2) *He declares all religions to be pernicious without making an analysis. He gives a few examples, and then makes sweeping statements.*
   Further than the nonsense accusation he maintains religion is and has been pernicious. The trouble is that Dawkins lumps extreme forms and moderate forms together.

3) *He makes light of evils coming from secular states.*
   He exempts atheism as a cause of evil. Atheism's record in the twentieth century was not great: Stalin's and Mao's brutality, imprisonments, murders, wholesale executions of priests and nuns, the 'Killing Fields' of Cambodia. Dawkins offers these an excuse: the bloodshed may have not been due to atheism itself, but he allows no such consideration to religions.

4) *He makes no effort to examine the good that has come from religion.*

5) *He is motivated by a preordained set of conclusions he is determined to arrive at.*
   He is not interested in anything positive about religion, and seeks to marshal all facts as arguments against.

6) *He is a scientific reductionist, deriding philosophical arguments, but his chief argument against a designer God is a philosophical one.*
   Dawkins maintains if God were to be the designer, he would have to be more complex than what he had designed.[41] This is very unlikely. So God is not the designer.

   Dawkins, is presenting a philosophical argument. He disposes of the design argument with the above consideration, and with the ensuing necessity of an infinite regress of ever more complex designers of designers. He deals with traditional philosophical arguments for God's existence mainly with dismissive eloquence. Philosophy is not a path to truth. But his own argument is a philosophical one. This should not be allowable for him. The conclusion should be unpersuasive as it does not come from the scientific method.

39. Shanahan, 238.
40. *Orr, ibid.*
41. Dawkins, *The God Delusion*, 113–114.

7) *The God he dismisses is not the God most theists believe in.*
God is transcendent, not to be equated with the complex material universe, the pure perfection of existence itself, the universal mind, the self-existent one, beyond our comprehension. Any concept of material simplicity cannot be applied to the simplicity of a transcendent spiritual Being.

8) *He makes no serious effort to engage with theological, religious, thought.*
His endorsements come from his other works, Carl Sagan, pop music, *Hitchhiker's Guide to the Galaxy*. He is willing to analyse and criticise other arguments, but does not subject his argument to similar analysis.

9) *He is an expert evolutionary biologist, but assumes authority in a number of fields in which he is not an expert.*
In this book Dawkins covers many disciplines. John Cornwell has written that 'the work embraces science, philosophy, psychology, religion, spirituality, anthropology, sociology, history and theology'.[42] But it cites very few authorities in any of these fields, gives very few references to noted academics in chapter and verse. One cannot be a master even of all aspects of one field, let alone be an authority in many separate arenas. He cites little from Judaism, nothing from non-Christian religions, and only one Christian philosopher of religion.

42. John Cornwell, *Darwin's Angel* (London: Profile Books Ltd, 2007), 29–30.

Further Reading

Ian G Barbour, *Nature, Human Nature and God* (Minneapolis: Fortress Press, 2002).

Christine Ledger & Stephen Pickard (editors), *Creation and Complexity: interdisciplinary issues in Science and Religion* (Adelaide: ATF Press, 2004).

Hilary D Regan & Mark Worthing (editors), *Interdisciplinary Perspectives on Cosmology and Biological Evolution* (Adelaide: ATF Press, 200).

Alister McGrath, *The Twilight of Atheism: The Rise and Fall of Disbelief in the Modern World* (London: Rider, 2004).

Hugh Montefiore, *The Probability of God* (SCM Press, 1985).

Chapter 9
The Christian God and Evolution

Chapter overview

- God is the Creator
- The Scriptures and evolution
- How does God act within time?
    - Deism
    - Intelligent Design
    - Continuing primal causality
- The pain of creation
- The God who saves
- Extension: Teilhard de Chardin

1. The Christian God—God is the Creator.

The God of Christianity is traditionally the God of the Jewish Scriptures (the 'Old Testament'), and the God of the New Testament in the person of Jesus Christ, and the Father to whom he bears witness.

1.1 Different creation narratives
The creation doctrine comes from the Jewish Scriptures in which the event is described in three (at least) different ways. There is firstly the seven-day version in which animals, birds, fish were created directly before the creation of humans; secondly, the Adam and Eve story in which the animals again were created directly, but after the creation of Adam, who named them, and before the creation of Eve; thirdly, God disposing effortlessly of the monsters of chaos.

A common background pagan narrative was this: the pagan gods had to struggle against chaos, and against the monsters which inhabited chaos, in order to bring about a coherent world. After the battle ended, the sea itself was a legendary goddess held back from sweeping civilisation away. In contrast, parts of the Jewish Scriptures picture God effortlessly quelling the fierce primeval monsters. This is an affirmation of the supreme jurisdiction of God. Various books speak of the monster *Rahab* and other monsters.

> Rahab seems clearly to be associated with or identified with the monster of chaos which is slain by the creative deity in ancient Semitic myths of creation. In the Old Testament this victory is attributed to Yahweh. Yahweh hewed Rahab in pieces, pierced the Dragon, dried up the sea (Is 51.9). He rules the raging sea, crushes Rahab (Ps 89.10). He stilled the sea, smote Rahab, slew the fleeing serpent (Job 26.12). The helpers of Rahab are bowed under his power (Job 9.13).[1]

The Psalmist speaks of another legendary monster *Leviathan.*

> By your power, you (Yahweh) split the sea in two,
> And smashed the heads of the monsters on the waters.
> You crushed Leviathan's heads,
> And gave his as food to the wild animals.[2]

1. John L McKenzie, *Dictionary of the Bible* (London: Geoffrey Chapman, 1966), 719.
2. Psalm 74:13–14.

> Leviathan . . . a monstrous being to be identified with the mythological monster of chaos, Lotan, 'the serpent slant, the serpent tortuous, Shalyat of the seven heads' slain by Baal . . .The victory of the creative deity is transferred to Yahweh.[3]

Yahweh with his finger holds down Behemoth and Leviathan, the forces of chaos. His angels are the pillars of heaven and earth. Humans between earth and dome praise Yahweh. [William Blake]

Whereas pagan mythologies had the gods battling seriously with the monsters, Jewish references in the Books of Job and Isaiah, and in the Psalms had God effortlessly disposing of them as part of the creation event.

1.2 The biblical teaching on creation

The underlying assertion of the creation stories is that God is the supreme master of the world, the skies. All has come from God. Everything is the result of divine action. The world and all that's in it was not made from something pre-existing. Not knowing actually how creation happened, the Hebrews affirmed it all came ultimately and seriously from God. In addition, everything God initiated was good; evil came from humans, from the disorder of the human heart. Creation accounts in chapters one and two differ; there is a firm belief in God the creator, but a readiness to entertain a variety of presentations as to how. There is a plan, there is a purpose.

3. McKenzie, *Dictionary of the Bible*, 505.

Question 1. The Jews were certain God was the Creator, but did not know how God created. What is the essential religious message of the various creation stories?

2. The scriptures and the theory of evolution

Does the Creator God of the Old Testament fit in with the scientific picture of evolution?

2.1. The Bible does not teach science
Literally, the Genesis creation accounts describe a sudden beginning, and a step-by-step build up of the cosmos and of living things. However, the Genesis picture is embedded in a primitive science, which knew nothing of the solar system, the Milky Way, or evolution; these are the fruits of today's science. The Bible does not teach science. The Biblical authors had to express their creation belief within the scientific understanding of the time. In the first creation account, it proposed that the whole cosmos as then understood was a step by step act creation by Yahweh. Other biblical books say if there were monsters of chaos, they were effortlessly disposed of by Yahweh, as a counter to the difficult battles with monsters proposed in pagan stories. We have to abstract the religious insight from the primitive cosmic understanding, and see whether this insight can stand with the evolutionary model.

2.2 The religious assertions of the Hebrew Scriptures
2.2.1 About God.
There is one unpicturable God. Everything that is, is ultimately due to this one God. It all came from nothing, chaos, trackless waste. God saves. God is primarily experienced as saviour. God chose the Hebrews in Abraham, rescued them from slavery through Moses, gave them the promised land through Joshua, delivered them from the Babylonian exile, gave them Saul, David, Solomon as kings.

2.2.2 About the world.
It is all good, until humans introduce evil. We can—and do—choose evil. All progress comes from humans—not from fate or gods.

2.2.3 Against pagans.
There is no mythological world of gods. The sun, moon, and stars are not gods. There was no prehistoric disconnected mythic era, in which great battles, were fought between deities or against monsters. Creation was effortless.The monsters of chaos are deemed irrelevant. In view of this stance against other mythologies, Genesis is a radical statement in the context of the times.

2.3 An answer to biblical literalism
The biblical account of creation, once the religious message is abstracted from the primitive science, does not conflict with the present understanding of cosmic origins. Biblical creation denies a preceding mythological age; it proposes a beginning through the action of a creator. It proposes a purpose given it by the creator. Mainstream science today proposes a beginning of the universe; the age of the universe is given as 13.7 billion years. The universe itself is thought to be 'contingent'—it did not have to come into existence, and it did not have to have the laws that it possesses. The universe can easily be understood as having a purpose imprinted on it as it has unravelled itself cosmically and biologically. There is no contradiction between this and the Creator God. In fact, the Creator God provides a good philosophical explanation.

> *A caution:* One must be careful not to attach one's creation belief to any current scientific picture. Present scientific models always await that observation which would cause their revision, and even replacement. The attachment of Church dogma to the medieval cosmic model led to the conflict with Galileo, and the subsequent tarnishing of the Church's image even to this day.

3. Beyond natural selection

The appearance of *homo sapiens* is the end point of evolution by natural selection. After the arrival of *homo sapiens* natural selection has had to take a back seat, as the mind and free choice take over. Humans pursue their own betterment or their own destruction by the free choices they make. Humans do not always make life hard for the unfit, but often look after the old, the sick, the poor. They respect and bury their dead. Rather than being pawns in the hand of natural selection, they become involved in future creativity. Such an intelligent being may have emerged elsewhere—we do not know. Once having emerged as free and reflective, *homo sapiens* is released from seemingly mindless natural selection and humans are enabled pursue life for their own betterment or destruction.

4. God and design

But can the process that led up to our emergence be a designed process? Can a process which was at the behest of chance mutations, continental drift, climate changes, ice ages be said to have been designed?[4]

4.1 Full knowledge of the laws not possible

We have only a partial knowledge of the laws of nature. Our knowledge of the reality behind the laws is partial. There may be a future observation which shows us our knowledge of the laws was more incomplete than we believed. However, we can understand it is laws of nature that have played a big part in shaping the cosmos and the biosphere, and these laws have enabled the progress evident in the story of life. The laws of nature include the susceptibility of DNA to chance mutations. Natural selection is the driving force of evolution, but the laws cannot do this without mutations: no mutations, no evolution. These occur at a regular rate, seem to have been factored in to the lawfulness of DNA. A mutation may be enough to confer a competitive advantage, or it may need a change in conditions to bring about a changed variation. The laws then select the mutations which will supply betterment.

4.2 Reason reflects on the laws

Philosophy and logic can be applied to the situation and say it is reasonable that there has been a designer at work. Science cannot argue that this has been designed, nor can it argue that it has not been designed. But meta-physically (meta = beyond) one can reflect on what science has revealed, compare the scientific picture with the Judaeo-Christian creation insight, and conclude they can well stand together. We can say such a collection of laws, of particles responding to pure mathematical 2nd order differential equations, of particles governed by 'the wave function', unpredictable in a single instance, but predictable given very large numbers of particles, of mathematical constants finely tuned to each other making life possible, we can say this fits in well with the idea of the Christian God and a final purpose for humanity.

<u>Question 2</u>. Many previous gaps in knowledge have been filled by science. Can you name any of these?

<u>Question 3</u>. There remain walls over which science can never climb, such as questions of cosmic purpose and human meaning. Is it legitimate to employ logic, philosophy, religion to scale these walls?

5. How does God act within time?

God's action can be thought of in three ways[5]:

- Uniformitarian—God selects the laws, and retires from the scene, allowing the laws to bring about the final result. This theology is named deism.

---

4. See chapter 8 section 7.1..
5. Ted Peters and Martinez Hewlett, *Evolution from Creation to New Creation: Conflict, Conversation, and Convergence* (Nashville: Abingdon Press, 2003), 118

- Interventionist—God is one efficient cause among others. Intelligent Design is the main interventionist theory at present.
- Non-interventionist—God acts in nature without contravening laws of nature.

5.1 Uniformitarian action: deism.
This is a God philosophy, but the God is not Yahweh who saves nor the incarnate Son of God, Jesus who is 'the way, the truth and the life'. God has not spoken to the world. God is accessed through reason. God is the unmoved mover of Aristotle, the overall designer. God could not be known through the church or the scriptures or miracles, or personal revelation. God can only be known through the providential design of the world.

> Aristotle observed that nothing starts to exist by itself. Its existence depends on something or someone else. An infinite series of beings, each depending on another for existence, could never get started except by a being who needs no one or nothing for existence. We call that self-sufficient being God.[6]

> Whoever admires a baby smiling and gurgling in his crib, whoever feels his heart beat and his lungs breathe, whoever foresees that this little guy will someday reason and love, whoever looks into his eyes has to believe that this baby's existence was planned, set in motion and guided by a supreme, intelligent being whom we call God.[7]

Deism's early adherents advocated replacing Christianity—ceremonies, supernatural aspects—with the cult of the supreme being. 'God gave us reason not religion' said the World Union of Deists.[8]

The French Revolutionaries renamed the Notre Dame cathedral 'the temple of reason'.

Deism maintains at the Big Bang, God endowed the creation with the required laws and suitable matter so that creation would eventually give rise to creatures with reflective intelligence. After this, God does not act within creation but leaves reality to create itself, nor does God reveal Godself to humanity.

Question 4. How does deism differ from Christianity?

5.2 Intelligent Design
5.2.1 God must be actively involved in evolutionary changes. As the accumulation of scientific findings made Creationism more and more untenable, a movement has arisen whose aim is to secure a presence for God as an active force in evolution. The evolutionary sequence is accepted, but it could not have occurred without the intervention of God alongside natural causes. Intelligent Design proposes that gradual change by natural selection operating on mutations could not have effected evolution.

5.2.2. Irreducible complexity. A key claim is that there are organs that are irreducibly complex. This means there are organs that consist of many parts which must work together to constitute the organ. The particular features necessary to establish a working eye cannot exist before the eye comes to be. There would be no purpose for an isolated optic nerve or lens without all the rest. The Intelligent Designer comes to the rescue and establishes all the parts at once. There are many times in the evolution of life where such organs with many necessary elements come to be, so that God is acting continually throughout creation to effect structures which exhibit 'irreducible complexity'.

Similarly the bacterial flagellum[9] is allegedly 'irreducibly complex'.

6. Raymond Fontaine, 'The Purpose of Life' at <http://www.deism.com/purposeoflife.htm>. Accessed 31 March 2009.
7. Fontaine, 'The Purpose of Life'.
8. http://www.deism.com. Deism defined. Accessed 17/4/2009.
9. en.wikipedia.org/wiki/E._coli. Accessed 17/4/2009

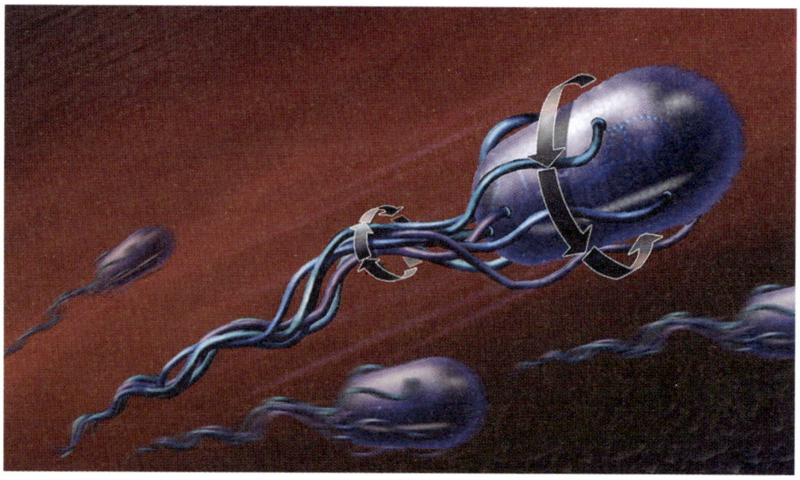

Escherichia coli cells use long, thin structures called flagella to propel themselves. These flagella form bundles that rotate counter-clockwise, creating a torque that causes the bacterium to rotate clockwise.

Intelligent Design proponent, Michael Behe, advances the cause of irreducible complexity. Francisco Ayala paraphrases Behe's assertion about this organ.

> The bacterial flagellum is irreducibly complex because it consists of several parts so that, if any part is missing, the flagellum will not function. It could not, therefore, have evolved gradually, one part at a time because the function belongs to the whole; the separate parts could not function by themselves.[10]

5.2.3 Response to irreducible complexity. Ayala rejects this explanation.[11] The evolution of the eye, and of any other organs showing alleged 'irreducible complexity' is a gradual process. The finished organ did not come to be all at once. It gradually became what it is today. The eye has evolved separately forty times[12] (See chapter 7, section 7.2). The necessary parts of finished organs have often been acquired by co-opting other elements and adapting them for new purposes. Three bones associated with human hearing were part of the jaw of earlier species.

5.2.4 Intelligent Design [ID] is not a science: Intelligent Design may be proposed and evaluated as a metaphysical conclusion, but not as part of science. Thus we may say firstly if the designer is a natural agent, we have the problem who designed the designer. This leads to the further problem of an infinite regress of designers who designed designers. An an undesigned designer disposed of this type of argument long ago. Secondly, if the designer is a supernatural agent, we are outside the realm of science. 'We cannot test or falsify this hypothesis using science'.[13]

5.2.5 ID claims evolution is a theory in serious doubt. It is one aim of adherents to Intelligent Design to have it located in the field of science so that it may be taught in American schools as a viable alternative to evolution by natural selection—this in the alleged cause of fairness. They have failed in a series of court cases to have Intelligent Design introduced into school curricula as an alternative scientific account on evolution.[14] They have adopted a new strategy: to attack evolution as a theory about which there is much doubt, thus staying within the bounds of science.

---

10. Francisco Ayala, *Darwin's gift to Science and Religion* (Washington: National Academy Press, 2007), 148.
11. *Ibid, 148-150.*
12. *Ibid*, 145.
13. Ted Peters and Martinez Hewlett, *Can You Believe in God and in Evolution* (Nashville: Abingdon Press, 2006), 50.
14. Glenn Branch and Eugenie C Scott, *The Latest Face of Creationism* (New York: Scientific American January 2009), 78–85.

> The fallback strategy amounts to substituting for creationism the scientifically unwarranted claim that evolution is a theory in crisis....evolution is unsupported by or actually in conflict with the facts of science.[15]

They proclaim a false dilemma implying evidence allegedly against evolution is evidence for some form of creationism. Evolution is not a theory in crisis. It is not scientifically controversial. Assertions that its fossil record is riddled with 'missing links' are false.[16]

5.2.6 God of the gaps is invoked to answer questions as yet unsolved
There is also the implied argument that if we cannot explain something naturally now, science will never explain it, and hence God is the explanation. There are organs whose development we are yet to understand; therefore, we need God's intervention to explain them. But science proceeds by solving problems one by one, and many problems that have previously seemed intractable have since been resolved. To explain natural processes we must look for natural explanations.

Question 5. What is Creationism? In what way is Intelligent Design another form of Creationism?

5.3 Non-interventionist.
5.3.1 Continual primary causality. God's continual causality is 'primary' causality. God acts within creation to sustain it in being, to keep its laws intact, and to make Creation free. God is outside of time and space, is transcendent being. The original creation event is an unfolding process for us, but for God, transcending past and present[17], it was—is—the one overall event.

Creation is not only bringing being from non-being, but it is a continuous act staying with creation to keep it from returning to non-being, and keeping its creative aspects in being. The initial laws having within themselves the potentiality to move matter on a progressive path were not merely dumped into the cosmos, but need to be continually sustained, as does the nature of matter itself with its spiritual potentiality need to be sustained. But for God, it all happens at once.

> The act of drawing the world from non-being into being is not limited to a once-for-all event in the past . . . The entire creation is still under construction, so to speak, yet to be completed.[18]

There is a Divine purpose for nature, not purpose in nature.

5.3.2 Possible quantum consideration. The universe is not a giant machine. Its ultimate constituents behave according to non-deterministic quantum theory. Some say God acts through giving quantum indeterminacy a nudge in one direction rather than another. The theory is well understood mathematically but what the reality is that behaves in its complex mathematical way is somewhat mysterious. Some say a door has been shut forever on our final understanding of material reality. So how God acts there may be also a closed book. God limits the divine power to give creation freedom so that random mutations and the laws of nature, and hence natural selection can act together.

6. The pain of creation

6.1 *Food chain*
The cosmos has given birth to life. But life is surrounded by suffering, the coming to birth of life and its progress have involved death. Species survive by killing other species. All life is condemned to death. Every living thing suffers. Creation is only possible because living things devour each other.

---

15. Branch and Scott, 82
16. For example, chapter 4 section 4, 'fishibians'.
17. When Moses asked God in the 'burning bush' what was his name, God replied 'I am He who is. This is what you are to say to the Israelites "*I am* has sent me to you".' (Exodus 3:13–14).
18. Peters and Hewlett, *Can you Believe in God and Evolution*, 161.

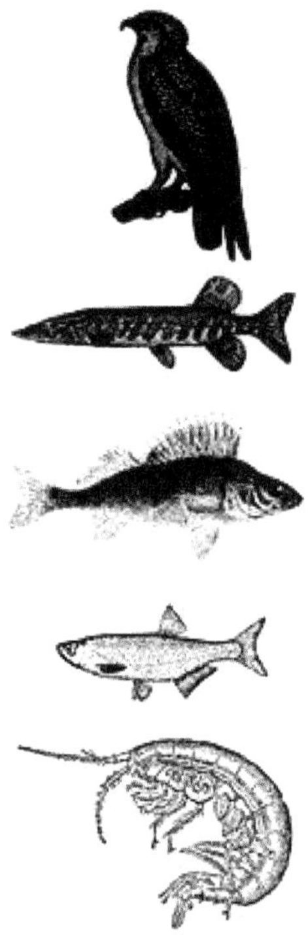

Living things feed on other living things. Even the one at the top of the chain must die.

Tennyson's oft-quoted lines[19] mirror the tortured face of nature:

> Who trusted God was love indeed
>
> And love Creation's final law
>
> Tho' Nature, red in tooth and claw
>
> With ravine, shriek'd against his creed

The place of men and women in nature is no better.

Every member of the species *homo sapiens* must die. This is often preceded by the infirmities of old age and painful illness.

> So runs my dream, but what am I?
>
> An infant crying in the night
>
> An infant crying for the light
>
> And with no language but a cry.

Tennyson did not leave the matter in such despair

> I falter where I firmly trod,
>
> And falling with my weight of cares

19. Alfred Lord Tennyson, *In Memoriam.* http://the other pages.org/poem/books/tennyson02.html. accessed 6.6.2009.

Upon the great world's altar-stairs

That slope thro' darkness up to God,

I stretch lame hands of faith, and grope,

And gather dust and chaff, and call

To what I feel is Lord of all,

And faintly trust the larger hope.

6.2 The God of the food chain

If we argue solely from nature to God, we argue from a nature riddled with suffering and death, from a Nature whose evolution has progressed remarkably, but nevertheless through the extinction of 99% of all species; and evolution has been dependent on climatic and extra-terrestrial calamities.

> The direction is from understanding nature to understanding God. The problem with such a natural theology, as we see it, is that the designer imagined can be nothing more than a designer of violence, suffering, death and enormous waste.[20]

Question 6. Is the fact of suffering, death and waste a convincing argument against the compassionate God?

7. The God who saves

7.1 Yahweh

The Jews' first and foundational experience of God was not as Creator but as Saviour. Yahweh rescued them from slavery in Egypt, (see footnote 16) and later from exile in Babylon, as well as giving them the promised land and, at one time, a strong nation under David. Christians inherit this experience, and its final fulfilment in God taking up residence among us, suffering as a human, suffering more than most are called upon to suffer. Perhaps God had to create in the way it was done, at least to ensure creation and ourselves had freedom, but the suffering and death necessarily intrinsic to creation is not the final end. God in Christ has marked out a divine purpose for nature, which may seem to be absent from nature itself.

7.2 Jesus Christ

7.2.1 Incarnation: God himself has joined this flawed creation

John's gospel begins in this way. 'In the beginning was the Word, the Word was with God, the Word was God'. Some verses later: 'He was with God in the beginning. Through him all things came into being, not one thing came into being except through him. Later in the same passage, John writes: 'and the Word became flesh, he lived among us, and we saw his glory, the glory he has from the Father . . .'[21]

Elsewhere in John, Jesus is quoted as saying 'in all truth I tell you before Abraham was, I am.[22] The author of the Letter to the Hebrews and St Paul affirm the divinity of Jesus:

> He is the reflection of God's glory, and bears the impress of God's own being, sustaining all things by his powerful command.[23]

20. Peters and Hewlett, *Evolution from Creation to New Creation*, 173.
21. John 1:1–2, 13–14.
22. John 8:58.
23. Hebrews 1:2–3.

> Christ Jesus: who being in the form of God, did not count equality with God something to be grasped. But emptied himself, taking the form of a slave, becoming as human beings are.[24]
>
> He is the image of the unseen God, the first-born of all creation, for in him were created all things in heaven and on earth; everything visible and invisible . . . all things were created through him and for him. He exists before all things and in him all things hold together.[25]

The person of Jesus, the incarnate Word, opens up different aspects pertaining to God.

7.2.2 Jesus: The compassion of God for suffering creation
By studying him in action we enter into the mystery of who God is. God is compassionate and understanding, cares about everyone, even the lowliest as Jesus demonstrated; God does not seek revenge, is incredibly dedicated to the human race as is evidenced in submitting to injustice and suffering and death, has taken upon himself the worst humans have to endure as a statement of understanding the reality of human suffering, and as a guarantee our inescapable suffering will also come to a happy conclusion; he has promised to all who are saddened by the certainty of dying new life in the model of his own resurrection. Jesus has emphasised the Almighty not so much as power, a threat, but as a Father. He addresses God as 'Abba'—an intimate word for father.

Question 7. Is Jesus' submission to an ordinary life, injustice, cruel suffering, painful death an adequate answer to the denial of God's compassion?

7.2.3 The Kingdom[26]
The emphasis of Jesus' message is the kingdom.
The kingdom is not a place. It is God's power and influence being felt, God's activity among the human race. It is a conflict between good and evil in which evil is overthrown; the overthrow of evil is symbolized by exorcisms, healings, changes of heart. It is God's power taking away sin and guilt, endowing us with the power to abandon the old ideas of survival of the fittest, revenge, prejudice and judgment, and enabling us to replace them with new attitudes.

It is obviously and completely present at the end of history, but it is anticipated here. Wherever we find true peace, active love of others, forgiveness, development of peoples, hope, trust, truth, conscience, honesty, care for the unfortunate, there the power of God is working.

8. Extension: Teilhard de Chardin.

8.1 de Chardin's stages of cosmic development.
Teilhard sees God acting within nature bringing about the remarkable evolutionary processes. *Geogenesis* is the development of the earth through water, its inner-structure, the influence of the sun. When the conditions are right, *biogenesis* takes over, life begins and progresses. Once a certain complexity has been established, *physcogenesis* takes over 'actuating a potential for a 'within' a sense of interiority'.[27] This does not include human consciousness, which is a huge step, differentiating humankind from all else. This is called *noogenesis*. Ultimately at a further step God will be revealed as all in all when creation reaches its final point through the agency of the God who has always been within it, the *omega point*. Teilhard certainly does not leave it all to natural selection.

Its further development now is in the coming together of human thoughts, the *noosphere*. The species thinks together, achieves a collective type of awareness.[28] It really was always there but depended on

24. Philippians 2:6–7.
25. Colossians 1:15–17.
26. See Chapter 10.
27. Peters and Hewlett, *Can you Believe in God and Evolution*, 127.
28. Teilhard de Chardin's Theology of Evolution<www.sheila-t-harty.com/Teilhard%20de%20Chardins%20Theology%20of%20Evolution.doc.>. Accessed 31 March 2009.

the complexification of matter to reveal its inner nature, its 'within'. The universe has been moving in a direction of more and more complexity, and hence greater and greater consciousness. It is being drawn along this path by *Omega.*

8.2 Omega[29]

- God acts within nature, not as an interventionist efficient cause, but acts as a final cause, drawing all things through *omega.*
    - *Omega* is the end to which everything is moving.
- *Omega* is already existing, attracting all things to itself. As Omega is also the actual cause of this movement, it is already existing. Like Aristotle's unmoved mover, it is a final cause, working through attraction.
- *Omega* is an intellectual, personal being. Things are becoming more and more personal, so what is attracting things this way is supremely personal. It is not an impersonal principle or force, nor is it an abstract idea.
- It is transcendent. It is attracting the universe to new levels of consciousness, so it is not part of the universe.
    - So it is beyond time and space, but reality must inevitably attain it. It is God.

29. Pierre Teilhard de Chardin, *The Phenomenon of Man* (London: Collins, 1959), 268–272.

Further Reading

Michael Ruse, *Can a Darwinian be a Christian?* (New York: Cambridge University Press, 2007).

K Miller, *Finding Darwin's God* (New York: HarperCollins, 2007).

Michael Ruse, *The Evolution-Creation Struggle* (Cambridge, Massachusetts: Harvard University Press, 2006).

Pierre Teilhard de Chardin, *Le Milieu Divin: An Essay on the Interior Life* (London: Collins, 1960).

Antony Flew, *There is a God: How the World's Most Notorious Atheist Changed his Mind* (New York: Harper Collins, 2007)

Chapter 10
Purpose in a Fractured World:
The Kingdom of God

Chapter overview

- Neither the developed world nor the developing world can deliver fulfilment
- Kingdom for all the world's fulfilment
- Naturalism
- Jesus speaks
    - For His hearers
    - For 21st century
- Jesus presents the kingdom
    - He calls for personal change
    - Jesus heals.
    - Performs miracles
    - Speaks in parables
- The Church and the kingdom
- Future kingdom
    - The gospels
    - The Book of Revelation
    - The final purpose

1. The fractured world

1.1 The developed world

In a minority percentage of the earth's population most people can almost be assured of adequate housing, amount and variety of food, clean water, employment, access to entertainments, communication, money for daily needs, and superannuation. Yet among these people there is a goodly rate of negative phenomena impinging on human happiness.. There are multiple failures in family life, alcohol problems, drug and gambling addictions, racial tensions, depressive illnesses, road trauma. There are robberies, murders, suicides. Then inevitably there is old age, sickness, the certainty of death. One can ask why do so many not discover real happiness, and is there an ultimate purpose.

1.2 The developing world

For the majority percentage of the Earth's population, there are all or some of the following problems: inadequate income, severe poverty, contaminated water, low standard of sanitation, poor housing (large numbers of slums and shanties surround many major cities[1]), malnourishment, illiteracy. Malaria is a debilitating and often deadly scourge. About thirty thousand children worldwide die every day from preventable disease. There are tens of million of people in refugee camps, fleeing armed civil strife, wars between countries. Should the majority aim to become like the minority and be faced with their problems? Is there a purpose?

1.3 The kingdom comes to all the world

To such a world comes the message of Jesus' kingdom. The kingdom is a realm within which people share, look after the poor and the sick, find peace, access respite from their own inner troubles, find a way to resolve conflict, and live together in peace, find a meaning in suffering, and lose the fear of

1. Geordie Williamson, 'A billion in one from Planet Slum', in *The Weekend Australian Review,* April 7–8 (2007): 15.

death. This realm is one which begins here on Earth and finds its fulfilment after death or at the end of time. This cannot come about by one's own efforts, but needs the activity of God among people.

1.4 The kingdom, a central theme in the gospels
Mark's gospel begins: 'after John had been arrested, Jesus went into Galilee. There he proclaimed the gospel from God saying 'the time is fulfilled, and the kingdom of God is close at hand' (1:14–15). The kingdom is mentioned fifty-one times in Matthew, thirty times in Luke, and fourteen times in Mark. The word was brimful of meaning for Jesus' contemporaries, but needs close examination to bring forth its meaning for today's people. The term is largely replaced in John by 'eternal life'.

1.5 The present earth cannot deliver true fulfilment
Can nature (the purely naturalistic view of reality) respond fully to the quest for meaning?
John Haught outlines the seven core teachings of the purely naturalistic view of reality (naturalism):

Seven core teachings[2]
- Beyond nature there is nothing.
- Nature is self-originating
- No overall purpose
- No soul, no post-death survival
- Emergence of mind and life accidental and unintended
- All causes are natural and accessible to scientific comprehension
- All features of beings explainable in Darwinian terms.

Haught responds in the negative to his question:
'We are meaning-seeking beings designed by evolution to seek communion with what is larger than ourselves'.

Question 1. How can human happiness be achieved?

2. The kingdom of God[3]

2.1 Dual aspect
After the resurrection, Christ reigns with divine power, creating aspects of the kingdom in the church and in humanity, and it will be fully revealed at the end of time.

The kingdom has a dual aspect: it begins now, it is fully revealed at the end of time. In the first sense, the kingdom now, the Spirit of Jesus provokes people to judge themselves, to choose life now or darkness, to confront evil, to embrace good. For Jesus, is this troubled world something to be escaped from? Buddhists say life is suffering: pain, disease, ageing, loneliness, frustration, fear, embarrassment, disappointment, anger. Get to the cause of suffering—desire. Quench, blot out all desire and you will be peaceful, happy. Seneca said think of the worst that can possibly happen, and you will never be disappointed. Plato counselled: be a philosopher, think deeply, resist pleasure, and at death your soul will fly happily back to the world of perfections whence it came. The Christian view is different. Recognise the presence of evil within oneself, and within the world, and meet it head-on. Transform the world and establish the beginnings of the kingdom in earthly life itself, and await the fullness of its revelation when God will transform creation.

2.2 What is the kingdom on earth?
The kingdom consists of:
- releasing people from the bonds of evil,
- calling people to a change of heart—calling sinners,
- the suffering—the sick, the maimed, the unfortunate—have value and need our support,

2. John F Haught, *Is Nature Enough?* (Cambridge: Cambridge University Press, 2006), 9.
3. Introductory note: chapter 9 section 6.1.3.

- free response to God's initiative,
- the danger of riches, the corrupting power of riches,
- don't back away from conflict in the quest for truth and justice, but violence is not the answer,
- the greatest commandment of all,
- God is Father: Abba—my Father, and your Father,
- love others as I have loved you.

The kingdom on earth comes about by the power of God.

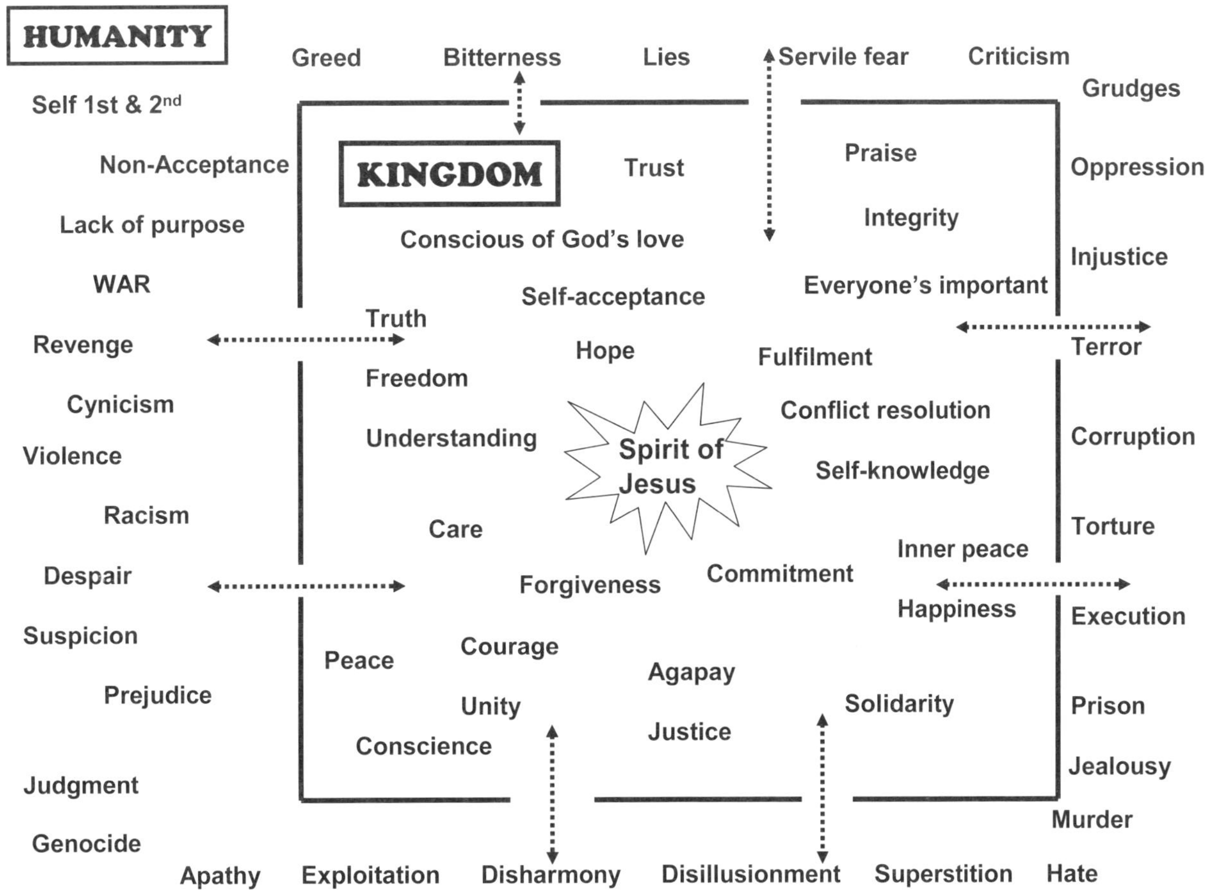

<u>Question 2</u>. Which of the above qualities of the kingdom would you select as essential?

2.3 Where is the kingdom?

> Asked by the Pharisees when the kingdom of God was to come, he gave them this answer: 'the kingdom of God does not admit of observation and there will be no one to say, 'look it is here, look it is there!' for look, the kingdom of God is among you' (Luke 20-21)

2.4 Relevance of 'kingdom'

2.4.1 To Jesus' hearers. Yahweh was earlier understood to be king of Israel, later as king over other nations, and later still as cosmic king, ruling over all creation in virtue of God's work as creator, and finally in the establishment of Yahweh's rule over Israel when God's salvation would appear in all its fullness. The theme was familiar to Jews of Jesus' time. The term meant much to his hearers, who looked back to David, and forward to a Messiah who would establish Israel as a power through the power of Yahweh.

2.4.2 To the third millennium.

So what do third millennium citizens make of Jesus' overriding theme 'the kingdom'? This word doesn't mean much to us. The phrase meant a lot to his contemporaries; that's why he used it. Some words or phrases mean a lot to us, have immediate associations: Oxford, Nazi, Woodstock, democracy, McDonald's, Gold Coast, Mandela, USA. I doubt whether 'kingdom' excites in us a whole lot of images; maybe a purely ornamental and symbolic English monarchy, or the chief of some third world backwater. And kings were not usually virtuous—they had to kill and imprison to survive;

WS Gilbert observed in the mouth of his Pirate King:

> Many a king on a first class throne
>
> If he wants to call that throne his own
>
> Must manage somehow to get through
>
> More dirty work than ever I do.[4]

For the kingdom now read the radical alternative, not radical in the sense of violent jihadist, or smoke-filled demonstrations, but rather a very different way of perceiving and living reality to the general view. Richard Dawkins says God's a delusion, that religion has caused all sorts of wrongs. Philip Adams dismissed the concept of God at an early age, although his continual return to religion and God in his weekly newspaper writings[5] makes one wonder whether he has really dismissed the concept of God. The radical view: there is a God, God matters, God matters so much that everything else has to be seen in relation to this reality. God wants to establish a better way on Earth and a final kingdom. God is close. At the centre of all reality is not a black hole but a Thou,[6] one you can address and trust, who wants you, but who leaves you totally free to respond, respects your individuality. Don't worry about getting old and grey or about dying young. God is not to be found in the ever faster software, but speaking within individuals, in families, in groups who are awake and who search. This has implications on the way we view life and live it out.

Question 3. What methods, experiences, of prayer can give a sense of God's closeness?

3. The kingdom as presented by Jesus[7]

We need to be saved in many ways: from our own inner demons, from despair when suffering is present, from the influence of the world around us luring us to greed, selfishness, violence, fame. The call of the kingdom is a present reality. Jesus proclaimed it, and acted it out in an understandable way suitable for the present, and proclaimed it fully and unequivocally by his death and resurrection; his Spirit makes it plain to this generation.

3.1 Healing of the person— forgiveness of sins

3.1.1 Jesus the one who calls for personal change.

Who is Jesus? In this context he's the man who calls people to a decision, reveals people to themselves, helps them see who they are, where they are going. He cuts through the rationalizing and self-deception. He breaks down the defences people throw up against self-discovery. In none of this does he do violence to the freedom or dignity of the human person. In this way he confronted the Samaritan Woman, Zacchaeus. He is unwavering in the determination to tell it like it is, no matter

4. Ian Bradley (editor) *The Complete Annotated Gilbert and Sullivan* (Oxford: Oxford University Press, 2001), 201
5. *The Australian Week-end magazine*
6. Andrew M Greeley, *The Great Mysteries* (New York: The Seabury Press, 1976), 11.
7. Thomas P Rausch, *Who is Jesus?* (Collegeville, Minnesota: Liturgical Press, 2003), 84–91.

what the cost. If this leaves him with few or no disciples, so be it. It's a trip through the narrow gate, and crowds need not apply.[8]

3.1.2 Our need for change.

Guilt, sadness for our past, unresolved features of former key relationships—some such inner trouble is often a feature of human lives, exerting negative influence on life. Remembrance of the past is combined with release from its grip when Jesus confronts us with ourselves, and changes us within, offering us self-acceptance and ultimately God's forgiveness. His influence leads to liberation from one's past, and to healing of relationships.

3.2 Miracles and exorcisms

These were necessary for his audience; sickness and infirmity were attributed to the power of demons and to sin. He had to show his power over what was believed to be the source of suffering and evil. 'If by the finger of God I drive out demons, the kingdom of God has come upon you' (Luke 11:20). We can think of his power over personal and societal evil today. As he exerted power over what people thought of as manifestations of evil in those times, he has power over evil today.

3.3 Shared meals—table fellowship

Jesus shared meals openly in the streets and market places with those deemed to be outside the acceptance of God—the sick, the obvious sinners, the poor, those who didn't keep the rules. Today to share a meal means acceptance of the other, and perhaps even more so in those days. God's saving activity was available to everyone; it proclaimed the opportunity for all to participate in the kingdom.

3.4 Parables[9]

- The Sower: The kingdom is accessible, but we need to respond.
- The Mustard Seed: it transforms life.
- The Buried Treasure: it is worth sacrificing all else for the kingdom; the person gladly gives up everything to cooperate with God's offer. Thus the response is total.
- The leaven in the bread: those who work for kingdom values have an influence that is hidden but real.
- The net cast into the sea: its benefits will surprise.

If God's kingdom had a future dimension, it was also present in Jesus' ministry. His parables proclaimed that God's reign was already active in the world. His exorcisms and healings, his proclamation of the forgiveness of sins, and his table fellowship showed God's saving power transforming the lives of the troubled, the sick, and the alienated, the tax collectors and sinners.[10]

8. Unpublished sentiments derived from American catechetical specialist James de Iacemo.
9. Matthew 13.
10. Thomas P Rausch, *Who is Jesus?*, 93.

The Pearl of Great Price

The Parable of the Talents

Question 4. Explain the meaning of the pearl of great price in life, and its further meaning.

3.5 Call for immediate response

Response means not only a confessional sorry for personal sin, but means think again, change your heart, your mind, your way of life; assume a new standpoint. 'Now' means there is an urgent need to respond immediately otherwise the chances are you will not get around to it in the course of time. Immediate action is exemplified in the parable of the talents.

Question 5. Explain the lesson to be drawn from the Parable of the Talents. Can you relate this to working for the kingdom?

3.6 Grace

You need to be born from above to see the kingdom. But then you need to personally respond. Jesus changed many in his time: Peter, Mary Magdelene, the Samaritan woman, Zacchaeus, Matthew. Others were untouched: Herod, Pilate, the rich young man, the chief priests and elders. Response must follow the offer of grace.

3.7 More than 'good news'

The kingdom message is not just the good news; it involves a commitment which can be difficult. It can also involve a judgment on those who failed to heed his words. 'Whoever is ashamed of me and of my words in this faithless and sinful generation, the Son of Man will be ashamed of when he comes in his Father's glory with the holy angels' (Luke 12:8–9). There is no soft message about God's unconditional love for all, God's final acceptance into heaven of all people.

Jesus as Judge of the Earth. Athens 1100

3.8 Future
'Thy kingdom come'. There is an essential future aspect to the kingdom. It is realized partially now, imperfectly in those who commit to it. There are many who adhere to other values which prosper the reign of evil. Life is a mixed bag. The parables of the mustard seed, the yeast, buried treasure, lost pearl, the net cast into the sea have a future interpretation when the full nature of the kingdom will be apparent. He makes this explicit when speaking of future judgment. This aspect takes on new meaning and importance after the resurrection.

<u>Question 6</u>. Have you a concept of life after death? Explain.

4. The church and the kingdom

The kingdom is not identified with the church, nor is it identified with an ideal political or social order. It is the churches' mission to proclaim the kingdom of God. 'The church receives the mission to proclaim and establish the kingdom, while the church itself represents its initial budding forth on Earth'. We know there are aspects of church that are not of the kingdom.

> Article 5 (of *Lumen Gentium*) underscored the common ground between the Church and the Kingdom of God, while making clear the two are not identical.[11]

In pre-Vatican II times, the Catholic Church often regarded itself as identical to the kingdom of God. Now, however, its task is to proclaim the kingdom, to help establish it, to witness to it by the quality of life of its members. Its imperfection and transitory nature is drawn attention to by the Vatican 2 Council

> Until there is a new heaven and a new earth where justice dwells, the pilgrim Church in her sacraments and institutions, which pertain to the present time, takes on the appear-

11. Richard P McBrien, *The Church, The Evolution of Catholicism* (New York: HarperCollins Publishers, 2008), 187.

> ance of this passing world. She herself dwells among creatures who groan and travail in pain until now and await the revelation of the sons of God.[12]

The Catholic Church no longer identifies itself with the realised kingdom of God, but sees itself as a servant of the kingdom on earth. Vatican 2 extended the concept of kingdom to reformed churches, other religions, and to all people of good will and conscience.

> Nor is God far distant from those who in shadows and images seek the unknown God, for it is He who gives to all life and breath and every other gift.
>
> Those also can attain to everlasting salvation who moved by grace strive by their deeds to do God's will as it is known to them through the dictates of conscience.[13]

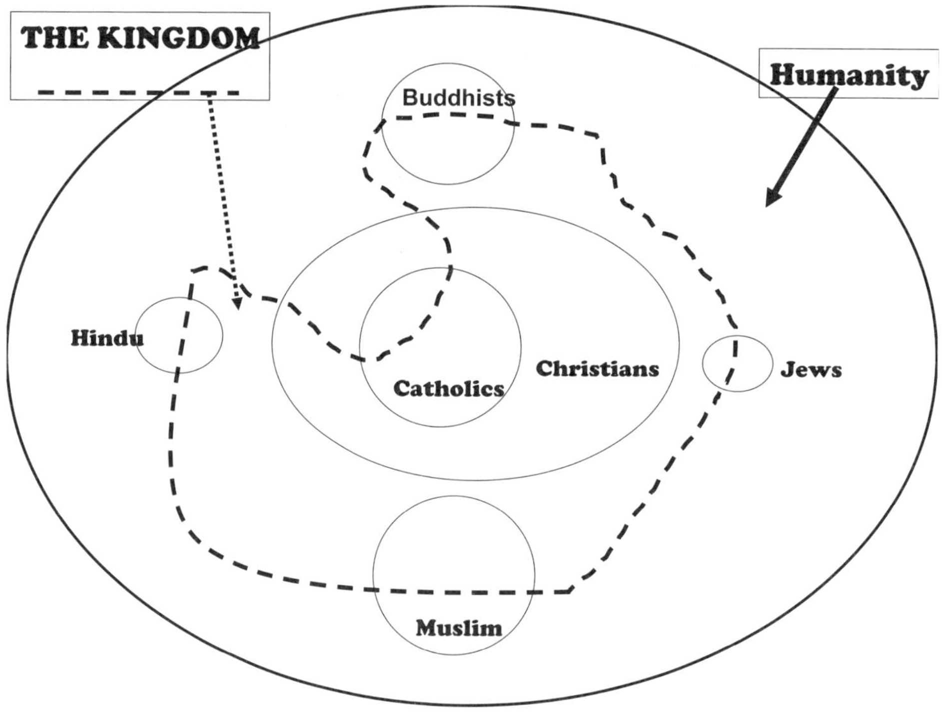

Today the kingdom is present in Christ-like compassion and service of others. The divine activity at the centre of all human life—'the human response universally valid of openness, acceptance, and commitment'. 'wherever people are being healed set free from oppression or dehumanising power of systems and made whole'.

5. Final kingdom

What is this final kingdom, which is the ultimate reason for Jesus' life and activity?

- Is it a transformation of the universe through a special act of God?
- Is it a further stage of the history of the universe? The different stages of cosmic evolution did not prefigure the next stage—who could predict a star manufacturing elements from swarms of hydrogen nuclei, helium nuclei, and electrons billowing outwards? Who could have predicted DNA from the early Earth? Is there, therefore, a further stage hidden within the laws of nature?
- Is it the creation of new heavens?

12. Documents of Vatican 2: *Gaudium et Spes*, n 48.
13. *Ibid*, n 16.

5.1 Transformation of the existing universe

5.1.1 The risen body

After the resurrection Jesus was not just a soul or a completely new being; he was recognisably Jesus, but different. He had been transformed. A number of resurrection stories portray him as the same but different.

Supper at Emmaus by Caravaggio

<u>Question 7</u>. Read the account of the meeting of the disciples with the risen Jesus on the Road to Emmaus. How does this story show Jesus is the same person, but transformed? (Luke 24. 13-35)

St Paul describes the risen state for faithful Christians:

> What is sown is perishable, but what is raised is imperishable; what is sown is contemptible but what is raised is glorious; what is sown is weak, but what is raised is powerful; what is sown is a natural body, and what is raised is a spiritual body.[14]

Our resurrection follows on the pattern of his:

> Christ has been raised from the dead as the first fruits of all who have fallen asleep.. through one man has come the resurrection of the dead.. In Christ all will be brought to life.[15]

5.1.2 The material universe

As the risen Jesus was the same Jesus but transformed, so too the entire Universe will emerge through the power of God as the same, but transformed. Just as the resurrection of Jesus was not the

14. 1 Corinthians 15: 43–44.
15. 1 Corinthians 15:20–22.

resuscitation of a corpse, so the universe will make itself anew out of the old. Science has a choice of dismal scenarios for the fate of the universe, but God's power will prevent the 'big crunch' or the 'big freeze'. New laws will be factored into its nature.

> Easter does not represent an intervention by God, which breaks the laws of nature, but an act of God which transforms the regular structure of nature into a new 'paradigm'[16], that of New Creation.[17]

St Paul speaks of the transformation of the present Universe:

> It was not for its own purposes that creation had frustration imposed on it, but for the purposes of him who imposed it—with the intention that the whole creation itself might be freed from its slavery to corruption and brought into the same glorious freedom as the children of God. We are all aware that the whole creation, until this time, has been groaning in labour pains.[18]

5.2 A further stage in the history of the universe

Looking back over the standard cosmological theory of the evolution of the cosmos, it is apparent there are distinct stages in this history; and that each new stage seems to be surprising given the previous stage. The great expanding hydrogen gas clouds do not seem to prefigure stars; stars do not intuitively produce higher elements; Earth does not seem disposed to bring forth life. Recently, a new surprise was revealed to researchers, as two independent groups came to an unexpected conclusion that the rate of expansion of the universe was accelerating. So far it defies present theories so that a new entity has been invented to explain it—the 'Dark Energy of The Vacuum'.

> 'it is not often that astrophysics challenges fundamental physics', Matt Mountain (the director of the Space Telescope Science Institute) told his guests. 'In the last 400 years you can count on one hand, maybe on two, when these instances have occurred' . . . 'This is game-changing science,' theorist Michael Turner repeatedly emphasised . . . it demands 'nothing short of a revolution in our understanding of fundamental physics'.[19]
>
> 'But what form does this energy take? If you know, reserve yourself a flight to Stockholm'.[20]

Whatever is causing this unexpected and relatively recent acceleration must have been factored into the laws of the universe at the Big Bang. Are there other yet to be revealed laws, hidden in the cosmos which will take it in the direction of a 'new heaven and a new earth'[21]? Science at present predicts either a final 'fry' or 'freeze' for the cosmos. Perhaps there is more to be revealed in nature itself.

5.3 A totally new creation

God will create a new realm for the saved—an alternative scenario.

The present pessimistic scientific predictions will be realised. The sun will expand to a 'red giant' in four or five billion years, incinerating Earth, and finally divesting itself of most of its contents. The Universe will continue expanding. In 100 trillion years all the available hydrogen will have been used up to provide nuclear fusion fuel for the stars. There will be no more stars. The result will be a realm of black holes and the 'big freeze'.

After 10^{100} years, protons have decayed, and black holes have evaporated. Only waste products from these waste processes remain: photons of colossal wavelength, neutrinos, electrons and

16. Steve Fuller, *Kuhn vs Popper,* (Cambridge: Icon Books, 2001), 19–22.
17. Robert John Russell, *Cosmology, Evolution, and Resurrection Hope* (Adelaide: ATF Press, 2006), 47.
18. Romans. 8:20–22.
19. Richard Panek, 'Going Over the Dark Side', in '*Australian Sky and Telescope*', April 2009, 45.
20. Panek, 'Going Over the Dark Side', 46. Stockholm has hosted conferences on Dark Energy.
21. Revelation 21:1.

positrons. For all intents and purposes the universe as we know it will have dissipated.[22]

Maybe the accelerating expansion will be reversed, and the universe will then implode to 'the big crunch'.

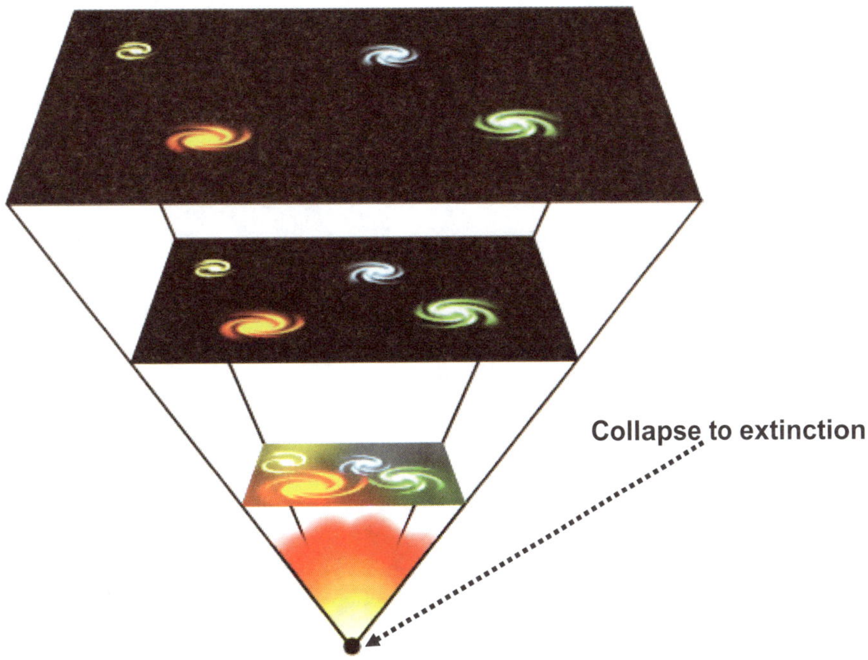

If science is right, whichever of these two scenarios eventuates, the universe dies. A new creation is needed.

6. Scripture on the end-time

6.1 The Last Judgment

Matthew 25:31–46. All humans will be gathered before the King who will judge them on how they have given themselves to others.

> . . .take as your heritage the kingdom prepared for you since the foundation of the world. For I was hungry and you gave me food, I was thirsty and you gave me drink, I was a stranger and you made me welcome, lacking clothes and you clothed me, sick and you visited me, in prison and you came to see me.
>
> Go away from me, with your curse upon you, for I was hungry and you never gave me food . . .
>
> And they will go away to eternal punishment, and the upright to eternal life.

This is a stark demarcation, with no mention of Church adherence, explicit faith.

John 5:26–29. Jesus is answering the Jews who are harassing him.

> As the Father has life in himself, so he has granted the Son also to have life in himself; and because he is the Son of man, has granted him the power to give judgment. Do not

22. http://www.pbs.org/deepspace/timeline/. Accessed 10/4/2009

be surprised at this, for the hour is coming when the dead will leave their graves at the sound of his voice: those who did good will come forth to life; those who did evil will come forth to judgment.

__Question 8__. **Describe the alleged features of the Last Judgment as shown in 'Christ Pantokrator'. What is your idea of the last judgment?**

6.2 The Book of Revelation

6.2.1 Earthly salvation from persecution. This symbolic book was written during a period of great persecution and suffering for Christians, as a statement of hope for them no matter what was happening. The book proposes an earthly salvation for Christians in the image of the four horsemen sent by God to remove the scourge of Rome. The Roman Empire was subjecting Christians to torture, and death. 'Revelation' foresees the Lord coming to their rescue.

In Zechariah 6:1–8, four horse-drawn chariots are despatched by God to enliven spiritually the land of the chosen people. In the same way, the four horsemen in *Revelation* are sent to prepare the overthrow of the Roman Empire, which was causing such grief to Christians.

The four horsemen of the Apocalypse[23].

Question 9. There are four horses? What does each represent?

6.2.2 Final salvation on the 'Day of Judgment'.[24] The author establishes a judgment scene which while somewhat dramatic really does nothing more than Jesus' accounts of the Day of Judgment: reward for the virtuous, punishment for the unrepentant, a new world. It is a final comfort for those suffering persecution.

> . . . then I saw a great white throne and the One who was sitting on it. In his presence, earth and sky vanished, leaving no trace. I saw the dead, great and small alike, standing in front of his throne while the books lay open . . . Anyone whose name could not be found in the book of life was hurled into the burning lake.
>
> Then I saw a new heaven and a new earth; the first heaven and the first earth had disappeared now.
>
> Then I heard a loud voice call from the throne. 'Look, here lives God among human beings. He will wipe away all tears from their eyes; there will be no more death, and no more mourning or sadness or pain. The world of the past has gone'.

23. Revelation, 6.
24. Revelation, from chapters 20 and 21.

> Theologian, Richard McBrien reflects: 'The last judgment will herald the final full flowering of the kingdom, where truth, goodness, everlasting life will flourish. After Jesus' public life, the resurrection and what was revealed of his newer existence changed how the disciples viewed the kingdom. Its full meaning is beyond death.
>
> The Church must recognize that the growth of the kingdom of God is moving toward the consummation of the earth and of humanity itself .'[25]

7. Reality's purpose

7.1 Response to physical and moral evil and building the kingdom
The overall purpose of reality is for humanity to bring to birth a foretaste of the kingdom, by firstly tackling evil in all its forms. There needs to be a compassionate response to physical evil: dealing with all forms of sickness, safeguarding society as much as possible against the effects of floods, droughts, earthquakes, tornados; bringing aid to victims of natural disasters. There needs to be an uncompromising response to evil afflicting others as a result of human choices: genocide, unfair trading practices, oppressive regimes, violence as a means of attaining ends. People are to strive to realise elements of personal peace and community peace, to establish justice, sharing, and so to contribute to real happiness.

7.2 Free choice replaces natural selection
This then is reversing the Darwinian law of 'survival of the fittest' through which we became intelligent beings. Rather than at the mercy of evolution,[26] we are to progress by free choice motivated by values of the kingdom and empowered by Christ's enlightenment and assistance. As life is short, and death beckons, we are invited by Christ to the ultimate destination of creation, the fullness of the kingdom which he will reveal. This overall purpose is clearly in harmony with the initial phases of cosmic evolution, and of the evolution by natural selection, which produced the human race, which now is in the position to direct evolution by free choice according to other values.

7.3 Jesus' resurrection illuminates the human situation
Jesus' resurrection gives the most profound insight into the human situation. It has revealed the provisional character of all worldly forms of fulfilments of life. Humans as humans are always something more than and extending beyond their present situations; one's destiny is not fulfilled in any given framework of one's life. God's reality experienced here and now is not only the ultimate source and guarantee of a present form of life, but points beyond every possible earthly fulfilment of existence.

William Stoeger looks for a consummation for creation:

> All creation now is groaning in one great act of giving birth – the life, suffering death of Christ, the life, suffering and death of humans, and the life, suffering and death of all creation is basically the same mystery connecting God and creation. 'Commitment' is ultimately expressed in death (surrender) leading to new life and fuller communion.[27]
>
> 'God continues to create and draw all things to completion through these intrinsic dynamisms, processes and relationships, which God has established with us and for us through the Word and the Spirit.[28]

---

25. McBrien, *The Church, The Evolution of Catholicism*, 197.
26. Steve Jones, *The End of Evolution*, in issue 24 of *Cosmos* December 2008. http://www.cosmosmagazine.com/features/2676/theendof evolution accessed 6.6.2009.
27. Bill Stoeger, 'Cosmology and a Theology of Creation', in *Interdisciplinary Perspectives on Cosmology and Biological Evolution*, edited by HD Regan and M Worthing (Adelaide: ATF, 2002), 144.
28. *Ibid*, 145.

Further Reading

John Polknghorne, *The God of Hope and the End of the World* (London: SPCK Press, 2002).

Bill Maguire, *A Guide to The End of The World* (Oxford: Oxford University Press, 2002).

Teresa Wong Yai-Chow *et al* editors, *The Cosmos in Becoming* (Adelaide: ATF Press, 2008).

Denis Edwards, *Jesus and the Cosmos* (New Jersey: Paulist Press, 1991).

William R Herzog II, *Jesus, Justice and the Reign of God* (Louisville, Kentucky: Westminster John Knox Press, 2000).

Paul Davies, *The Last Three Minutes* (London: Weidenfeld and Nicholson, 1994).

John Stenhouse and Brett Knowles, editors, *Christianity in the Post Secular West* (Adelaide: ATF Press, 2007).

Ronald Modras, *Ignatian Humanism* (Chicago: Loyola Press, 2004).

George V Coyne SJ and Alessandro Omizzolo, *Wayfarers in the Cosmos: The Human Quest for Meaning* (New York: The Crossroad Publishing Company, 2002).

Gerald O'Collins, *Incarnation* (London: Continuum, 2002).

Wolfhart Pannenberg, *Jesus–God and Man* (London: SCM Press, 1976).

Jack Dominian, *One Like Us: A Psychological Interpretation of Jesus* (London: Darton, Longman and Todd, 1998).

Richard Swinburne (editor), *Miracles* (New York: Macmillan Publishing Company, 1989).

Ted Peters, Robert John Russell, Michael Welker (editors), *Resurrection: Theological and Scientific Assessments* (Grand Rapids: Eerdmans, 2002).

Epilogue

- Classifying the truth value of scientific theories
- God and chance revisited
- Can natural selection be extended beyond biology?
    - * Cosmology
    - * Altruism
- Further questions
    - * Outstanding human qualities not necessary for survival
    - * Alien intelligence
- Final words

1. Classifying scientific theories

Sir Roger Penrose classified scientific theories, dividing them into three categories, superb, useful and tentative[1]. A superb theory is one which applies accurately to a broad range of phenomena. A useful theory is one which works well but whose accuracy and predictive power falls somewhat short. A tentative theory is one which so far has lacked 'any significant experimental support' such as string theory. Tentative theories may eventually be abandoned, or may contain within themselves 'seeds of a new substantial advance in understanding'. I hesitate to elaborate on Penrose's examples of theories fitting into these categories as the idea was published in 1989; except to say that at the time of writing (1989) General Relativity is classified as 'superb', Big Bang origin of the universe as 'useful', and string theory as 'tentative'. Speaking of evolution (close to the reference in footnote 1) he says:

> 'Perhaps the theory of natural selection, as proposed by Darwin and Wallace, comes closest (to 'superb'), but it is still a long way off'.

The point here is to be wary of such throw-away lines as 'only a theory'. Given the length of geological time, the fossil evidence, the findings of gene chemistry, and observations of bacterial development of resistance to previously effective drugs, evolution by natural selection is a well established theory of biological science. It cannot be lightly dismissed.

2. God and chance revisited

Does the incorporation of chance events into the theory place in jeopardy the idea of a transcendent God, one of whose functions is the design of the universe? Firstly, this is not the meeting of two opposing scientific theories. The God idea springs from philosophy and religion, and hence is non-scientific. This does not mean it is unreal—philosophical ideas underpin cultures, morals, and science itself. The question then becomes, does the chance aspect of Darwinian evolution deny any relevance to further philosophical speculation on the results of Science? Clearly, no: science has nothing to say about the validity of further speculation.

Secondly, the chance aspect is not purely chance. Chance delivers mutations in the DNA. But it is then the unchanging laws of nature that operate on the chance occurrences. If the chance occurrence does not confer an advantage, it is ignored. The determining factor ultimately is the unchanging laws of nature. Also chance changes have been factored into the nature of DNA. Deleterious ones are ignored, or condemn the possessor to extinction.

1. Sir Roger Penrose, *The Emperor's New Mind* (Oxford: Oxford University Press, 1989), 152–155.

3. Extensions of natural selection

Natural selection is a well-established tenet of evolution of life. Because of its success here, it has been applied elsewhere.

3.1 Cosmology

Lee Smolin[2] proposes an evolutionary development of universes. The universe is very well fitted by means of the laws inherent in it to form stable creative structures—stars, elements, life and intelligence. He asks how could this have happened. It could not be chance, the possibility is far too remote. Rather there has been a series of universes progressively becoming more and more specialised towards stability and creativity by means of cosmic natural selection. Many of these universes may have a lifetime of much less than a trillionth of a second. The ones which develop more black holes are those more on the path to becoming stable and creative. It is difficult to see how something creative could emerge from black holes which are the end of matter, time and space.

3.2 Human altruism

Natural selection is invoked to explain how the human race became altruistic.

> . . . we can start to see the beginnings of a coherent answer to our original question of how humans – driven as we are by selfish genes – have evolved such a complex capacity as morality.
>
> In an environment where cooperation such as reciprocal altruism is beneficial . . . our selfish genes allow for the evolution of cooperative behaviour[3].

This aspect flies in the face of the law of the jungle in which the food chain is maintained by an equilibrium between uninvited dying and successful killing, and species in the long term survive because they can outperform or dispose of other species, outlast them in the quest for resources or habitats. How could something diametrically opposed to survival of the fittest result from survival of the fittest?

It is better to restrict natural selection to its tried and true region of mindless evolution of life, rather than deify it and fasten upon it as applicable elsewhere, often in the quest for a materialist explanation of life.

4. Further questions

4.1 About homo sapiens

4.1.1 Rapid attainment of intelligence. There remain other questions. Why did the evolution to intelligence happen so quickly? Evolution from bipedal Australopithecenes to *homines sapientes* needed only 3.5 million years[4], the brain exploding in volume from 450 to 1330 cubic centimetres in a geological twinkling of an eye.

4.1.2 Presence of qualities not necessary for survival. Why did evolution result in features not necessary for survival? *Homo sapiens* sits atop the food-chain which begins with numerically dominant prokaryotes; *Homo* not only survives and out-survives all other species of animals but has developed properties not needed at all for survival. *Homo sapiens* reads books, writes poetry, composes music, reflects on the origin of the universe; members can give their lives to causes not involved with survival. Servant ants do the same, but their existence and activity is factored into the DNA of the species for the benefit of general thriving and surviving of the more dominant members.

---

2. Lee Smolin, *The Life of the Cosmos* (London: Weidenfeld and Nicholson, 1997), 90–106.
3. Tim Dean, 'Right and Wrong: Tim Dean Finds that Cognitive Psychology, Evolutionary Biology and Gametheory are Offering Fresh Insights into one of the Most Perplexing of Human Capacities, Morality', in *Cosmos*, 17 (Oct/Nov 2007): 53.
4. Dan Jones, 'A window on the Past', in *New Scientist*, 2705, (25 April 2009): 30–31.

4.2 Extra-terrestrial life and intelligence[5]

4.2.1 Search so far negative.

Has evolution ever happened anywhere else? Is the vast universe teeming with life, even intelligence, even perhaps technically advanced civilizations such as ours?

Search for Extraterrestrial Intelligence (SETI) has been going on for fifty years and no evidence has been forthcoming. The age of the universe indicates conditions for an earth-type geological and life evolution could have been present elsewhere billions of years ago. Civilizations could have come and gone many times. There is no evidence in the electromagnetic spectrum so far. It is even said, had a civilization developed a billion years ago, they should have developed the technology to pay us a visit. The argument goes 'If intelligent life is abundant, where are they?' But absence of evidence is not evidence of absence, and the search goes on.

4.2.2 Conditions necessary for the evolution of life.

- The planet must be in a habitable region of the galaxy. Some regions have stars with too few elements, some are too close to lethally active sources of radiation, some have too many stars per cubic light year.
- The planet must be in the habitable zone of its solar system. The temperature has to be between 0^0 and 100^0C.
- Included in the solar system must be a Jupiter-like planet not too close to the planet. Jupiter's large mass and its subsequent high gravity ensures it captures most of the rogue comets and asteroids.
- The planet must have enormous supplies of water.
- The planet must be gifted with tectonic plates. Recycling of matter between the surface and the molten interior is essential.
- There must be a significant satellite such as our moon. The moon's gravitational effect on the earth ensures the axis of rotation is stable. Without the moon the earth's axis of rotation would swing unpredictably through large angles. This would vary conditions too much to allow for the slow process of natural selection.
- The planet must have a magnetic field. There are dangerous energetic charged particles whizzing around the galaxy. The magnetic field exerts forces on these which propel them away from the earth.

4.2.3 Rare or common?

Thus it is argued, life may be unique to earth, or may be a very rare phenomenon. On the other hand there are more stars in the universe than grains of sand on all the earth's beaches; even an ultra-small chance could well be successful elsewhere. Once the conditions on earth were right, life arose very quickly. Given the chance elsewhere, it must happen, so it is said.

If life has only occurred once, does not this mean it is a vastly unlikely event? That its presence is meaningless in such a vast universe? However, if life were to emerge it would have needed the time for stars to form and earth to form. For this to have happened, for time to be so extensive, the universe had to be as large as it is. Smaller universes would have too short an existence to produce stars and life.

Simon Conway Morris's book *'inevitable humans in a lonely cosmos'* investigates this question, and his answer is in the title. Paul Davies answers differently[6].

> 'If so, (biogenesis factored into quantum nature of molecules),biological determinism might at last receive a convincing theoretical underpinning, justifying the popular belief we inhabit a bio-friendly universe in which we are not alone' [7].

---

5. Margaret Turnbull, 'Where is Life Hiding? Location Holds the Key to Finding Extraterrestrial Life', in *Astronomy*, 34/10 (October 2006).
6. Paul Davies, 'Life Force', *New Scientist* (18 September 1999): 27–30.
7. *Ibid*, 30.

5. A final word

Every philosopher has an unproven starting position.
One cannot base all one's conclusions on deductive or inductive logic. There have to be starting positions which are taken as given. The atheist may declare that the theist begins with a gratuitous and unproven assertion about the existence of a supreme being. The materialist's assertion of scientific reductionism leading to a denial of anything beyond the material is equally unproven. The materialist may assert that chance does away with the theist's starting position. The theist may well respond that the extraordinary evolution from mindless matter to intelligence contradicts the meaninglessness implicit in the atheist's overview, and that the evidence of most of humanity desirous of goodness but unable to realize it communally or personally is indication of something beyond, answered very well in the life death and resurrection of the incarnate Son of God.